*Women and Reform in a
New England Community,
1815–1860*

Women and Reform in a New England Community, 1815–1860

Carolyn J. Lawes

THE UNIVERSITY PRESS OF KENTUCKY

Publication of this volume was made possible in part by a grant from the National Endowment for the Humanities.

Published by The University Press of Kentucky
Scholarly publisher for the Commonwealth,
serving Bellarmine College, Berea College, Centre
College of Kentucky, Eastern Kentucky University,
The Filson Club Historical Society, Georgetown College,
Kentucky Historical Society, Kentucky State University,
Morehead State University, Murray State University,
Northern Kentucky University, Transylvania University,
University of Kentucky, University of Louisville,
and Western Kentucky University.
All rights reserved.

Editorial and Sales Offices: The University Press of Kentucky
663 South Limestone Street, Lexington, Kentucky 40508-4008

04 03 02 01 00   5 4 3 2 1

Library of Congress Cataloging-in-Publication Data

Lawes, Carolyn J., 1958-
    Women and reform in a New England community, 1815-1860 / Carolyn J.
Lawes.
        p.   cm.
    Includes bibliographical references (p.   ) and index.
    ISBN 0-8131-2131-0
    1. Women social reformers—Massachusetts—Worcester—History—19th
century. 2. Women political activists—Massachusetts—Worcester—History—
19th century. 3. Women's rights—Massachusetts—History—19th century.
4. Children's Friend Society—History. 5. Worcester (Mass.)—History—19th
century—Sources. 6. Worcester (Mass.)—Social conditions. 7. Worcester
(Mass.)—Politics and government. I. Title.
HQ1439.W67L39   2000
305.42'097443—dc21   99-28840

For
Robert B. and Jane G. Lawes

Contents

Illustrations follow page 118

Acknowledgments

This study began as a dissertation in the Department of History at the University of California at Davis, under the direction of the late, and greatly missed, Paul Goodman. Whatever insights the following pages might offer are due in no small measure to his example of thorough and nuanced scholarship. I am also deeply indebted to F. Wilson Smith, professor of history emeritus, and to Karen Halttunen, professor of history, for their generous guidance, unyielding standards, and constant support. The Department of History provided many years of financial support through liberal teaching assistantships and the Emmanuel Ringleblum Fellowship in History. The Graduate Division of the University of California at Davis funded the preliminary work upon which this study was based with a Humanities Graduate Research Award and a Humanities Institute Dissertation Fellowship.

The vast majority of the archival research for this book was conducted at the American Antiquarian Society in Worcester, Massachusetts, a premier library of American history. At the AAS I was privileged to be selected as a Kate B. and Hall J. Peterson Fellow, which not only supported my research financially but introduced me to a congenial scholarly world I scarcely imagined existed. Among the society's unparalleled professional staff, I wish to thank John B. Hench, Joanne D. Chaison, Marie Lamoreaux, Thomas Knoles, Caroline F. Sloat, and Laura Wasowicz for their many efforts on behalf of this project.

Other individuals in Worcester also eased this study along. Kenneth J. Moynihan, professor of history at Assumption College, took an early interest in my work. He not only shared with me his extensive knowledge of local history, but graciously read the manuscript and saved me from several errors. Kenneth and Mary Jo Moynihan also welcomed me into their Paxton home and made my after-library hours something to which I greatly looked forward. My thanks as well to Nancy Gaudette of the Worcester Public Library, Theresa B. Davitt of the Worcester Historical Museum, Mary Kate McMaster, formerly of the American

Antiquarian Society, Jane B. Griesheimer and Amy Cardullo of the Worcester Children's Friend Society, and the staff of the Pitt Theological Library at Emory University for their assistance.

The research foundation of Old Dominion University provided a Spring Faculty Grant in 1994 and a Summer Faculty Research Grant in 1995 which together enabled me to return to the Worcester archives for two successive summers while I expanded my dissertation into a book. The dean of the College of Arts and Letters, Karen Gould, generously funded the book's illustrations.

I would like to thank Deborah van Broekhoven, one of the readers for The University Press of Kentucky, for her cogent suggestions.

Certain friends and colleagues have been instrumental in helping me to stay focused over the years. To Scott E. Casper, Mona J. Danner, Anita Clair Fellman, J.C. Johnson, Jeff Kolnick, Jane T. Merritt, Sujata Moorti, Sandra Pryor, Michael L. Smith, and Alan S. Taylor, I offer my deepest appreciation for your aid and comfort.

To several individuals I owe still more. Daniel L. Letwin was present from the beginning and heard me out with great patience. David J. Garrow offered constant encouragement while this book took shape. Karin Wulf has redefined the very meaning of friendship. Finally, without a lifetime of unwavering support from my sisters, Susan J. Lawes and Julie Goodson-Lawes, and my father and mother, Robert B. and Jane G. Lawes, nothing would have ever been possible or even imaginable.

Materials from the collections of the Worcester Historical Museum and the American Antiquarian Society are used with permission. Portions of chapter 1 are excerpted from the author's essay "Trifling with Holy Time: Women and the Formation of the Calvinist Church of Worcester, Massachusetts, 1815-1820." *Religion and American Culture* 8, no. 1 (1998). © 1998 by *Center for the Study of Religion and American Culture*. By permission.

Introduction

The Mother at Home! The amount on't is, she's never at home!
                            — Worcester resident Joseph Boyden,
                        on the 1835 bestseller, *The Mother at Home*

In 1835, Joseph Boyden, a Worcester, Massachusetts, jeweler and something of a local wag, remarked upon a common antebellum contradiction. On the one hand, American culture assumed that women—primarily middle-class, northern, urban white women, although this was usually left unstated—were wives and mothers and that they were at home. On the other hand, the reality was that although most antebellum women were indeed wives and mothers, they often were someplace else. *Women and Reform in a New England Community, 1815–1860,* explores that someplace else and argues that a close examination of the many organized activities of women in antebellum Worcester clarifies the ways in which women held prominent leadership roles in their community. From the churches to the sewing circles, from the nursery to the orphanage, and from feminism to female employment, women in this antebellum city were notably absent from home and hearth.

Over the past thirty years, historians of women and gender have developed a significant body of literature examining women's roles in American society, and the impact upon scholarly narratives has been impressive. In the late eighteenth and early nineteenth centuries, many historians now agree, a new ideal of femininity emerged that assigned to women the chief responsibility for shepherding social morality and purveying civilization unto the next generation in order to ensure the virtue of the new American republic. Domesticity thus became the "sphere" of the true antebellum woman, and while most historians are careful to emphasize that this was an ideal, not necessarily a reality, it was nonetheless a dominant cultural symbol. The emergence of the market economy in the early nineteenth century further relegated women to the domestic sphere by marginalizing their contributions to the family economy. A gendered separation of "public" and "private" meant that real women remained at home, their lives increasingly narrowed by a pervasive ideology of feminine passivity and weakness. Indeed, so thoroughgoing was this cult of domesticity, some historians suggest, that partly as compensation for their social and political invisibility, and partly because it was expected of them as the "religious avatars of embattled altruism" (to use Charles Sellers' phrase), middle-class women devoted themselves to their families, denying their own hopes and ambitions so that others might prosper.[1]

Historians from a variety of perspectives have embraced the rhetoric of domesticity and rigid gender spheres, and thus routinely characterize the antebellum middle-class family as "secluded," its female inhabitants isolated from the "real" world. However, such characterizations have significant negative implications for the study of history because they assume that women stood on the sidelines of what truly mattered in nineteenth-century America: politics, economics, and the power the two conveyed. The paradigm of separate spheres therefore permits scholars to continue to disregard women in their analyses of the vigorous antebellum political system. If the women were kept at home with the children, after all, what significant role could they have played?[2]

Some of the earliest work in women's history addressed just this question by arguing for the rise of "domestic feminism." Not only did antebellum women find comfort in a shared "woman's culture" and the bonds of sisterhood, this argument held, but a consciousness of gender difference inspired them to participate in social reform, leading ultimately to the women's movement. Subsequent historians, however, finding little evidence for such a trailblazing role, moved the field in a new direction by arguing for the importance of class in stimulating antebellum women's social activism. Mary P. Ryan's influential study of Oneida County, New York, argued that not only were women instrumental in the formation of the middle class but that they both accepted gender spheres and used their organizations to defend their class interests. Nancy Hewitt concurred in her study of Rochester, New York, describing the distinctive styles of activism that divided women's organizations and arguing that rather than working together out of a shared gender consciousness, women worked alongside the men of their class in opposition to the women and men of other classes. By the end of the 1850s, Hewitt concluded, women's groups had lost their independence and were subordinated to men's organizations, a finding echoed in Suzanne Lebsock's study of Petersburg, Virginia.[3]

There the discussion of women's local activism stood until recent scholarship refocused the field once more. Current work seeks to revise the paradigm of separate spheres by integrating women back into the public, for example, by exploring women's participation in the political system. Still others reject the public-private dichotomy entirely and focus upon the role of gender and class in motivating nineteenth-century women to participate in national movements, such as the abolition, temperance, and suffrage campaigns.[4] The interest in re-examining women's alleged exclusion from the "public" sphere is proving quite fruitful and will likely prompt a general reassessment of the relationship of women and institutional politics in the nineteenth century.

The developing literature on antebellum American women's history has, however, created a discordance between characterizations of what women were doing at the local level and what they were doing more broadly. How do we explain the solid evidence of women's grassroots participation in political campaigns, and their high profile in several national reform movements, at the very time local women were "meekly" ceding control of their own organizations? In addition, analyses of women's role in their communities raise important ideological questions. If antebellum women's social activism was chiefly class-oriented and ultimately male-dominated, then wherein lies its significance for the history of women? More to the point, did antebellum women, as women, gain nothing from their own organizing efforts? Is the notion of a reforming "sisterhood" historically invalid? More fundamentally, is it logical to expect that well-educated, experienced, and clear-eyed individuals consistently worked so hard to improve the fortunes of others—but not their own? Or is it possible to reconcile the indisputable gendered limits of antebellum women's lives with their class interests and with women's leadership in their local communities?

The answer to the last question is yes, and that is what this study attempts. *Women and Reform in a New England Community, 1815–1860,* analyzes the organized social activism of (mostly middle-class, urban, white) women in antebellum Worcester, Massachusetts, and finds that women were at the center of community life and leadership. While no community may accurately be said to reflect all others, an argument for

Worcester's suitability as a test case for antebellum women's social activism can be made. A shire town and the self-described "heart of the commonwealth," neither frontier nor densely urban, Worcester encountered the stresses common to so many communities in the northeast as it developed and diversified, economically, demographically, and religiously. Situated at the crossroads of several stage and railroad lines connecting metropolitan Boston to the West, antebellum Worcester was the site of numerous social and political conventions, including the first and second national women's rights conventions, and its citizens, male and female, participated actively in the era's various political, social, and religious reform movements. Being a smallish but growing urban center gave the antebellum city its special character: large and diverse enough to accept change but small and cohesive enough to remember community.

Just as important for the historian, Worcester is especially well suited for studying women due to the unusually rich local history collections available at the American Antiquarian Society. Founded in Worcester just after the War of 1812, the American Antiquarian Society's unparalleled archival and manuscript records make it possible to overcome the chronic scholarly problem of past women's invisibility, and to permit the kind of fine-grained analysis necessary to root women's history in the interpersonal dynamics of community life. The study that follows is based upon a close reading of the extensive local records of antebellum Worcester. It draws heavily upon institutional sources, such as the records of the town, churches, voluntary societies, businesses, tax and census data, and vital statistics; published sources (for Worcester was a publishing center), such as government documents, newspapers, pamphlets, books, broadsides, biographies, autobiographies, and reminiscences; as well as unpublished sources, such as diaries, letters, and family papers. I do not pretend that the list is exhaustive, though assimilating it certainly was exhausting.

This study proceeds from the assumption that human beings, regardless of their particular circumstances, seek to maximize their autonomy and self-control. It is not my goal here to document the many ways in which overcoming new and traditional gender barriers remained difficult, at times even impossible. Such an exercise would be, at this state of the literature, pointless. Rather, this book examines *what women were able to do and why* and seeks to reinterpret American women's history by demonstrating how the complexities of antebellum life affected both the limits and the possibilities of individual and group efforts to change themselves and their society. To this end, this study examines women's organizations from several angles and finds that a combination of gendered and class instability united the middle-class women of Worcester in defense of their interests as women and in defense of their roles as active members of the community.[5]

One note of caution. Although it is the prerogative of the academic historian to impose order on an unruly past, to do so runs certain risks. First and foremost, we risk holding to contemporary standards of belief and behavior people who lived very different lives. As will hopefully become apparent, the concerns of the antebellum world, in particular the suddenness and propinquity of death and economic failure, are not ours; indeed, much of the daily reality of their lives is simply unimaginable in America today. As a consequence, this is not a study of the inevitable march of progress from darkness into the light; it is, rather, a story of individuals making their own order out of chaos. Similarly, although change over time is apparent in most of the women's organizations studied here, theirs is not a tale of the linear unfolding of ideas and events from small to large, from provincial to universal, from local to national, from confinement to freedom. The internal lives of women's voluntary societies ebbed and flowed in response to particular situations, first heading in one direction, then sailing in another, much as individual lives do. While the groups usually ended up at a different place from where they started, they did not necessarily intend to go there, and to impose a chart on their wanderings is to miss the significance of the process. Finally, although I do emphasize the importance of gender in shaping antebellum women's lives, I do so as a corrective, not as an explanation of how gender trumps class. Both were important because, as others have argued, gender differed by class and because, as I hope to illuminate, class differed by gender.

That being said, on with the show. We begin with the breakdown of the town's central communal institution, the First (Congregational) Church, and examine the feminization of religion in a moment of community crisis. We also explore the interplay of women and the institutional church during the era of disestablishment by analyzing financial, membership, and disciplinary records. Denominational challenges to the Standing Order during the Second Great Awakening, combined with Worcester's chaotic growth, led to the breakdown of traditional sources of male authority even while women emerged as the moral arbiters of acceptable social and religious behavior.

In chapter 2, we address the most ubiquitous form of women's organization, the constitutional, permanent, for-profit sewing circle, which was for antebellum women what the political party was for antebellum men: a forum for good fellowship, mutual improvement, and social activism. We look at six of the sewing circles of antebellum Worcester and examine one in depth, following the development of its members' political interests from a concern for supporting missionaries with in-kind donations to supporting local and national reforms by making and selling goods for a profit. We trace the sewing circles' evolution from parochial rivalries to mixed-sex community organizations involved in pressing social issues, from sewing clothing for fugitive slaves to taking up the massive soldier relief efforts needed during the Civil War.

Next we explore women's organized activities on behalf of the community's welfare and study how gender affected the ways reformers conceptualized and addressed social ills. Chapter 3 examines the growing problem of poverty and how women in Worcester came together in a citywide effort to assist the community's poor. The history of the Children's Friend Society (CFS), founded in late 1848, describes how well-meaning women initially sought to rescue the children of the intemperate, the poor, and the immigrant. But the CFS, which at first appeared to emphasize the class interests of its relatively privileged founders, soon found that gender and class instability, rather than privilege, were the women's daily realities. Life in general was growing more precarious in the antebellum period, affecting CFS members' families as well as those of the less privileged members of their community. But genuine empathy for the problems of other mothers, and not bourgeois condescension or a desire for social control, brought women together in the CFS.

Chapter 4 examines more broadly the role of the Children's Friend Society within the Worcester community and argues that an ideology of maternalism, which focused upon the uniqueness of the child and the importance of the mother, was the bedrock of the social welfare policies of the antebellum city. Although it was a private women's society, the CFS served as Worcester's quasi-official child welfare department. At the same time, the CFS's legal power was curtailed both by its ideology of maternalism and by the parents of Worcester, especially the mothers, who utilized the society's services to suit their own purposes.

In 1850, the first national women's rights convention took place in Worcester, and it returned the following year. Chapter Five examines the connections between the national conventions and their host community, as well as the ties between the national movement and local women's organizations. Analysis of the membership of the 1850 convention reveals that many who formally subscribed to the antebellum feminist movement were also active in the women's organizations of Worcester. Not only did the women of Worcester not lose control of their organizations during the 1850s, but they solidified and expanded their leadership in the city. The book concludes by arguing that an emerging feminist sensibility both undergirded existing local women's organizations and inspired new ones.

Thus, throughout the antebellum era the organized women of Worcester played prominent roles in their community's affairs. In the 1810s and 1820s, women focused on the religious institutions that were the traditional centers of small-town New England life. In the 1830s and 1840s, years of dramatic economic and demographic development, the sewing circles emerged as centers of community life when women joined together to redefine their place in a rapidly growing and secularizing city. By the late 1840s and the 1850s, women's voluntary societies had assumed an official role within the city and were working to further the goals of the antebellum feminist movement by expanding women's political, educational, and employment opportunities in their city. Joseph Boyden's wry comment in 1835 that the mothers of Worcester always seemed to be out and about thus pointed to a local tradition of community involvement that united the disparate women's groups of antebellum Worcester and that implicitly rejected gendered distinctions of public and private spheres of life and labor.

1

Keeping the Faith

Women's Leadership in
an Orthodox Congregational Church

> I believe that those who are once regenerated and united to
> Christ by a true faith will never finally fall away, but will be
> preserved, by divine power, and in fulfillment of God's
> eternal purpose of grace, unto final salvation.
> — Articles of Faith and Covenant,
> adopted by the Calvinist Church in Worcester, 1834

It was half past nine on a quiet Monday night in April 1818. Elizabeth Tuckerman Salisbury, known throughout Worcester as "Madame Salisbury" in deference to her family's wealth and social position, was passing a serene evening at home with her niece and adopted daughter, Eliza Weir. Her husband Stephen, a merchant and the town's wealthiest citizen, was away on business. The Salisbury mansion's drawing room was pleasant, graced by Elizabeth's harp and a piano bought expressly for Eliza.[1]

Suddenly the peace was shattered as something crashed violently against the front window. Salisbury immediately "call'd in the people" (the servants) for protection. Venturing outside, they spotted no one lurking about, but did find two good-sized stones, one weighing over half a pound. Peering out into the now still night, Elizabeth Salisbury noted that "it was very dark, & no one appeared to be in the street. [Y]ou may suppose I did not recover my tranquil[l]ity very soon."[2]

The next morning Salisbury summoned her nephew by marriage, Daniel Waldo, a merchant and investor, and the town's second-wealthiest citizen. Waldo hurried to her side with disturbing news of his own: "he had his trees broken *that* night, & the one *preceeding* [*sic*], he supposed by the same person or persons" who had thrown the rocks. Musing over the broken trees and shattered glass, Waldo suspected a political motive behind the attacks, which had occurred on the evening of an election to decide whether he retained his seat in the state senate. Waldo explained that "there had been great exertions made by some disaffected *person*," costing him not just a few trees but one hundred votes as well. If indeed the vandalism had been linked to the election, it would cease now that the votes had been cast. Heartened by Waldo's conjecture, Salisbury wrote confidently to her husband that there was no cause for alarm, since "there is not the least probability of [the attack] being repeated." A reward of one hundred dollars for information about the "evil-minded" vandals yielded no suspects, and the night visitors were never identified.[3]

Yet if the destruction of Waldo's property was indeed an act of his political opposition, then why the attack on the Salisbury home? None of the Salisburys was active in politics, nor could the women vote. But the senate election was not the only source of intense conflict in Worcester. In the spring of 1818, Daniel Waldo's unmarried sisters, Rebecca Waldo and Sarah Waldo, and their aunt, Elizabeth Salisbury, were embroiled in a feud that threatened to tear apart the community's oldest institution, the First (Congregational) Church. From 1815 through 1820, the three women defied gender conventions by challenging the authority of their church and their minister. Rather than "trifle with holy time," as Elizabeth Salisbury expressed it, the women withdrew from the First Church to found the orthodox Congregational Calvinist Church, sparking an acrimonious debate over the nature of religious authority.[4]

As Anne Hutchinson had two centuries before, these women laid claim to religious autonomy and self-determination, and exercised the power implicit in their spiritual equality to command and to criticize the male church leadership. Unlike Anne Hutchinson, however, they were able to do so while remaining within the fellowship of Congregational churches. The Worcester dissidents were assisted in their revolt by their unusual wealth which, in the era of disestablishment, gave them considerable power. By 1820, the dissidents and their male allies had founded the orthodox Congregational Calvinist Church, whose tax structure and disciplinary practices reveal the significant leadership role religious women played in the antebellum church.

CHALLENGING THE BRETHREN

In 1815, after twenty-five years in the pulpit, the minister of Worcester's First Church, the Reverend Samuel Austin, announced his intention to assume the presidency of the University of Vermont. As was true for many congregations at this time, the harmony of the First Church dissipated in the course of settling upon a successor.[5] At the eye of the maelstrom were Rebecca and Sarah Waldo, and Elizabeth Salisbury. The Waldos and Salisbury were unusual women in that each controlled a sizable fortune in her own right. The unmarried Waldos had inherited large sums of money from their father, a merchant, and by 1827 each was worth more than $35,000. Rebecca Waldo, moreover, was an active capitalist who put her inheritance to work: like her brother Daniel, Rebecca was an important local moneylender who invested in farm mortgages. Elizabeth Salisbury was even wealthier; in 1846, her estate was appraised at more than $125,000. Their fortunes not only landed Rebecca Waldo, Sarah Waldo, and Elizabeth Salisbury at the very top of local tax lists, far ahead of almost all of the men in Worcester, but also among the nation's elite.[6] Barred by their sex from holding formal positions of leadership and power, these economically independent women asserted themselves in the church. They thus did not hesitate to speak out when the Reverend Austin's replacement, Charles A. Goodrich, proved disappointing.

Through no fault of his own, Goodrich's ministry in the First Church began under a cloud. Samuel Austin was a preacher of firm and outspoken beliefs, a New Divinity Calvinist who once declined a post because the congregation refused to repudiate the Halfway Covenant. He had prepared for the ministry under the theologian Jonathan Edwards, Jr., whose father's works he later collected and published, and was married to Jerusha Hopkins, daughter of renowned conservative theologian Samuel Hopkins. In his commanding appearance and "fearless spirit and firmness," Austin reminded his parishioners, for good or for ill, of the Puritan martyrs of old. A minister of local and national prominence, much in demand as a speaker, Austin had set a precedent of forceful and austere spirituality that might have proved difficult for anyone to equal.[7]

The task facing his successor was all the more trying because Austin did not officially vacate the First Church's pulpit. The growing heterodoxy of Protestantism had prompted calls from dissenting sects for the disestablishment of Congregationalism and raised the question of who owned the ministerial lands that had long since been set aside to support the town's church. In 1815, the First Church was in the midst of protracted litigation with the Second (Unitarian) Church over the disposition of Worcester's ministerial lands. As joint plaintiffs in the lawsuit, Austin and the First Church considered it improvident to sever their official connection until the case was resolved. Thus, although settled in Vermont, Austin remained the official pastor of the First Church, a technicality that would spawn numerous complications. When the Reverend Charles A. Goodrich rode into town in the autumn of 1816, it was as junior pastor to an absent and, to some, a greatly missed patriarch.[8]

Signs that Goodrich's tenure would be contentious first arose during the year-long search to fill the pulpit. According to the church's version of events, the Waldos proved "unusually solicitous" about Austin's replacement, forcing the congregation to pay "a scrupulous regard to the views, feelings and advice of this family."[9] The Waldos could command such deference because of their critical financial support. Although Congregationalism was not formally disestablished until 1833, Massachusetts passed the Religious Freedom Act in 1811 requiring towns to apportion the church tax among its denominations according to the size of each church's membership. Some towns, such as Worcester, ceased collecting the tax altogether, compelling churches to raise money on their own by levying a tax on the property of communicants who were heads of households.[10] The Waldos were by far the wealthiest taxpayers in the First Church and their financial contributions were considerable: in 1816, the year the schism began, the Waldo family alone supplied slightly more than one-quarter of the First Church's tax revenues. (As a married woman whose husband did not belong to the First Church, Elizabeth Salisbury was not subject to its tax.) Money bought the Waldos influence, prompting bitter complaints about those whose "claims to consideration over most others are founded entirely on property."[11]

The new minister thus had good reason to court the endorsement of the Waldos. Goodrich boasted that he had been selected with their blessing because they had had "a presentiment . . . that he would come up to their prescribed standard of excellence." In fact, Goodrich insisted, the family was so pleased that it offered "to furnish the pulpit with a curtain and cushion." It was thus all the more shocking when Daniel Waldo, on behalf of his sisters and Salisbury—who, as women, were not entitled to vote—cast his ballot against hiring Goodrich. But the church decided "it was now time to act with decision and independence" and soundly outvoted Waldo, sixty-four to two. The Waldos and Salisbury found themselves increasingly isolated within the church that, under Austin, had shown deference to and respect for their social and economic standing.[12]

The election of Goodrich over the objections of the Waldos and Salisbury sparked a four-year battle for control of the First Church. The dissidents' aversion to Goodrich formally focused upon their suspicion that he was insufficiently orthodox, a potentially serious allegation. Yet they could name no specific breach of Congregational doctrine. When pressed, they offered only vague examples. At tea one day, the Waldos declared, Goodrich had disparaged John Calvin and derided "those who wanted *the cords of orthodoxy as large as cart-ropes.*"[13] The Waldos vehemently denied ever having championed Goodrich; his "frequent visits at our house," they charged, were merely the result of his clumsy attempts to curry their favor. Daniel Waldo insisted that the family had treated Goodrich with the civility due a gentleman and no more; perhaps, he insinuated, Goodrich was unaccustomed to simple respect. The Waldos denied unduly influencing the search committee and haughtily rejected the implication of bribery.[14] The dissidents then accused the new minister of taking lightly his duties as spiritual shepherd. Goodrich frequently absented himself from the pulpit, they alleged, recycled his sermons, ignored the sick, neglected to baptize children, and seldom attended religious conferences. Such a minister, the Waldos and Salisbury concluded, was "unworthy [of] our esteem and confidence."[15]

Amorphous though these charges were, they were potentially devastating. In New England's orthodox Congregational churches, a sinner's redemption depended upon the intensely personal process of spiritual development and conversion. Only God could save a soul but the minister played a pivotal role. It was his responsibility to promote an awareness of sin in the unconverted, to guide the penitent through conversion, and to keep the converted on the path of righteousness through example and constant exhortation. A minister who did not inspire his congregation was the wrong minister for it, regardless of his doctrinal fitness. Thus the accusation that Goodrich's ministry was ineffectual was, quite literally, a damning one.[16]

Most important in stimulating and driving the dissent, however, was gender. By tradition, Congregational women had no formal role in the governance of the church; the selection of ministers, disciplinary proceedings, and questions of doctrine were the unique province of the brethren. The Waldos and Salisbury did not explicitly object to their secondary status but their acceptance of gender subordination proved contingent upon the minister meeting their definition of ministerial masculinity. The women and the brethren of the First Church agreed that a minister rightfully exercised "paternal watchfulness" over his flock and acted "as a father and a friend." In return, he could command their deference. But the middle-aged Waldos and Salisbury found it difficult to accept Goodrich, only twenty-six years old, in this role. Although the Waldos and Salisbury never objected specifically to Goodrich's age, they referred repeatedly to his undeveloped character, a likely synonym for youth. In comparison, the dissenters were close friends with the slightly older Austins.[17] The Waldos and Salisbury also found Goodrich's style of discourse unimpressive. Accustomed to Austin's trenchant preaching, which was notorious for being "of that sort which permits no hearer to be indifferent," the Waldos and Salisbury described Goodrich's prayers as "cold and heartless" and scorned his sermons as "*pretty*," never "*sound, weighty, and impressive.*" The dissenters criticized what they viewed as Goodrich's "lightness of mind" and "foolish and extravagant conversation," which to them was a mode of expression more suitable to the parlor than the pulpit. Goodrich was "a lover of pleasure more than a lover of God," Daniel Waldo wrote implacably, and was once spied dallying "in a mixed company" when he was supposed to be leading prayer services.[18]

For their part, the Waldo sisters enjoyed a reputation for piety and stern sobriety that even family friends found intimidating. When the formidable "Misses Waldo" went calling, neighbor women not feeling up to the task of hosting were known to hide behind their curtains, and "were not visible or did not choose to be." Similarly, Rebekah Dean Salisbury, Elizabeth Salisbury's daughter-in-law, once described to her sister a friendly discussion of the doctrine of total depravity. Salisbury confessed her admiration for John Locke, prompting her to wonder, "What would the Miss Waldos say to me?"[19]

At the heart of the ensuing schism was the role these women could legitimately play in their church. Their wealth, their reputations for piety, and their unmarried status placed the women in an anomalous position: full church members and wealthy taxpayers who nonetheless were excluded from church decision making. As far as the brethren of the First Church were concerned, the problem was nakedly one of the power of wealth. From their perspective, "the peace and harmony of the Society . . . were nothing: the almost unexampled unanimity of the Church and Parish, after such a succession of Candidates, was nothing: the estimation in which Mr. Goodrich was held by neighbouring Pastors and Churches was nothing—so long as *they were not gratified.*" Throughout the dispute, the brethren staunchly maintained that the Waldos' objections "would have sunk into its merited insignificance, had it not been for the money which upheld it."[20]

In a sense, they were correct: the dissenters' money *was* a critical element, for had they not been wealthy the dispute would likely have ended in disciplinary proceedings against the women as "disorderly walkers" for trampling on the covenant. The covenant was the theological and constitutional foundation of the decentralized Congregational churches. By owning the covenant, church members signified their acceptance of the authority of the congregation to pass judgment on their spiritual and temporal lives. In theory, the church was a gathering of spiritually equal souls. In reality, religious authority was reserved for the brethren alone. By withdrawing from worship and refusing to accept that the "decisions of Providence" had been manifested by the election of the Reverend Goodrich, the women repudiated the presumption of male authority and, in essence, denied that the brethren spoke for God. In this contest over who rightfully exercised authority within the church, the women's wealth gave them a measure of power.[21]

Unwilling or unable to take seriously the women's protest at their exclusion from church decision making, the brethren insisted that the dispute was fundamentally a question of the control of the majority by a wealthy minority. Indeed, the church was forced to focus on their money because the Waldos and Salisbury had comported themselves impeccably. Not for them was the fate of Betsey Flagg of the neighboring town of Boylston. In 1814, Flagg expressed her dissatisfaction with the pastor of her church "in an improper and injudicious manner & in a way calculated to irritate and offend," thus shifting the discussion from the minister's conduct to her own. An ecclesiastical council, of which Samuel Austin was a member, successfully mediated the dispute but not before requiring that Flagg apologize to the offended Boylston brethren.[22] In sum, the schism of Worcester's First Church occurred with the two sides fighting different battles. For the dissidents, the issue was a question of gender, the right of spiritually equal *women* to decide their own religious futures. For the brethren and the new minister, the issue was a question of democracy, the right of the (male) *voting majority* to decide the future of the church, including the women's religious futures.[23]

Throughout 1817 and into 1818, a stalemate ensued as Goodrich solidified his position, conducting a revival that brought in eighty new members, and organizing a Sunday School. Confident of his support, Goodrich denounced his detractors from the pulpit. The Waldos sat in the family pew silently fuming while Goodrich "frequently pointed at us in his publick discourses."[24] The tension broke one Sunday in the spring of 1818, when Goodrich addressed the congregation on the "nature and obligations of their Christian vows," which, he explained, required all to accept meekly the discipline imposed by the church. Certain that the sermon was intended as a public rebuke, the Waldos had had enough. Joined by Salisbury, they stalked out of the church and went to worship with the recently arrived Baptists, whose services the Waldo sisters and Salisbury had taken the precaution of observing. There the dissidents "felt much happier than at our own meeting-house."[25] A week later, Daniel Waldo ran for reelection to the state senate and the stones flew.

During the summer the dispute took a new turn when the lawsuit over ministerial lands was finally settled. The church prepared to formally dismiss Austin and promote Goodrich to full pastor, a role he was, for all practical purposes, already performing. But it seems Austin was unhappy in Vermont and proposed to return to the Worcester pulpit since he was, technically, still its senior pastor. Seizing upon the opportunity to rid themselves of the despised new minister, the Waldos and Salisbury organized a campaign for Austin's return. Austin actively encouraged them, informing the First Church that he would accept dismissal only if "a *large proportion* of the Church" requested it and if they "assign *sufficient reason* therefore." The absent minister underscored his position by signing his letters to the church "Your affectionate copastor." Austin also stepped up the pressure by demanding a Mutual Council to arbitrate his claim, as was his right under Congregational church rules.[26]

The Mutual Council, composed of five clergymen jointly agreed upon by Austin and the church, met the following November. They read a pro-Goodrich majority report pointing out that Austin had left willingly and that Goodrich had been properly installed. The lack of a formal dismission was due to the novel complication of Austin being a party in the lawsuit, which did not fundamentally alter the circumstances. The Council also read a pro-Austin minority report that sought to return Austin and, in effect, to fire Goodrich. The minority relied largely upon a legalistic argument: they wanted Austin for their shepherd, he wanted them for his flock, he was still the senior minister, and to their minds he had done nothing to merit dismissal.[27]

However, the Mutual Council was persuaded by the principle of majority rule and by a determination to uphold ministerial authority and "strengthen the hands of him that is set over [you] in the Lord." In December 1818, it formally dissolved Austin's connection to Worcester's First Church and ordered the dissidents to "return to the stated ministrations of their worthy Pastor." The Mutual Council concluded its report with a prophetic warning against the likely outcome of continued dissension: "It is to be feared you may plunge into a series of difficulties, of which we cannot see the issue. You may lay a foundation for dissensions and evils which may extend to generations yet unborn. Remember, you are acting for yourselves, and not for us."[28]

The Mutual Council's decision forced the dissenters either to admit they were wrong and return to the First Church or to go elsewhere. The Waldos and Salisbury took temporary respite with the Baptists but were soon journeying to Boston's Old South Church, eight hours away by stagecoach. This solution was untenable in the long term and, unwilling to yield to the First Church, the dissidents resolved to form a church of their own. As a first step, Rebecca Waldo, Sarah Waldo, and Elizabeth Salisbury sought dismissions and recommendations from the First Church, the process by which individuals transferred their membership from one church to another. To forestall their leaving, a subdued Goodrich wrote to Salisbury with "the most pacific views" to request "a personal and friendly interview."[29] When Salisbury refused to meet with him, Goodrich and the First Church dismissed the women but would not recommend them, a very public declaration that the dissenters, although full church members, were not worthy Christians. The First Church thus formally censured the female dissenters for their impertinence in passing judgment upon the minister and for repudiating the male church authorities.

The Waldo sisters and Salisbury were not about to tolerate any further humiliation. These women were full church members; that is, each had undergone conversion and experienced the saving grace that only an omnipotent God could bestow. Conversion assured them of their worth, for who could be more qualified than God to judge them? Moreover, because their identity and social status were linked to their reputations for piety, Goodrich's refusal to recommend them struck at the heart of who they considered themselves to be. As they demanded in a petition to the First Church, "Are the Church, who have witnessed the constancy, cheerfulness, and solemnity with which the disaffected have heretofore attended with them, on the duties of publick worship, prepared to question their sincerity, and denounce their repeated avowals, as assumptions, affectations, and hypocrisy?" They insisted that the church "hold us blameless.—We say blameless. . . ." The Waldos and Salisbury were women of considerable means, unusually free to govern themselves. When the new minister dared to bring them to heel, their consciences, and likely their pride, compelled them to rebel.[30]

To a woman, the Waldos and Salisbury denounced Goodrich and the First Church and unequivocally asserted their right to determine for themselves their religious fates. If they were uneasy with the minister, they implied, it must be he who was at fault. Trusting in their "feelings and the impressions which have been made on our minds," the Waldo sisters explained in a joint letter to the First Church that under Goodrich they had "failed of receiving . . . religious satisfaction, comfort, and improvement." With a nod toward the majority, they conceded that their opinions might seem erroneous to some, but declared frankly that "still [our opinions] are real and fixed in our minds" and were not going to change. It was a duty they owed to themselves as Christians, the women argued, to seek "comfort and happiness" where they could find it.[31]

Elizabeth Salisbury concurred in a separate petition. To Salisbury, the fiery Austin had been "a burning and a shining light." Goodrich lacked Austin's passion and thus, to her mind, Austin's devotion. Salisbury granted that her assessment might be subjective but maintained that such was "not now the question: it is sufficient that [my objections] have prevented me from receiving that improvement and edification from attendance on publick worship, which are the ends of its institution." The new minister had failed to uplift and enlighten her, Salisbury declared, and "rather than . . . trifle with holy time" she would do as she deemed fit.[32]

The Waldos and Salisbury followed up their individual petitions with a joint statement to the First Church reiterating and elaborating upon their views. After demurely reminding the brethren how "painful . . . it must be to females to submit their religious sentiments to the animadversions of contending parties," they went on the offensive. Goaded by the church's repeated attempts at "solemn expostulation, if not of admonition," the women articulately attacked their critics. They un-equivocally rejected the authority of the minister and the deacons to dictate to full church members, and maintained that only they were quali-fied to judge their own minds. It was the privilege and the obligation of all Christians to trust their consciences: "of our own happiness and af-flictions, of our own enjoyments, sufferings and trials, and of the means of promoting them, especially of a religious nature, we are, and from necessity, must be, the best judges." As the church knew well, they ar-gued, Christian introspection "can never be performed by substitutes, or yielded to any other person." According to the three, what was at stake was their inalienable right to religious autonomy in the face of a tyranni-cal authority.[33]

They then launched a multi-pronged offensive against the men who were trying to discipline them. They insisted that the Mutual Council's decision to uphold Goodrich's ministry cast in doubt its "wis-dom, foresight, affection, and sincerity." How could its verdict be just, the dissenters demanded, when they had been "condemned . . . unheard, undefended, and even unapprized of the process against them." In fact, the women could hardly have been "unapprized" of the actions of the Mutual Council. Such a statement may have been a way to emphasize their sense of grievance, but it also reflected their disdain for a court of appeal that men controlled, and from which they, as women, were ex-cluded from direct participation.[34]

The real issue, it seemed to them, was not whether they had acted improperly but whether others had. In the process the Waldos and Salisbury recast the debate by protesting the efforts of a majority to trans-gress the rights of a disempowered minority. Turning the argument in a new direction, they accused church authorities of trying to silence righ-teous opposition. Did the First Church have the right to use Congregationalism's "Law, Constitution and Platform" to "support its measures, however intolerant, illiberal and severe they may be . . . ?" The women concluded: "We are informed otherwise." A religious minority, they insisted, was entitled to rely upon "the perceptions and affections of [their] heads and hearts," which after all were "the vitals of religion and piety." The women insisted that natural law, "a law paramount to all other laws" because it was "impressed by the finger of God," superseded human law and granted them freedom of thought and action. True reli-gious principles, they concluded, must be "spontaneous, self-efficient, voluntary, unforced, uncorrupted, and unawed by foreign energies." The women's assertion of the right to dissent had thus developed into a declaration of religious independence.[35]

The Waldos and Salisbury did not explicitly link their criticisms of church authority with a protest against gender subordination. But the arguments they marshalled presumed a position of equality in the church, as did their refusal to accept the decisions of the church leaders. Moreover, by registering dissent as Christians, rather than as Christian women, they implicitly repudiated religious distinctions based on gender. Although only men held formal positions of leadership in the Congregational churches, it does not follow that women had no voice in church decisions, particularly where they formed a majority of full church members. Still less does it suggest that women accepted without question or protest the decisions of male church leaders. In Worcester's First Church, the Waldos and Salisbury reserved the right to veto decisions with which they did not agree, and they repeatedly refused to recognize the authority of a minister whom they neither supported nor respected. For the Waldos and Salisbury, the church was an assembly of believers whose power was contingent upon the voluntary submission of each member. This submission could be justly withdrawn—indeed, *must* be withdrawn—if the congregation strayed from the path of righteousness.

Economically independent, clearly well educated, and the daughters of families of standing, the Waldos and Salisbury were accustomed to deference from those around them, male and female, clergy and laity, and were well armed to assert and to defend their autonomy. At their insistence, a second ecclesiastical council met, overruled Goodrich and the First Church, and granted the recommendations that restored their status as Christians. Free to transfer to another church, the dissidents found none to their liking. Pointing out that "none of us can enjoy the ordinances of the Gospel with convenience; and some of us can no longer enjoy these ordinances at all," the dissidents elected to found a new church.[36] In May 1820, over the strident objections of the First Church, yet another council of ministers met to consider whether to convene the "come-outers" as a regular church. The rancor within the First Church was "most delicate and interesting," the council noted diplomatically, and it appeared no compromise was possible. It seemed to be best for the peace of religion to accommodate the desire for independence. The council was also reassured that the wealthy come-outers were "able and disposed to support publick worship by themselves." After scrutinizing the proposed church's Articles of Faith and Covenant for conformity to orthodox tenets, the council unanimously pronounced the dissidents no longer outcasts but "a regular Ch[urc]h of Christ." The council ended its report by beseeching Worcester's faithful to halt the internecine squabbling: "Brethren, be of one mind; live in peace, and the God of love and peace be with you."[37]

Four years after the onset of strife within the First Church, the dissidents were officially sanctioned as the Calvinist Church of Worcester. The Waldo sisters and Elizabeth Salisbury had led a rebellion against established religious authority and had rejected the sanctioned governance of their minister. Not only did they successfully defend their religious independence, but they were able to remain within the Congregational church. The forces of heterodoxy had transformed the church of the Puritans, which two centuries earlier had tried and banished Anne Hutchinson for criticizing the clergy. It was now more accepting of the demands of individual conscience, even from women. Moreover, the Worcester dissidents enjoyed a degree of self-confidence that enabled them to stare down their opposition. Their faith granted them equality, their conversions fortified them with conviction, and their wealth accustomed them to independence. In 1820, they left the church where they had worshiped for many years, where they had experienced God's saving grace, and built another.

In view of the acrimony that preceded the split, it was not to be expected that the parties would easily follow the council's plea for harmony. A number of Worcester's citizens had staked their reputations upon a favorable resolution and were sorely disappointed. Nor did the new church separate graciously from the old, as was indicated by its choice of a name. When a town boasted more than one congregation per sect, they distinguished themselves by number or by geography. Worcester's Unitarian Church, for example, was known locally as the Second Parish, while Boston had its North and South Congregational churches. The Worcester dissidents took a third route, christening themselves along doctrinal lines as the Calvinist Church. Thus they signaled that they were the true believers and that the First Church had strayed from orthodoxy. When tempers cooled in the late 1820s, the new church reverted to custom and began to refer to itself as the Centre (or Central) Church, after its location in the center of town.

The rash behavior of some also periodically fanned the embers of religious strife. Moses Child, a farmer, was one of the founders of the Calvinist Church. Child's intense dislike for Goodrich led him to accuse the minister of embezzlement, a baseless charge that prompted Goodrich to sue for slander. Child apologized after Goodrich won the suit, but the incident is evocative of the bitterness that poisoned the religious atmosphere in Worcester.[38]

Still, the First Church's continuing animosity is striking. The old church scorned the Council's decision. It insisted that the Calvinist Church was not a true church. It refused to dismiss and recommend members to it. Samuel Austin exaggerated only slightly when he accused the First Church of engaging in "zigzag proceedings" that were "entirely unprecedented and unwarranted." As the Council itself had acknowledged, the dissidents had not, after all, done anything wrong. Since the Council of 1820 had accepted the Calvinist Church into the fellowship of Congregational churches, the First Church could not refuse to dismiss and recommend its members to it. And yet it did. As Austin queried, "Cui bono?"[39]

The belligerence between Worcester's orthodox Congregational churches continued into the 1820s when it became clear that most of those seeking to transfer to the new church were women. It was bad enough when extraordinary women, such as the unmarried and moneyed Waldos and the enormously wealthy Salisbury, led the attack on Goodrich. It was worse still when they thwarted the First Church's attempts to discipline them, and founded a new church. But it was intolerable when other women followed their example and began to exercise their spiritual autonomy, thereby rejecting the presumption of female submission to the male church hierarchy.

Both men and women left the First Church to join the new Calvinist Church, but the procedure differed by sex as a result of the gender inequities of church membership and taxpaying. The First Church dismissed without recommending five individuals—Sarah Waldo, Rebecca Waldo, Elizabeth Salisbury, Rebekah Richards and her husband David Richards—but refused to dismiss seventeen others, maintaining that they were still part of the First Church. Subsequently, the men of this group found a loophole: they filed certificates to transfer their tax liability to the Baptist Church, as was their right under the Religious Freedom Act of 1811. Although the First Church initially opposed the men's actions, ultimately it accepted their departure. But this option was available only to taxpayers. Because only heads of households were taxpayers, married women, and most single women, could not use the loophole. Thus, for women, institutional affiliation remained an open and contentious question in the more ecumenical environment created by the Second Great Awakening and the disestablishment of Congregationalism. The crosscurrents of gendered beliefs and loyalties were played out in the cases of Anna McFarland and Lydia Taylor. William McFarland, a wealthy farmer, and Samuel Taylor, a clock maker, were among the original subscribers of the Calvinist Church. Both were church trustees; Taylor was also a deacon. In the fall of 1820, their wives, Anna McFarland and Lydia Taylor, wrote to the First Church respectfully requesting dismissions and recommendations to the Calvinist Church on the grounds that they wished "to become members of the same church to which our husbands belong." The petition raised a thorny issue: what should a pious Christian woman do when confronted with conflicting patriarchal claims upon her loyalty, one from her husband and the other from her church?[40]

The Protestant churches prized the religious unity of married communicants. To the orthodox, marriage embodied divinely ordained gender relations, which justified and strengthened the patriarch's position as the head of a family. More prosaically, couples were a boon to a church's finances. Disestablishment compelled parishes to become self-supporting, but because churches maintained the traditional tax structure, only heads of households were liable for the church tax. A married woman whose husband did not belong to her church was not taxed for its support, and her membership, while spiritually vital, was less likely to be economically helpful. Only when a woman was widowed was she reclassified as a head of household, becoming a church taxpayer. But the poverty or reduced circumstances that all too often accompanied widowhood limited the contributions of most women to the church coffers. At the same time, ministers were increasingly judged by the number of converts won and sustained. The loss of a communicant to death or resettlement was no reflection upon a minister; not so his or her removal to the church across the Common. It would be especially galling, we might imagine, if the rival church belonged to the same sect. Antebellum churches and ministers thus had both practical and theological reasons to respect and to foster the religious unity of married communicants. The financial health of the church depended upon the fidelity of its congregation, while the minister's reputation was built upon a demonstrated respect for his ability and authority.[41]

Such was the dilemma facing Charles Goodrich upon receiving McFarland and Taylor's petition for a dismission and recommendation to the Calvinist Church. Hesitant to encourage wives to disregard the divinely sanctioned authority of their husbands, yet unwilling to lose two parishioners to the despised new church, the minister trod a fine line by simultaneously acknowledging the women's dilemma while rejecting their solution. He began by commending McFarland and Taylor on their conscientious efforts to do what was right. The church "must highly respect" their desire to worship with their husbands, Goodrich wrote, for marriage was a sacred relationship "of a nature most tender." Still, the Calvinist Church was not "a regularly formed Church of our Lord Jesus." The new church was an assault upon the order and discipline of the Christian community, Goodrich insisted, and he denied their request to transfer. Should McFarland and Taylor persist, the minister warned, "this Church will consider you as . . . cutting yourselves off from the priviledges [*sic*] of Members of the Church." In sum, Goodrich argued that a Christian woman's obligation to her soul took precedence over her social (and legal) obligation to her husband. A woman who did not defend her spiritual autonomy risked excommunication and eventual damnation.[42]

Goodrich's ultimatum forced McFarland and Taylor to decide whether to follow their minister or their husbands; they could not do both. Shortly after receiving Goodrich's letter they asked that the Calvinist Church accept them as full members despite the lack of recommendations. In this petition, they made no mention of a desire to worship with their husbands but instead professed their devotion to the orthodoxy of the new church. "The First Church is divided," the women explained, "and our views and feelings are with that part, which have taken the name of the Calvinist Church." The new church, predictably, promptly received them.[43]

The McFarland and Taylor controversy suggests the means by which orthodox women could be brought to act upon the possibilities inherent in their acknowledged spiritual equality. It seems likely that McFarland and Taylor anticipated that their request would excite a conflict—in light of the hostility between the churches, it would have been naive for them to believe otherwise—and their first impulse was to deflect trouble by relying upon the shield of patriarchal gender relations. They thus justified their request by insisting that they wished to follow their husbands, as good wives should. But Goodrich rejected this argument and urged the women to act independently. For the sake of their souls, he commanded them to follow him, to repudiate the ruling of the Council of

1820, and to defy their husbands. Obliged to be decisive, McFarland and Taylor spurned their minister instead. They declared that their consciences would properly guide them and made their choice based upon their "views and feelings." Through his own intransigence and that of his congregation, the Reverend Goodrich unwittingly provided the opportunity for female parishioners to reject the spiritual authority of men and to enact the spiritual autonomy of women.

The situation confronting McFarland and Taylor was increasingly common as the number and kinds of Protestant denominations proliferated in the first half of the nineteenth century. But whereas McFarland and Taylor joined their husbands, other women made other choices. Elizabeth Salisbury left the First Church to organize the Calvinist Church even while her husband and son continued to worship with the liberal (and, to an orthodox trinitarian, the heretical) Unitarians.[44] Between 1820 and 1830, sixteen married couples joined the Calvinist Church as full church members. The total number of new church members in this decade was 108, including sixty-two females and forty-six males. It is likely that most of these were adults and that they were married. If so, then slightly less than thirty percent of the members of the Calvinist Church worshiped alongside their spiritually equal spouses, while slightly more than seventy percent did not. Of those who did not, forty-six, or sixty-one percent, were women; thirty, or thirty-nine percent, were men. Especially in churches torn by dissent, the decision of church membership was more than a manifestation of a culturally prescribed feminine piety. It was an assertion of autonomy from the dictates of the male church hierarchy.[45]

GENDER, MONEY, AND DISCIPLINE— THE POWER BEFORE THE PULPIT?

Founded by dissidents in 1822, the Calvinist Church rapidly became an anchor of orthodox Protestant religion in Worcester. Within ten years, the church had blossomed from a handful of contentious rebels into one of the more popular and fashionable churches in town.[46] But as the Calvinist Church matured, it was forced to come to grips with developments that altered the practice of organized religion and expanded the status and role of women. The first major issue confronting the fledgling Calvinist Church involved its economic foundation. A church's financial structure could act as a conservative force that bolstered the tradition of male authority. But the church had great difficulty getting men to pay their taxes, even while the town's chaotic growth forced church officials to expend more time and energy simply organizing and maintaining a semblance of order in the parish. One consequence of the churchmen's preoccupation with collecting taxes and tracking down nominal members was to open up space for the women to engage in social reform and political activism. A second aspect of new church organization concerned discipline. The discipline of errant communicants was a liberalizing force that encouraged a moral belief system women found easier to live by than men and reinforced orthodox women's confidence as autonomous moral agents.

The first order of business for Worcester's newest church was to secure an economic foundation. To overcome their reputation as a band of querulous dissenters, the founders sought to encourage new members by declaring a five-year moratorium on church taxes. The cost of running the church in the interim was borne by a group of five male subscribers, Daniel Waldo chief among them. As a letter from Waldo to the church's first minister, the Reverend Loammi Ives Hoadley, makes clear, the offer was explicitly intended to encourage recruitment. But in 1827, when the tax-free period ended and the church became self-supporting, a recurring problem was the struggle over who should support the church and how.[47]

The expansion of religious liberty in Massachusetts eliminated the traditional tax system and left churches at the mercy of voluntary payments from its not always reliable communicants. From the seventeenth through the eighteenth centuries, churches had been divided between members of the parish (that is, all town residents, who were required by law to attend services and to pay a church tax) and members of the church (that is, those who had experienced God's saving grace). The disestablishment of Congregationalism and the proliferation of denominations during the Second Great Awakening complicated the categories of membership based on conversion with distinctions based on gender. Most Americans exercised their freedom from religion to remain outside any particular church's sphere of influence—and beyond the reach of a church tax collector. Others, such as the founders of the Calvinist Church, left established churches to organize new ones. As a consequence, in the antebellum era fewer people were supporting more churches, and those who remained within a church found their share of the tax increasing. Moreover, most church members did not pay any taxes because most church members were married women. Thus in the wake of disestablishment, male church members carried a heavier tax burden. Historians have noted that men were much less likely than women to join an antebellum church. Many considerations no doubt weighed into this decision; however, it is important to recognize that for men, but not for women, going to church was becoming more expensive.

Understanding the antebellum church's financial support is critical to understanding women's role in New England congregations. The financial structure originated at a time when everyone belonged to the town's one church, and all heads of household were legally required to pay a church tax. The head of household represented all members of the family and the tax was computed as a percentage of his or her real and personal property. Since husbands and wives were one unit, the husband's contribution stood for both. No matter how wealthy they were, women were not liable for the church tax unless they were unmarried or widowed; in other words, when they were heads of households. This customary formula continued to define the financial obligations of church membership even after disestablishment. In the Calvinist Church, heads of households were assessed an annual tax equivalent to six percent of the reduced value of their real and personal property; adult males also paid a poll tax of $1.50. One of the church's male members was assigned the unenviable role of tax collector and visited taxpayers to solicit payment.[48]

The financial structure of antebellum churches therefore acted as a conservative force, reinforcing the tradition of patriarchy. As vital as women were as parishioners, they were not expected to contribute much economically. Nor did they. Of the seventy-seven heads of households assessed for the Calvinist Church's first tax in 1827, only six, or less than eight percent, were women. Three of the six were extremely wealthy: Rebecca Waldo, Sarah Waldo, and Elizabeth Waldo, each a single woman, each holding property assessed at $35,500. The other three women taxpayers were poor or getting by: Duty Austin's personal property was estimated at $100, Sally Flagg's at $500, and Dorrance Wilder's at a more comfortable $750; none owned any real estate. Ten years later, of the 117 heads of households assessed, eight, or less than seven percent, were women. These eight included the three Waldo sisters and Elizabeth Salisbury; the unmarried Waldos were now worth $43,500 each, while the newly widowed Salisbury was in a league of her own at more than $120,000. Of the four remaining women, only Sarah "Widow Sally" Avery was a woman of substance, whose real and personal property totaled $7,800. The other three women taxpayers were destitute or financially modest: Welcome Washburn had no taxable property, the widow Betsey Gates owned $700 in real estate, and Sally Flagg had $900 in personal property.[49]

By 1845, the limited means of the church's non-elite taxpayers had been further eroded by the general economic decline of the late 1830s. Of the 124 heads of households assessed, eight, or less than seven percent, were women. Elizabeth Waldo, Sarah Waldo, and Elizabeth Salisbury were in better shape than ever, with the Waldos' estates valued at $61,100 and Salisbury's at $132,000. Sally Flagg, too, was prospering. In 1837, she held personal property worth $900 but by 1845 she was worth $2,400, most of it in bank stock. The other women were not as fortunate. "Widow Sally" Avery's estate was estimated at $4,000, a sharp decline from its value of $7,800 in 1837. In 1837, the property of Calvin Darby, a stonecutter and gravestone maker, was assessed at $3,350, but when his widow Lydia Darby appeared on the tax list in 1845, the estate's value had been reduced to less than half. Mary Eager, a schoolteacher, had $300 in the bank earning interest, while the widowed Mary Wheeler was more comfortable with $3,000 in personal property. The percentage of churchwomen who were also church taxpayers actually declined over time, from a high of eight per cent in 1827 to a low of under six per cent in the 1840s, as more women of average means became members.[50]

Tax data therefore reveal that the church rarely expected women to contribute financially, because only a handful were heads of households. Moreover, with the exception of the spectacularly wealthy Waldos and Salisbury, few of those who were heads of households had much to tax. The church's financial health therefore rested upon the shoulders of the men. At the same time, women benefitted most from the church's welfare policies. Charity for the needy was an integral part of the covenant, and while the Calvinist Church's charity was limited and unsystematic, it comforted those in want. The church doled out small amounts of cash, usually less than five dollars, distributed in-kind donations, such as cords of wood for heat during the winter, and boarded the sick and enfeebled in private homes. Almost all of those assisted were women. The church paid a nurse nine dollars to care for Betsy Tracy in 1833; delivered cords of wood to Mary Cogswell during the winter of 1838 and gave her fourteen dollars in cash in 1839; and subsidized a room for Sarah Harrington, a schoolteacher, during the winter of 1845–1846.[51]

The female face of the welfare recipients reflects in part the numerical dominance of women in the congregation—women composed approximately seventy percent of the church's membership in the antebellum period—as well as their generally less secure financial status. Since the poor were more likely to be female than male, and the church was composed of many more women than men, it is not surprising that the parish needy were mostly women. The economic roles of men and women within the church thus mimicked their secular roles: men were the breadwinners and women were the dependents.

There were, however, significant countervailing trends that undermined the influence of men's financial contributions. Chief among these was the constant problem of getting anyone to pay his or her taxes. It had never been easy to extract church taxes from an often cash-poor congregation, as many ministers woefully attested.[52] The separation of church and state not only freed individuals from the burden of supporting a church, it also failed to provide a mechanism to collect the now voluntary taxes or to ensure that subscribers met their assessed contributions. As a result, in the wake of disestablishment a complicated church bureaucracy sprang up to track down the wandering, argue with the errant, and try to get those who had pledged to support the church actually to do so.

Churches adopted various strategies to coerce their communicants to pay up. The Calvinist Church followed the example of the town and offered abatements to those who paid their taxes promptly: a six percent abatement for payment within thirty days; four percent within sixty days; two percent within 120 days. The abatements benefitted those with the heaviest tax burdens and inspired timely payment from those who could best afford it. To persuade the less affluent, the church tried to give the impression that the civil government stood behind the parish by paying an agent to collect the church tax at the same time he collected the town tax.[53]

Securing the funds to support the church was a constant battle that pit the mostly male taxpayers against the all-male church hierarchy. The magnitude of the problem is suggested by Daniel Waldo's 1838 estimate that of the hundreds who attended the worship services each Sunday, only one in six or seven was also a taxpayer. The problem was caused in part by the tactic of including among the ranks of taxpayers anyone who had ever signed the church's membership log, known as "the Book." Long lists of signatories of the Calvinist Church's Book indicate that promises made, perhaps during the intensity of a revival, were forgotten or ignored when religious zeal waned.[54]

The high rate of transiency also created a constant state of flux. Worcester's population more than doubled between 1840 and 1850, and tripled between 1840 and 1855. Moreover, the swirl of people moving in and out of the city was much greater than these absolute figures indicate, and by 1850 the turnover rate of Worcester residents was nearly twice what it had been in 1800.[55] The city's constantly shifting population made it necessary for churches periodically to comb through their books, identifying and purging the names of those who were included but should no longer be, and appending those who were not included but should now be. Among these were individuals who had not attended services recently but whose absences were unaccounted for, as well as those who were attending but had somehow managed to avoid signing the Book.

To the faithful, the failure to claim membership in the church and to pay a share of its expenses was intolerable. Unlike secular groups, which organized for social or political reasons, churches existed to save immortal souls. They were thus a peculiar kind of antebellum voluntary society, and the mantle of church membership could not, at least according to the churches, be worn lightly nor simply shrugged off when oppressive. To herd the wandering back into the fold and keep them there, churches turned to the Standing Committee. Composed of from three to five male church members, the Standing Committee existed originally for theological purposes but soon assumed the responsibility for business of a far more practical nature. The Calvinist Church created its Standing Committee in the 1830s and charged it with examining the religious credentials of prospective members. But before long, the Committee's primary function became to scrutinize the correctness not of church members but of church membership lists.[56]

Accurate lists were essential for religious and tax purposes, but keeping them up to date was increasingly complicated. Members who no longer wished to support the church were required to file a Certificate of Dismission, and extant certificates suggest a variety of reasons for resigning. Some came to prefer other churches. William Harrington, a merchant, left the Calvinist Church to join the Baptists in 1826 and transferred his financial support to them. Others left the church altogether, such as Joseph Boyden, a watchmaker, who resigned in 1843. Still others were removed by geographic mobility. During the depression of 1837, Luther Harris, a cordwainer, left Worcester and the Calvinist Church in search of better opportunities elsewhere. Widows seized

the freedoms offered by their new status as heads of household to dis-
avow responsibility for the church tax. Upon his death in 1837, Jeremiah
Harrington's widow, Betsey, executrix of his estate, declared that "said
Estate may no longer be taxed by said society & hereby withdraws from
any membership thereof." A disgruntled Lucy Prentiss Hastings, a widowed mother of seven, wrote in 1847, "you will please erase from your
list my name, as I decline paying a Parish tax this year. I should not have
withdrawn had my tax last year been a reasonable one."[57]

Hastings' complaint highlighted the recurring problem of collecting taxes from those who had once agreed to pay them. From 1822 to
1827, there were no taxes to collect due to the Waldo family's subsidy.
When the church became dependent upon the membership it immediately spiraled into the red, as operating expenses exceeded revenues by
nearly $500. From 1827 through 1830, between one-half and three-
quarters of the taxes went unpaid and by 1829 the deficit had reached
$1413. The situation was resolved eventually, though not happily, when
the tax collector, merchant William Chamberlain, went bankrupt in 1831
and lost not only his own business but $82 of the church's money as well.
Replacing Chamberlain were more economically secure, and apparently
more persuasive, collectors who brought in a greater percentage of the
monies due, although large amounts consistently went unpaid.[58]

Also undermining the Standing Committee's attempts to set the
church's business affairs in order was the high rate of mobility. A diligent search for absent members in 1850, for example, revealed that, un-
beknownst to the church, Catherine M. Parker had relocated to New
York, married, and joined the Methodists. The Committee was also cha-
grined to discover that Dolly Goddard's failure to attend services was a
natural result of her having "died some years since." Both women were
dropped from the membership list.[59]

Absentee members were not a minor annoyance but an impediment to the creation of a sense of community within the church. In
1841, the Calvinist Church decided to ascertain the magnitude of the
problem. An ad hoc committee counted 261 nominal communicants; of
these, seventy percent were women and thirty percent were men. But
only two-thirds of the members resided in Worcester; the remaining
one third were "nonresident members," that is, they had either moved
out of town or their current whereabouts were unknown. Wherever they
were, they were beyond the church's influence even while technically
under its "watch and ward." But what did church membership mean if it

was extended to those who, for whatever reason, were not subject to worship services, prayer meetings, and ministerial guidance? Nor attended the communal rites surrounding communion, baptisms, marriages, and funerals?[60]

In the late 1840s the Standing Committee determined that "about 50 individuals" currently considered members "ought not to be reckoned so." Displaying a touching faith in the power of its Committee, the church ordered it to "use its influence" to convince nonresident members to transfer to a more convenable church, and "To report the names of all resident members of the Church who absent themselves from communion with it, also to report what church, if any, such residents commune with."[61] Whether absent members had migrated out of town or were lurking about Worcester backsliding, the church believed all would eventually be accounted for and neatly swept into one of the city's many churches. But such a goal proved beyond the power of the Committee. After nine months' effort, only four of the fifty unresolved cases were closed: one communicant was confirmed dead, one had relocated, one was discovered communing with the Unitarians, and one was cast out due to chronic religious apathy. Frustrated by its inability to regulate the membership on a one-to-one basis, the Calvinist Church finally conceded the task was hopeless and voted to solve the problem of nonresident members by fiat. Henceforth, anyone absent from communion for a period of ten years would be automatically stripped of membership.[62]

Just as disruptive to a religious community as the nonresident members were the nonmember residents. Those who signed the Book but neglected to attend services aroused the church's curiosity and concern. But those who attended services yet failed to sign aroused its frustration and resentment. Such people received the benefits of Christian fellowship and worship but did not commit themselves to the church's financial well-being. In 1835, the church made its position explicit. Six months—a year at the most—would be the measure of its patience for those afflicted with the "pernicious habit" of grafting off the spiritual generosity of others. "It is not the duty of the Church," the Calvinists stated sourly, "to permit [such] persons to commune [with us]." Signing the Book and paying taxes were among the prerequisites for communing with any church, they insisted, and "we regard no one as a member of the Parish who refuses to join, by entering his name on our Parish Books and meeting its responsibilities."[63]

Russell Fay, a carpenter, discovered that the church meant business when he answered the door one day and found the tax collector. Fay hastily requested that his name be struck from the Book. Although records indicate that Fay had joined the church seven years earlier during a revival, he insisted that ". . . I never signed the book . . . I do not consider myself as a member."[64] The truly artful might maintain their tax-free status even while enjoying services by periodically migrating from one church to another. By the late 1830s, there were six Protestant churches in Worcester: three Congregational, plus a Unitarian, a Methodist, and a Baptist. By 1860, there were more than a dozen of various denominations. Individuals wishing to attend services or to mingle with those who did, but unwilling to commit their souls to a particular theology and their wallets to an annual tax, could deftly play the ends against the center by claiming membership in one of the churches they were not currently attending. If some individuals felt social pressure to attend services, there apparently were ways to achieve the desired effect without incurring spiritual or financial obligations.[65]

Taxpaying was therefore a source both of financial support and of friction within the churches. Male heads of households were the primary source of church tax money, which validated the tradition of male church authority. Yet separating taxpayers from their money was seldom easy. Despite the Waldo family's endowment, the Calvinist Church faced recurrent financial crises due to the necessity of relying upon an often unstable pool of male taxpayers. The tax collectors, tithingmen, and Standing Committee worked tirelessly but often unsuccessfully to locate and cajole members into making good their pledges. Thus, while men's role as breadwinner supported traditional male influence in the church, the aggravating slowness with which taxes were paid, and the numerous attempts to shirk responsibility, undermined the moral authority of men even while throwing into greater relief the moral fidelity of women.

Women, moreover, supported the institutional church in other ways, particularly through pew rental. Pews were a traditional badge of status in New England. Wealthy families coveted the most desirable pews and decorated them with pillows and rugs in a manner befitting their social rank. Pews were a form of real estate, sold at auction to the highest bidder, and were carefully recorded in the Town Registry of Pews. It was not necessary for a pew owner to be a member of the church that housed the pew; Samuel Jennison, a lawyer, owned pews in both the First (Congregational) Church and the Second (Unitarian) Church, although he attended services only at the latter. Pews were not cheap and, depending upon their location, might sell for hundreds of dollars. Churches therefore permitted staggered payments of half the money down, with the balance due in three annual installments. Owners who defaulted could expect to have their pews repossessed. As real rather than personal property, pews were bought, sold, and swapped; were offered as collateral for loans; and were included as part of a woman's dower rights so that pew sales required her signature. Because pews also conveyed symbolic value, enlarging the meetinghouse necessitated delicate negotiations so that the status of the old pew was reflected in the placement of the new.[66]

Through most of the nineteenth century, attending church services therefore meant paying the price of a seat in a pew. The Calvinist Church reserved a few pews, those in the least desirable locations, for the use of the parish poor and the town's African Americans. For parishioners unwilling to sit among those whom they considered their social inferiors, but unable to afford a pew, the alternative was to rent one. Women made up more than two-thirds of the congregation but owned less than one-tenth of the pews. However, if buying and selling pews was mostly men's business, using them was women's. The desire of many antebellum women to attend church, when combined with their usually limited means, thus yielded a market for pew rentals, and it was with female tenants in mind that some individuals invested in multiple pews.[67]

Since pews were expensive, and were auctioned off but a few at a time, the antebellum market in pew rentals was brisk and was an important source of revenue for the Calvinist Church. In the late 1820s and early 1830s, income from pew rentals equaled the income from church taxes. As late as the 1850s, attorney Alfred D. Foster willed his pew to Worcester's Union Church to be used as rental property.[68] Churchwomen also contributed to the church in other ways. Women's groups, such as sewing circles, both donated their labor and organized fundraising drives. Such contributions were not recorded as income in the account books, but church records indicate that contemporaries were well aware of the money that the women saved the congregation.[69]

The relationship between the financial support of antebellum Protestant churches and women's role was therefore complex. On the one hand, women did not contribute to the same extent that men did, both as a result of traditional notions of gender relations embodied in the practice of grouping families under the (usually male) head of household, as well as the more prosaic problem of women's economic disadvantage vis-à-vis men. On the other hand, men's influence was undermined by the myriad difficulties the church faced in trying to collect the taxes. Furthermore, women's dedication to religion and their desire to attend services generated a market for pews to rent out to the large number of women who could not afford to own one. Thus, while the mostly male taxpayers fostered frustration, the mostly female pew tenants and sewing circles generated revenues.

MARKING THE STANDARD OF CHRISTIAN BEHAVIOR

The primary reason for Christians to gather into a church was to promote "love, watchfulness, and purity" and to guard against the ever-present threat of "ungodliness and worldly lusts."[70] The way to do this was through firm but loving Christian discipline. Accordingly, the records of the Calvinist Church reflect a pervasive awareness of and concern for the behavior of its parishioners. But who was disciplined, what they were disciplined for, and whether they were disciplined at all varied by gender and over time.

The difficulty in keeping track of its communicants led the leaders of the Calvinist Church to hold occasional summit meetings with other churches in the hope of rooting out the spiritual freeloaders. At issue in the conclaves was not just money but fear of dissent in an increasingly heterogeneous society. Soon a more militant tone crept into the suspicion of outsiders. In the 1840s, the church began requiring of all new members a Certificate of Dismissal and Recommendation, the letter of transfer issued by the church one was leaving and addressed to the church one was joining, and printed up batches of blank certificates to supply its own members with the proper religious credentials. Apparently some individuals appearing on the church's doorstep with a Certificate in hand had indulged in a spot of spiritual fraud, for the church also instructed the Parish Clerk to verify that all Certificates were authentic.[71]

Such bureaucratization of church membership reflects the passing of other, more personal methods of discipline. Transgressions of the church's moral code tended to be sins of commission rather than sins of omission; that is, the machinery for discipline engaged when individuals acted wrongly, not when they failed to act rightly. The distinction was a morally conservative one and reveals the church's essentially static approach to social control, which operated through accusation, confession, and redemption. It was also a thoroughly gendered conception of moral crime and punishment. Men were more likely than women to breach the code of acceptable behavior; men were also judged guilty of a wider variety of offenses than women. Similarly, the types of sins committed were usually gender-specific. In part, this was a result of men's greater freedom in antebellum America: men had more opportunities to do wrong. But it was also a result of a moral code that women found easier to live by than men, and implicitly testifies to their role as the moral arbiters of an orthodox community.

When the Calvinist Church was founded, its members swore to uphold the covenantal obligation to "walk with you in all brotherly watch-fulness and kindness, hoping that you and we shall become more and more conformed to the example of our divine master, till we, at last, come to the perfection of holiness. . . ."[72] Such "watch and ward" was exercised in two ways. On occasion, one communicant would openly confront another. All the known instances of such direct accusation involved men accusing other men. Francis F. Woods, an ornamental painter who joined the Calvinist Church when he moved to town in 1831, took seriously his religious duties. He helped to organize and recruit members for the Sunday School and served on several church committees. Woods also took seriously his obligation to keep an eye on his neighbors. He informed the congregation when William H. Oaks left town without first arranging for a dismissal and recommendation, and reported Erastus B. Rice for defecting to the Methodists. Woods's zeal for surveillance apparently aroused interest in his own affairs, for he was himself called on the carpet for unspecified charges and ultimately excommunicated in 1847.[73]

The more familiar method of accusation was known as "common fame," which was essentially the institutionalization of rumor, of gossip, of knowledge that was commonly known.[74] The great majority of those disciplined by the church were brought up on common fame charges. Common fame had the virtue of distancing the accuser from the accused, and thus offered a way for churchwomen to exert institutional power. Intemperance, a charge used mostly to discipline men, usually originated as a common fame accusation. The women of the church, who composed nearly three-fourths of the full members, were rarely accused of intemperance. In 1841, common fame charges were leveled against Sarah Matthews, who admitted having indulged in "strong drink" in the past but insisted she had quit the year before. Perhaps fearing that her reputation undermined her credibility, Matthews brought in an expert witness, her physician, to corroborate her testimony.[75]

Those accused of violating the church's moral code were examined by a committee of two or three of the brethren, who were empowered to dismiss the matter, to investigate further, or to pronounce the accused guilty as charged. If the last, the condemned was required to confess and to repent, the confession was read to the church, and the congregation indicated its acceptance of the confession by standing, as if to welcome the sinner back into the fold. If, however, the guilty party refused to confess or to repent, he or she was given the opportunity to reconsider the wisdom of defying the church while enduring suspension from communion for a specified period of time. Continued intransigence could lead to banishment from the church, also known as excommunication.

The machinery of discipline ground slowly, and it was not unusual for an entire year to elapse between the initial accusation and the resolution of a case. In 1825, Benjamin Goddard, a machinist, was suspected of "the intemperate use of ardent spirit" and was summoned before the committee to explain himself. Unlike Sarah Matthews, Goddard was unable to raise doubts about the charges. The committee found "the complaint is supported" and suspended Goddard for one year. Eight months into the suspension, Goddard confessed and repented, and was accepted back into the community three months later. Two years after David and Julia Cutter moved to town and joined the Calvinist Church, whispers of common fame suspected David Cutter of intemperance. By the following spring the congregation was sure of it. Suspended "till he gives evidence of penitance & amendment," Cutter was excommunicated a year later for "continued intemperance & for forsaking his family." Julia Cutter, meanwhile, remained a full church member until she moved out of town in 1850. Accusation was not synonymous with conviction, however. David Dakin, a farmer, was acquitted of haying on the Sabbath; similarly, the "reports in circulation" that accused Benjamin Conant, a mason, of unnamed transgressions were determined to be groundless.[76]

No one escaped the watchful eyes of the overwhelmingly female congregation. William McFarland was a wealthy farmer, a founding member of the church, and the president of its board of trustees. But in 1829 a "special meeting" convened to consider common fame charges lodged against him. The nature of the complaint was circumspectly omitted, but it was sufficiently serious to warrant formal censure. When a three-month suspension failed to induce McFarland to confess, the church dispatched a committee "to labour with him and endeavor to reclaim him." A defiant McFarland still failed "to give satisfaction" and was again suspended. The church was evidently reluctant to excommunicate McFarland, perhaps in recognition of his past service, or possibly because it considered him yet salvageable. McFarland was left in a state of permanent suspension. A full ten years later, as McFarland lay dying and in fear for his immortal soul, the news of his "agitated mind" reached the church, likely through the agency of his wife, Anna Davis McFarland, who was still a full church member. The outcast was reportedly convinced he was bound for hell and was "in danger of sinking into confirmed melancholy or complete despair." McFarland "penitently asked their forgiveness," and the church agreed, "provided he continues in the same temper of mind." Two weeks later, the congregation "with unfeigned pleasure" voted unanimously "to cordially and formally extend to him forgiveness and receive him back to their communion and fellowship," and McFarland died in peace.[77]

Church discipline sought not only to protect the individual from incurring the spiritual consequences of sinful behavior, but also to shield the institution of the church from the temporal folly of its members. There were a number of ways an individual could cast aspersions upon the church's good name. In 1821 Moses Child's untoward slander of Charles Goodrich provided ammunition for the new church's critics. Disciplined for his zeal, Child apologized for "the reproach [my actions] have brought upon religion, and the injury it has occationed [*sic*] to you." Men ran afoul in other ways. The church did not usually intrude upon the business activities of its parishioners, with the exception of its decision in 1833 to "abstain entirely from the use of ardent spirits . . . and also from traffic in them." However, the business activities of parishioners occasionally invaded the church, primarily in the form of bad debts. In 1835, beset by creditors, Otis Chapin scandalized the congregation by sneaking out of town and refusing to disclose his whereabouts. The church censured Chapin for his "unchristian conduct . . . and for borrowing money, neglecting to pay his just debts and *secretly* leaving town and retiring to some place unknown. . . ." The exploits of William D. Fenno were even more outrageous. Fenno was a jeweler whose advertisements prophetically described his business as "nearly opposite the Bank." Fenno owned pew number thirty-six in the Calvinist Church, which his mother used for worship and he used for more secular purposes. Fenno offered the pew as collateral for so many loans that eventually its mortgages grossly exceeded its value. In 1841, Fenno defaulted on the loans and skipped town. The Calvinist Church was faced with the undignified spectacle of the sheriff of Worcester County repossessing one of its pews, and was dragged into the dispute when Fenno's creditors issued warrants to slap liens against the pew.[78]

Taking to the road was a favorite means by which men not only eluded their creditors but avoided the wrath of the congregation as well. The church's repeated attempts to censure William H. Oaks proved fruitless when he left town without notice and without leaving a forwarding address. Communicants also dropped out of sight with less nefarious intent, as when they neglected to obtain a dismissal and recommendation. Charles B. Townsends, who joined the church in 1831, wrote from Boston in 1840 to request a belated dismission when he wished to join a new church. Before acceding to his request, the Calvinist Church required that Townsends account for his "walk and conversation" during the intervening years. Others were religious dissenters. William Howard was excommunicated for renouncing the Christian faith; Theophilus Brown and John Taylor were thrown out for refusing to attend services; Albert Howe was banished for attending the wrong services—he preferred the Unitarians.[79]

If churchmen practiced a variety of sins, churchwomen excelled at two: fornication and separation. Fornication, or nonmarital sexual intercourse, was by definition a female crime against morality. Only one man was accused of fornication. In 1833, Horatio L. Carter and Julia A. Lyon were suspended from membership, but were restored to communion when they confessed and married the following September.[80] For women for whom there was no reputation-saving marriage, the accusation was potentially ruinous. In 1832, "charges publicly circulated" that Nancy Barber, a thirty-eight-year-old single woman who had undergone a conversion experience four years earlier, had committed fornication. Although condemned by "unquestionable proof"—pregnancy?—as well as "by her own confession," Barber refused to agree that she ought to be ashamed of herself. There was to be no grace period for this "erring professor;" Barber was "immediately excommunicated" from "the ch[urc]h of Christ which she has so wickedly dishonored." On a somewhat gentler note, the church promised to "again receive this excommunicated member" if Barber would only admit her sin and repent. (She did not.)[81]

Women's second major transgression, religious separation, was an outgrowth of their oft-noted religious devotion. The congregation's willingness to countenance the loss of some of its members to other churches did not include tolerating beliefs it considered beyond the theological pale. In March 1844, two years after joining by confession, twenty-two-year-old Sarah Marie Moore declared that she no longer shared the beliefs of the Calvinist Church and wished to be dismissed to another, unspecified denomination. The church was unconvinced of the sincerity of Moore's change of heart and postponed a decision until its committee could attempt to reclaim her. When Moore persisted in her new beliefs she was excommunicated. That same month Harriet Fales Hutchinson asked to be dismissed and recommended to the Unitarians. The orthodox trinitarians of the Calvinist Church flatly refused, stating it would be "inconsistent with our rules or our sense of duty" to sanction the desire to embrace what was to them a heretical church. Still Fales persisted and, like Moore, was excommunicated. Nor were individuals free simply to leave the church. In 1842, twenty-two-year-old Fidelia Perry Peckham, who had joined by confession at the age of sixteen, asked to be dismissed because "her views on the doctrines of the Gospel had changed." She stopped attending services but did not request a recommendation to another church; in effect, Peckham had declared her religious independence. The Calvinist Church would not accept this decision, and dispatched its committee to "visit and labor to reclaim her." One can only imagine Peckham's reaction when the earnest brethren kept turning up on her doorstep hoping to persuade her of the error of her secular ways. For two full years the church puzzled over the case before ultimately banishing Peckham. As it had with Nancy Barber, the congregation propped the door open for Peckham's return should she give "satisfactory evidence of repentance & sincere piety." (She did not, either).[82]

Excommunication was strictly a religious punishment with no direct consequences in the secular world. However, those who flouted the church's moral code occasionally did find it interfering with their plans. This was especially true for women, whose youthful sins acquired new meaning when they became wives and mothers. Like Nancy Barber, Mary Stearns was accused of fornication, refused to repent, and was suspended from communion. But since the church would not banish a sinner without giving her the opportunity to make amends, Stearns avoided Barber's fate, excommunication, by leaving town. Eight years later, Mary Stearns was Mary Holder, married and more settled in life, and wished to join a church in her new town. To obtain a dismissal and recommendation from the Calvinist Church, Holder had to resolve her uncertain status, left pending when she decamped years before. Holder made her confession by mail and was duly dismissed. Similarly, at some point Melinda Goodale Clark had been suspended from the church, an act whose consequences she ignored at the time. When she later sought to transfer to a church in New Braintree, the Worcester church pointed to her outstanding suspension. Clark dutifully confessed her sin by letter and was dismissed and recommended within a few months.[83]

Sinners who could not be redeemed in person or by post risked excommunication, a drastic and final solution that the church employed sparingly. The stakes were high: for the faithful, banishment meant spiritual death. But if excommunication was generally rare, it was far more common for men than for women: men composed fourteen, or nearly two-thirds, of the twenty-two excommunications in the antebellum church. The number of men excommunicated is still more striking in light of the comparatively small number of male communicants. Although churchwomen outnumbered churchmen by at least two to one, men were twice as likely as women to be banished from the church. Thus, while women composed the majority of the church, men composed the majority of the disciplined.[84] The disproportionately male face of those drummed out of the church further emphasizes women's institutional leadership. Although they were not permitted in the pulpit or on the Standing Committees, churchwomen utilized common fame accusations to exercise institutional power and to set and maintain the standard of Christian behavior.

The practice of church discipline in the orthodox congregational Calvinist Church reveals that while the congregation assumed that women were more pious than men, and held female communicants to a higher standard of sexual purity, it was willing to reinstate those who confessed and repented their transgressions. The goal of discipline was not simple punishment but conformity to the female-dominated group. Sinful lapses had to be confronted and admitted but would not dog one's steps forever, as Mary Stearns Holder and Melinda Goodale Clarke eventually discovered. The church did not expect communicants to always behave well. But it did demand that they acknowledge the mostly female congregation's authority to pass judgment. In a church in which women were a decided majority, and in which most accusations arose informally as common fame charges, women were instrumental in establishing and maintaining the standard of Christian behavior.[85]

BUT CAN SHE VOTE?

One final area of organization offers further evidence of the often convoluted nature of women's power in the antebellum churches. As we have seen, churchwomen had no official part in the selection of ministers. The charter of the new Calvinist Church explicitly reserved the right to "elect ordain and settle" a minister to the brethren, three-fourths of whom had to agree upon a candidate. There was, however, an exception to the rule of men: the charter specifically granted to the Waldo women the right to nullify ministerial elections. The Waldos do not seem to have exercised their unique veto power, although it might not have been necessary for them to do so. Daniel Waldo sat on all ministerial search committees and presumably would have gained his sisters' prior approval of candidates.[86]

But the Waldos were not the only women of the church to have a voice in the selection of the minister. Despite the charter's limiting clause, women voted in every ministerial election in the antebellum Calvinist Church. The church's first election in 1823 set the precedent when the women joined the men in standing to show their unanimous support for the Reverend Loammi Ives Hoadley. The women's endorsement was thereafter sought for all new ministers. The extension of the vote to the women of the church provoked no recorded comment or criticism; nor do church records indicate when the decision was made, or by whom. While such an act did not violate church laws or covenants, it was a decided break with tradition. Moreover, while some of the brethren occasionally voted against confirmation, the sisters invariably voted unanimously to confirm the choice of the male search committee.[87]

The meager evidence of women's voting suggests at least two contrary interpretations. On the one hand, the extension of the vote to the women of the church, as well as their tendency to vote as a bloc, may indicate that women wielded real power in the decisions of a church in which they were a decided majority. Only men sat on the search committees and only men negotiated the terms of settlement. But the women of the church had numerous opportunities to air their criticisms and to express their preferences during the lengthy search process, which required candidates to meet with the parish and to audition for the pulpit by delivering sermons, often over a period of several months. The women's unanimous support for the successful candidates may reflect extensive lobbying that eliminated unacceptable applicants prior to the final vote. On the other hand, it is possible that the churchwomen's sanction of ministers was purely perfunctory, essentially a hollow affirmation of a choice that had already been made by the brethren.

Still, at a time when American politicians were extending the suffrage to most white men, but expressly not to women, it is significant that churchwomen voted at all and that they did so alongside the men. Moreover, the women's vote was considered sufficiently formal for the tally to merit inclusion in the church records. The participation of women in the antebellum Calvinist Church's ministerial elections likely was a result of its origin in dissent. The belief that a religious community existed only with the declared consent of each member, male *and* female, had been the purpose in forming the Calvinist Church. In their petitions protesting the actions of the First Church, the Waldos and Salisbury defended their rejection of Charles Goodrich by stating that, since they had not consented to his election, they were not bound by his authority. The church these women founded sought to avoid the same mistake and thus required all church members to participate formally in the choice of a minister. At the very least, the congregation acknowledged that women had the right to help decide the future of the church, and demonstrated confidence in women's ability to vote wisely. In the wake of the Second Great Awakening and the disestablishment of religion in Massachusetts, orthodox Congregational churches could thus be more democratic in practice than they appeared in principle.[88]

Whereas Worcester's churches were a focal point of community life in the late teens and early twenties, capable of generating passion sufficient to launch stones through Elizabeth Salisbury's windows, by the 1830s such was no longer the case. Indeed, religious animosity and religious fervor waned simultaneously. In 1827, the First Church and the Calvinist Church reestablished friendly relations; in the 1840s, they jointly founded a third orthodox Congregational church, the Union Church. At the same time, diversity increasingly characterized Worcester's religious community. The Methodists organized in 1834, the Universalists in 1841, and the Episcopalians in the mid-1840s. The town's African Americans founded an African Methodist Episcopal Zion church in the late 1830s, although some continued to worship with the older churches. The Protestant monopoly broke when the Irish arrived in the 1830s, and the first Catholic church was erected in the early 1840s. In 1852, religious liberals organized the city's first free church, which became a bastion of progressive politics when it hired as its pastor the abolitionist Thomas Wentworth Higginson. By the 1850s, orthodox Congregationalists organized a downtown mission to minister to the poor and the intemperate. The churches themselves became umbrella organizations that included an expanding number of voluntary societies, some mostly social, others explicitly political. Women figured prominently in these voluntary associations, such as sewing circles, that both shaped and were shaped by religious women's moral code.

In the early nineteenth century, New England's Protestant churches were important centers of community life in which women were the majority and men the minority. The question was no longer when, or if, one experienced conversion but within what church and on whose terms. The much-noted feminization of American Protestantism did not result from women's numerical dominance, for they had long been the majority of church congregations. Nor can it be inferred from the more sentimental religious expression of the Second Great Awakening, for both sexes were drawn to the New Measures. Rather, religion was feminized when disestablishment confronted pious women with the unprecedented freedom and necessity to choose. It was this new opportunity to express themselves that gave force and meaning to women's numerical majority.

The schism in Worcester's First Church illustrates how the ability of a few wealthy women to contest the election of a minister served as an opening wedge in cracking men's control of church affairs. The travail of the beleaguered Charles Goodrich demonstrates that, in an era of theological controversy and new religious options, male church authorities had to earn the respect of the women of the church, they could not assume it. A preacher who failed to grasp this lesson could find his ministry—and potentially his masculinity—assailed as "pretty" and unimpressive. The founding of the Calvinist Church also suggests that pious women did not shy from challenging male authorities when confronted with what they perceived to be a threat to orthodoxy. Dissenting women drew upon their acknowledged spiritual equality to criticize, even to disparage, the governance of a minister whom they did not respect. Their actions strengthen the argument for the feminization and democratization of orthodox New England Protestantism, not just in terms of theology and numbers of converts but also in practice.

2

Missionaries and More

Women, Sewing, and the Antebellum Sewing Circle

> It is in the churches and chapels of the town that the ladies
> are to be seen in full costume; and I am tempted to believe
> that a stranger from the continent of Europe would be
> inclined, on first reconnoitering the city, to suppose that the
> places of worship were the theatres and cafes of the place.
> —Frances Trollope, 1832

"'The 'Sewing Circle' has just departed, leaving nothing behind but confusion and disorder," Caroline Barrett of Worcester wrote wearily in her diary in March 1850. Despite the disarray of her home, the twenty-one-year-old schoolteacher, newly arrived in the city, was pleased with the gathering. She noted reflectively, "I have formed some new and pleasant acquaintances. . . ." But the sewing circle whose untidiness Barrett lamented was not only an avenue for friendship; it would also introduce her to new ideas and experiences. The histories of several of the sewing circles of antebellum Worcester reveal that the circle functioned for women as the political party functioned for men: it was a vehicle for expressing interests and concerns that embodied community, gender, and class loyalties.[1]

Historians have recognized the importance of sewing circles in antebellum women's lives, as well as their financial support of numerous social causes. Antislavery sewing circles and their fundraising fairs have attracted particular scholarly attention. By the mid-nineteenth century, organizations such as the Boston Female Anti-Slavery Society stood at the apex of a pyramid of local antislavery sewing circles, whose members were educated in the goals and principles of the national campaign. Yet by the late 1850s, BFASS and the Boston Antislavery Fair fell under male control, while antislavery feminists developed an autonomous women's rights movement.[2]

Sewing circles that were *not* dedicated to antislavery, however, were far more numerous and were similarly complex historical creations. Yet historians almost always characterize the benevolent sewing circles as traditional and ameliorist, as charitable organizations set apart from politics and rooted in a separate "woman's sphere." A study of women's organizations in antebellum Boston found that while the groups raised "sizable sums" for their churches, they were limited, ad hoc, and dependent upon ministerial leadership. The Channing Circle of the United Federal Street Church, for example, "rarely made its own unassisted decisions." Mary P. Ryan's study of Utica, New York, argues that the sewing circles were part of a welfare network that helped to create and sustain the working class, yet the members "were only half aware of the social and economic implications of their altruism." Nancy Hewitt's analysis of Rochester, New York, finds three competing networks of social activism—benevolent, evangelical, and radical—and argues that only the radicals embraced controversial social issues. The others "did not, in fact seek social change at all, but continuity." In the 1850s the women's organizations were also subordinated to men's organizations. Finally, a recent overview asserts that, as the wives of local mercantile elites, benevolent women "were not at all inclined to rock the boat." Scholarly interpretations thus tend to separate women's activism into the radical few, those interested in political reforms such as antislavery and feminism, and the conservative many, whose local and ameliorist benevolence was a male-controlled expression of class loyalties.[3]

And yet the ubiquitous sewing circles themselves—and *not* the fairs they sponsored or the causes they supported—are rarely the subject of scholarly scrutiny. But it was precisely the internal dynamics of the community sewing circles that encouraged an interest in local and national reforms. Analysis of women's individual and group sewing in antebellum Worcester finds that by the late 1820s this most traditional female labor had been both politicized and institutionalized, with significant implications for women's political development.

Essential to the maintenance of a family's health and imbued with cultural notions of respectability, sewing was time consuming, demanded great skill, and involved women from every social class. Not all women married and not all women had children. But virtually all women, young or old, rich or poor, free or enslaved, sewed. Indeed, for most of American history, the ability to sew was a benchmark of womanhood. Thus the antebellum redefinition of sewing signified the redefinition of womanhood. In the colonial era, women gathered to work in informal settings known as sewing bees; in the revolutionary era, they sewed for the patriot cause. In the early nineteenth century, however, a new institution appeared: the organized, constitutional, for-profit sewing circle. Its emergence reveals a fundamental transformation in women's perception of their social place. Through the sewing circle women laid claim to the right to participate in the political and social development of the community, the nation, and the world.[4]

Analysis of six of the sewing circles of antebellum Worcester reveals how this quintessentially feminine labor assumed political and social significance. During the crisis in the First Church from 1815 to 1820, the members of the Female Reading and Charitable Society and the Praying Society, rival sewing circles, wielded their needles in defense of their chosen minister. In 1824, as partisan fervor waned, churchwomen founded a new sewing circle, the Worcester Female Association, to act as a conduit for donations to foreign missions. Three years later, the Worcester Female Samaritan Society, an organization that was gender-, age- and class-conscious, invited the women of the town to work together for the greater social welfare. In 1839, apparently chafing under the leadership of their elders, the "young ladies" of the Calvinist Church founded the Centre Missionary Sewing Circle. Its unusually comprehensive records permit an in-depth analysis of the group's social and intellectual development as it moved away from a narrow focus on missionaries toward a broad interest in society, and added production for profit to production in kind. Also organized that same year was the Worcester Anti-Slavery Sewing Circle, a society that was not only profit-oriented but explicitly political, and whose membership figured prominently in the national women's rights conventions held in Worcester in 1850 and 1851. When the Civil War began, the many sewing circles of the city and county united under the banner of the Worcester Soldiers' Relief Society to support the Union war effort.

The story of the sewing circles of antebellum Worcester does not find that women's groups necessarily followed a linear evolution from an interest in the parochial to a concern for the universal, although this was the case for some. But neither did they represent distinct nor competing networks with fixed class and social interests. Rather, the sewing circles were overlapping and occasionally cooperative efforts; indeed, a woman might belong to several at once. By the 1850s the women's groups were supporting municipal reforms, such as the Children's Friend Society, and even the most conservative among them played a role in the city's emerging antislavery consensus. Employing the metaphor of the circle, which symbolically linked each woman to every other to create the one from the many, the women of Worcester participated in social and political activism within an association that both honored women's work and enjoyed the sanction of custom.

THE QUINTESSENTIAL FEMININE LABOR

Through most of American history sewing was central to the female life. Learning to sew was an integral part of the training for womanhood and entailed painstaking hours of practice under the guidance of a mother, a relative, or a teacher. At the age of six or seven, girls began to make "samplers" of the various stitches and techniques demanded of a competent seamstress. As their skills progressed, they turned to making miniature versions of adult clothing for their dolls. In 1829, seven-year-old Louisa Jane Trumbull of Worcester noted in her journal with satisfaction, "I have made my doll a pretty pelisse with points before and behind." Mastering the art of sewing was a rite of passage, a sign that a girl was mastering the skills of womanhood. Sarah Bigelow of Worcester was only six years old when her father wrote to her mother, "Your little darling Sarah is a good girl, and almost a little woman. I am glad she thinks of me so much, and that she employs so much of her time to make me a shirt." Sarah's father promised the child a new dress if she completed the project. Even as adults, women continued to refine their talents and learn new techniques, turning to one another as well as to traveling teachers, such as Mrs. Windsor, who came to town for three weeks in 1826 to teach the "Ladies of Worcester" how to work lace.[5]

Keeping the family neat, clean, and presentable was a woman's job, a practical necessity imbued with social meaning. Sunday schools offered sewing lessons because it was a useful skill and because neatness was a badge of virtue. Louisa Jane Trumbull also associated sewing with good character when she reflected that her big sister ". . . is quite a nice girl though rather lazy I must confess about sewing." In 1851, a Worcester paper intoned solemnly, "when one sees a family of children going to school in clean and well mended clothing, it tells a great deal in favor of their mother; one might vouch that those children learn some valuable lessons at home . . . ." By these terms, social respectability depended not on wealth but on a woman's labor. In 1847, Abby Kelley Foster, an abolitionist and a feminist, wrote to her husband of her plans to return to their Worcester farm. She sought to dissuade him from cleaning the house, writing "I would suspect whether you had not better wait till I come." Foster hoped to arrange for the assistance of a cousin, Avilda Ballou, "a very capable business girl," in setting the household in order. Topping the list of things to do was sewing: "Sewing, fitting up furniture, cleaning house, cooking, in fine every thing. . . . Avilda and I can make [our home] *decent* and perhaps *comfortable*." For Abby Kelley Foster, as for other Americans, making a home respectable and homelike was a woman's job, and sewing was chief among its requirements.[6]

Women of all economic and social classes were expected to manufacture garments and to mend the inevitable rents and tears. Nancy Avery White was the daughter of a minister and the wife of a farmer in rural Westboro, Worcester county. Throughout her long life (she died in 1863 at age 79), White kept a diary of her activities, which revolved around cooking, cleaning, going to church, and constant sewing. In April 1808, White noted, "Friday 20. Mended some and clean'd house a little. Saturday 21. Bak'd in the forenoon & mended in the afternoon. Sunday 22. Went to the meeting in the afternoon. Mr. Huntington preach'd. Monday 23. Scour'd pewter—finished a couple of gowns." Sewing was both a chore and a pleasure, a task easily put down and picked up again while she coped with the rigors of farm and family life. One day found White dropping her work to extract the brindle cow from the cellar of the ice house where it had fallen on a rainy afternoon; on another she sewed while keeping an anxious eye on her baby, who was "very unwell." Similarly, Eliza Earle Chase of Salem wrote to her family in Worcester that she had nursed her son through "a very severe attack of croup." For five long days she "did not leave him, day or night." When little Eddie began to recover, a relieved Chase "went to the sewing circle for an hour and a half. . . ."[7]

Sewing also was a preoccupation of women in highly privileged circumstances. In the eighteenth century, decorative or "fancy" sewing, such as embroidery, became the hallmark of a true lady. But plain sewing continued to consume the time and energies of many wealthy women, at times to the exclusion of other interests. Although Elizabeth Tuckerman Salisbury was a wealthy woman married to an even wealthier merchant—

at his death in 1829, her husband's estate was worth more than $300,000—she made much of the wardrobe of her only surviving child, Stephen Jr. While at Harvard, young Stephen frequently wrote home asking for special foods, more money, and more clothes. Salisbury responded to the last by thriftily making over one of her husband's silk waistcoats to fit her son, warning him that his "old loose gown will do, till I have time to make the new one." When Stephen burst his pantaloons while exercising, he sent them home for his fond mother to repair (along with his soiled laundry). There were limits, however, to Salisbury's maternal devotion, and when her son failed to appreciate her labor she was quick to correct him. When two pairs of made-over pantaloons were greeted with the comment that he would soon outgrow them, Salisbury replied, "I was disappointed that my present to you last week, of 2 pr Nankin pantaloons, were not rec'd with gratitude—more especially as they were made of an article which was not new, & intended merely for the present season—I hope you will acknowledge to me that you have found them very comfortable—." Further in the letter she softened, writing "Supposing as the weather has been very warm, that you have worn your Gown, a good deal, and of course that it is dirty, I have made you another . . . ," which prompted her son to issue a graceful apology. Nor was Salisbury willing to work when she thought it unnecessary. To her son's repeated pleas for privacy curtains for his ground-floor dormitory room, Salisbury replied that he had no need for them as long as he remained "in the path of duty."[8]

Rebekah Scott Dean was the daughter of a well-to-do family from Charlestown, New Hampshire, who married a grown Stephen Salisbury and became Elizabeth Salisbury's daughter-in-law. Despite her husband's immense wealth—Stephen Salisbury II inherited the bulk of his father's estate—Rebekah Dean Salisbury described to her sister Catherine Dean Flint her plans to make his New Year present. But for Rebekah Salisbury, as for her mother-in-law, sewing was more than a hobby. It was a duty that took precedence over other activities, including her correspondence with her cherished older sister. As Salisbury wrote to Flint in 1841, "I believe I will not fill my letters with apologies for not having written you for so long a time, my dear Sister 'tho I think I am naughty. I have had a sewing fit come over me & have lived myself each day so that I have not felt like writing." Lydia Stiles Foster, a neighbor, knew whereof Salisbury wrote. The wife of a wealthy lawyer and politician, Foster enjoyed the assistance of servants in running her home. But it was her responsibility to sew for the family. In 1838 Foster explained to her sister, Mary Stiles Newcomb, "I do not feel at all in the mood of letter writing this morning, as I have been obliged to sew a good deal of late, and, as usual, my eyes suffer for it." Even among the wealthier antebellum women, sewing for the family was an enduring occupation.[9]

One of the great virtues of sewing was its flexibility, which enabled women to fit domestic production into the interstices of other pursuits. Sewing was especially well suited to cultivating the intellect since it occupied the hands in productive labor but left the mind free for contemplation. Nancy Maria Hyde, a schoolteacher, pondered the meaning of literary texts as she worked her needle, and later set down her fully articulated thoughts in her journal. Of *World without Souls* Hyde commented, "While I regret the personal and general depravity, which justifies a satire of such severity, I am led to doubt the efficacy of the weapon employed against it." Not long before her death from scarlet fever, Maria Allen of Worcester sewed while a friend read aloud from Shakespeare. Over the span of "a fortnight," or fourteen days, the young women assiduously read their way through the plays of Richard II, Henry IV, Henry V, and Henry VI. Allen wrote to a friend that they had discovered "this part of English History is very interesting and I feel desirous of making myself thoroughly acquainted with it." She then quizzed her correspondent, "What are you reading now? Have you seen an essay of MacAuley's on Frederick the Great? I am sure you would enjoy reading it." In early 1849, twenty-two-year-old Ann Jennison Barton of Worcester, newly married and settling into her role as wife and housekeeper, noted briefly in her diary, "Attended a sewing and reading meeting of the High St. neighbors." *Godey's Lady's Book*, a popular mass-circulation magazine, combined reading and sewing in a single format, publishing patterns alongside its short stories and serials. The early national and antebellum eras witnessed an explosion of interest among middle-class women in reading and writing, with significant long-term consequences. Many factors contributed to this development, including the ease with which women combined reading, sewing, and neighborliness.[10]

Sewing was also one of the few skilled occupations open to women. Although dressmakers, milliners, mantua makers and "tailoresses" were notoriously underpaid, theirs was a profession in which only women catered to women. Moreover, dressmakers and milliners were also merchants who sold wreaths, fake curls, trimmings, artificial flowers, ribbons, laces, plumes, handkerchiefs, shell combs, and, as one Worcester advertisement declared, "a variety of other articles too numerous to mention." Eliza Bancroft, the daughter of a renowned Unitarian minister, worked as a milliner. In 1812, she charged $1.57 for "making and tacking [a] gown" and preparing the "lining for sleeves." Bancroft also ran the town's first "exclusive" dry goods store before her marriage to Whig politician John Davis. Dressmakers also had apprentices to whom they taught the trade. Twenty-two-year-old Caroline Cloyes, a milliner and mantua maker, recruited young women through notices in the local press indicating that she "Wanted: Four Young Ladies, to learn the above business." A competitor, milliner Nancy Wesson, sought only two apprentices.[11]

Women who were not professional dressmakers also turned their skills to profit when the situation presented itself. One frontier woman raised the capital to establish the family farm by sewing shirts for Indians and gloves for soldiers. Rosalie Roos of Sweden, who toured the United States in the early 1850s, wrote home that she was running low on money and so had devised a plan: "I am going to make a vest in cornflower blue, have bought the material and silk for it, but not for the pleasure of giving it to one of my dear ones, but in order to try to sell it so that I may have some way of obtaining a little money." Adelaide Isham Crossman, a busy farm wife in South Sutton, Worcester county, made money sewing for the hired hands. In 1847 she recorded in her diary, "I cut a pair of pants for Jess Leonard. . . . I sewing on pants. . . . I finished Jess pants, .40." For much of her life, Crossman noted, "I sewing on one thing & another."[12]

Because learning to sew took years of effort and involved hours of tedious work, girls and women who did not expect to ever turn their skills to wage labor nevertheless valued their talents and proved reluctant to work without some compensation. Louisa Jane Trumbull grew up in comfort as the daughter of the cashier of Worcester's Central Bank. In 1834, at age thirteen, she was invited to visit a family friend, where, she noted, "I intend spending a week or two and I am to sew for her she said she would give me ninepence a day." Her mother, however, disapproved of Louisa Jane charging a friend for sewing, to which Louisa stoutly replied, "If I cannot I am sure I shall not waste my strength little as I have got in sewing for any one save myself. So unless I have some prospect of a remuneration be it ever so small for my services go I shall not." The quintessential feminine labor, sewing taught girls such as Louisa Jane Trumbull the values of discipline, hard work, and pride in their abilities.[13]

So central was sewing to women's lives that, according to contemporaries, a woman and her sewing were seldom parted except perhaps in church (although women did sew or knit during Bible classes). "American women, throughout all the backwoods, are the most industrious females I have ever seen," an English visitor remarked admiringly in the early 1820s, "the American farmer's wife makes every article of clothing for her whole family." City women were no slouches either, and combined sewing with urban amusements. At one lyceum history lecture, half of the women sewed while the other half took notes. Indeed, a sewing basket was so much an extension of its owner that the loss of hers prompted one Worcester woman to place a newspaper ad offering a reward for its return. The ad indicated that the sewing basket was also a purse in which the owner stashed such personal items as a bank note, several coins, two handkerchiefs "one silk and the other cotton," as well as "several other articles of no use to any one but the owner."[14]

Frances Trollope, an English woman who toured the United States in the late 1820s and early 1830s, described how American women were perennially sewing and commented tellingly, "The plough is hardly a more blessed instrument in America than the needle. How could they live without it?" Americans sewed even when company was present, the disdainful Trollope wrote, conceding that women did attempt to disguise the prosaic nature of their work, in one case absurdly insisting that a shirt was actually a pillowcase. Still, Trollope agreed that sewing was a fault line of civilized womanhood, and to her mind an exhibit of Indian needlework proved that "they are perfectly capable of civilization." Similarly, English tourist Marianne Finch sought to rebut accusations that Paulina Wright Davis, a leader of the American women's movement, was "coarse, masculine, [and] overbearing" by emphasizing that Davis was "an excellent housekeeper, and an indefatigable needle-woman."[15]

Sewing also engaged the time of women in rather unusual circumstances. In 1835, Philadelphia's city officials grouped almshouse women by sewing skill: ward one housed "aged and helpless women in bad health"; ward two was reserved for "aged and helpless women who can sew and knit"; ward three was for "aged and helpless women who are good sewers"; ward four held the more energetic "spinners." Similarly, Worcester's Lunatic Asylum, the first in the state, accommodated several hundred women in a second-floor "female gallery." In 1841, a trustee touring the facility noted that "A considerable portion of the females were absent from the galleries attending a sewing party," which the trustee hoped would calm them. (Apparently it did not always work, and one woman put her sewing notions to a different use: "She hung herself with a skein of yarn while many from the gallery were gone to church.") So interconnected were sewing and nineteenth-century womanhood that the inability to sew served as a marker of mental incompetence; New York City prostitutes sewed for their favorite customers; enslaved women used their needles to express their creativity; Emily Dickinson reversed the process and wrote poems about sewing. Sewing was, in sum, a badge of femininity expected of virtually all antebellum women.[16]

Sewing also brought women together for communal labor. Sewing circles were the oldest and most common form of New England women's voluntary associations. The colonial Puritan economy depended upon the informal networks of exchange of its "good wives," and quiltings and sewing "frolics" were common. The American Revolution prompted women to offer their associated labor in the service of the nation. "Spinning bees" spun wool into cloth to substitute for British imports while sewing circle members raised money for the cause, helped to clothe the revolutionary army, and wove patriotic themes into their needlework. After the Revolution, sewing circles continued to provide a venue for socializing and afforded farm women the all too rare opportunity to spend time with other women. However, in the antebellum years the sewing circle assumed an even greater importance as it emerged as a permanent, constitutionally based organization with explicit ties to social activism. From sewing to benefit one's family to sewing to benefit society was a charge many women eagerly embraced.[17]

THE RISE OF THE FOR-PROFIT SEWING CIRCLE

Diaries and letters from the early nineteenth century reveal a shift in the location, organization, and purpose of sewing as women increasingly associated it with non-domestic interests. The life of Nancy Avery White again exemplifies the pattern. Initially White integrated sewing into her domestic affairs, manufacturing her family's clothing by herself. When her daughters assumed the dress of adult women, White began to bring in others to assist her, for the production of gowns demanded more labor and greater skill than did children's more shapeless clothing. White's desire to dress her daughters in a manner befitting their station prompted her to alter her routine, making sewing not an individual but a group enterprise. In the early 1830s, White joined her first sewing circle. Until her death nearly thirty years later, the sewing societies were a central focus of her life. "I went to the sewing society and church meeting," White recorded in 1837 and again, "I went to the sewing society and prayer meeting." For Nancy White, and especially for her daughters, membership in a sewing circle became synonymous with interest in temperance, foreign missions, and relief for the poor. "Catherine and [I?] collected money for the Missionary society," White wrote in 1838, and in 1839, "Catherine and Louisa and Avery went to hear a lecture by Dr. Channing read by Mr. Fisher." The sewing circle served a similarly politicizing function for Lucy Stone of rural Brookfield, Worcester county. Stone recalled a visit by educator Mary Lyon, the founder of Mount Holyoke College, who urged circle members to support her proposed female seminary. Angered by Lyon's description of gender inequality in education and employment, Stone tossed her sewing aside and went on to a career as an abolitionist and feminist lecturer.[18] The sewing circle thus linked women such as White and Stone to contemporary social issues as they reinterpreted sewing as a public act.

By the 1860s, several generations of New England women had experienced sewing and social causes as two sides of the same coin. Indeed, where the sewing circle ended and the reform society began was usually blurred. In the spring of 1861, White noted "Mr Lincoln was inaugurated" and a month later, "Elizabeth went [to collect] for the missionary cause—Mary went to sew for the soldiers." White's daughter Mary was but one actor in a cast of thousands. During the Civil War, sewing circles across the North churned out immense quantities of clothing and bandages for Union soldiers, held fundraisers, and filled barrels with desperately needed garments, blankets, medicine, and food. During Reconstruction, women's groups continued their work, sewing clothing for the freed slaves of the South. Beginning in the early national period, and with increasing momentum in the decades thereafter, the sewing circle moved women's labor beyond the realm of domestic production to connect with larger social concerns.[19]

DUELING NEEDLES AND SOCIAL POLITICS

The process by which many women became involved in social reform can be seen at work in Worcester. As early as 1815, the sewing circles of the First (Congregational) Church emerged as arenas for religious rivalry. In that year, the American Board of Commissioners for Foreign

Missions (ABCFM), a national organization supporting Protestant missionaries, hit upon an innovative plan to encourage donations to its schools
in India. The ABCFM announced that "any person, or society, may cause
an orphan to be selected and educated, by paying thirty dollars, annually,
till his education is completed." The genius of the scheme was in the
details: along with the donation came the privilege of naming—or, more
accurately, of renaming—the recipient of the scholarship. The opportunity to make such a personal statement on behalf of religion sparked the
formation of Worcester's Female Reading and Charitable Society
(FRCS). The FRCS was a sewing circle composed of approximately
fifty "Young Ladies, divided into several Associations" who wrote a constitution, elected a slate of officers, and met twice a month to engage in
"some useful employment" while listening to books read aloud. The
members sold what they made at the circle and collected subscriptions, and by 1817 had enough money to christen an ABCFM mission
school child. As "a testimony of respect" the women decided to honor
their minister, and named the child after the Reverend Charles A.
Goodrich.[20]

The choice of name was significant for it signaled the women's
loyalties in the crisis then unfolding within the First Church. In 1816,
the selection of Goodrich to fill the pulpit upon the apparent resigna-
tion of the Reverend Samuel Austin had split the parish into highly
acrimonious pro-Goodrich and pro-Austin factions. While the men of
the church fought it out with the dissenters in numerous ecclesiastical
councils, the women of the church took a more symbolic tack. By naming the mission child after Charles Goodrich, the members of the FRCS
both supported an international religious campaign and unambiguously
declared their allegiance to the pro-Goodrich majority. Meanwhile, a
pro-Austin women's group, calling itself the Praying Society, retaliated
by raising money to name a child after Samuel Austin. By 1817, a little
Charlie Goodrich and a little Sammy Austin studying at mission schools
halfway around the world were living emblems of the duel between the
rival sewing circles of Worcester's schismatic First Church.[21]

In the mid-1820s, the difficulties in the First Church were settled
and the FRCS evolved into the Worcester Female Association (WFA),
known variously as the Ladies' Association and the Worcester Female
Foreign Missionary Association. Once more names proved symbolic,
for although the sewing circle laid claim to local preeminence by titling
itself the *Worcester* Female Association, in actuality it was composed of

members of the First Church. Its goal was similarly ambitious: "to convey light and knowledge to that part of the earth that now dwells in darkness and in shadow" by supporting ABCFM missions. Yet whereas the earlier sewing circles had been producers, the women of the WFA were hunter-gatherers, who concentrated upon collecting money from other church members. For these women, the sewing circle was simply the most obvious way to organize; it was not itself a vehicle for production and members neither made goods for sale nor held fundraisers. They did, however, serve in office, and the WFA's leadership structure consisted of a president, a vice-president, a treasurer, a secretary, and more than a dozen collectors. Moreover, the women eventually took over the leadership role initially filled by the minister. Until 1836, the minister opened the group's meetings with prayer, but afterward the officers assumed this responsibility. The WFA thus provided women with hands-on organizational experience, a function every sewing circle served. Not only was a generation of women in Worcester thus accustomed to viewing other women as leaders, but many themselves bore the title "Madame President."[22]

Although the members of the WFA appear to have been assertive within the sewing circle, the group was not otherwise especially ambitious. Only once in the WFA's first twenty-five years did the annual collection exceed one hundred dollars, and usually it averaged far less. Nor at first did the women control the money; indeed, they did not even send it to the ABCFM themselves. Rather, the treasurer turned the collections over to "its parent society," the all-male Worcester Central Association Auxiliary for Foreign Missionary Societies, the local branch of the ABCFM. In 1848, for example, WFA Treasurer Hannah J. Brooks noted that she had forwarded their collection to the "Gentleman's Association" and "consequently, *your* Treas. is unable to report from that District." In return for the donation, the WFA received the *Missionary Herald* and copies of the ABCFM's annual reports. But their lack of control over the money gave the women a sense that it had disappeared into a void. In the early 1850s, the WFA voted to cut "its parent society" out of the loop and although the money ultimately arrived at the ABCFM, it made a few stops along the way. In 1852, for example, the circle spent most of its annual collection to make Margarette E. Smith, the widow of the former pastor, an honorary member of the ABCFM; in 1854, they did the same for Helen James, the wife of the current pastor. By the 1860s, the women had run out of ministers' wives to honor and began to make *each other* honorary members. From lauding the efforts of others to recognizing the work of their own, the women of the WFA increasingly acknowledged the value of their own contributions.[23]

The Worcester Female Association, which concentrated on accumulation rather than production, was one model for a benevolent society for which the sewing circle dictated the form but not the function. A sewing circle formed three years after the WFA adopted the more aggressive tactics of the Female Reading and Charitable Society and the Praying Society. In the fall of 1827, the *Spy* announced the formation of the Worcester Female Samaritan Society (WFSS). Headlined "TO THE BENEVOLENT," the notice stated that requests for assistance from the needy of the town had led "the Ladies of Worcester" to propose the formation of a society "the object of which shall be to inquire into the situation of such as apply for relief, and thereby render the distribution of charity more equal and more effectual." All those interested were to meet in the vestry of the Calvinist Church the following Monday afternoon "in order to adopt a Constitution, and elect Officers to manage the concerns of the Society."[24]

The association that was organized that Monday in October was a combination of a sewing circle and a welfare society, and although the newspaper notice suggested that it was an interdenominational effort, in reality the WFSS was dominated by members of the new Calvinist Church. Declaring "it is a well-known fact that the poor inhabitants of our village have increased within a few years," organizers concluded that welfare in Worcester was both inadequate and ineptly administered. Whereas "in some cases of distress the relief afforded has been short of the actual wants," the women maintained, in other cases "the supply has exceeded what the case required." It was their intent to "render the distribution of charity more equal and more efficient." Thus did the women of the WFSS explicitly criticize the handling of a vital social service by the officials of their town and assert that they could, and would, do better. The "Ladies" proposed to "clothe the destitute, to provide bedding and other necessaries for the sick, and occasionally to assist in purchasing fuel." They took aim at assisting not the terminally indigent—the almshouse was more appropriate for them, the women noted—but those in temporary need of assistance, "who in health supported themselves, but in sickness require aid which must be immediate to prove availing. Strangers too come under our consideration, nor are the widow and fatherless to be forgotten." However, it was not the poor in general in whom the WFSS was chiefly interested, but poor women, as indicated by their exclusive use of the feminine pronoun to refer to those in need.[25]

The organizers of the WFSS created a liberal leadership infrastructure of a president, a secretary, a treasurer, twelve assistants, and a Prudential Committee "selected from the elderly ladies of the church," which was to swing into action when "there is a doubt as to the expediency or propriety of relieving the object, who has applied for assistance." At the monthly meetings the members of the circle were to "cut and prepare garments" for the needy, and if the demand for assistance were great "those members who have most leisure" must agree to work overtime. Each member was also personally responsible for certifying the eligibility of applicants and "for the safe return of all articles loaned," such as bedding and blankets.[26]

The WFSS catered primarily to the interests of the better established, older women of the Calvinist Church, such as Elizabeth Tuckerman Salisbury. The annual membership dues, fifty cents, were relatively steep compared to other women's groups; moreover, the repeated references to the membership as "ladies," as opposed to "young ladies," as well as the restriction of the Prudential Committee to the "elderly ladies," emphasized the group's class and age hierarchies. Although the WFSS had been announced with a great fanfare in 1827, the circle subsequently kept few records and by the 1840s was eclipsed by another organization associated with the Calvinist Church. In 1839, the younger generation founded its own sewing circle, which was at once more democratic, more egalitarian, and more ambitious than those that had come before. Its unusually extensive records permit a rare in-depth reading of the ways in which a sewing circle stimulated antebellum women's interests in social and political reform.[27]

A Case Study: The Centre Missionary Sewing Circle

On November 21, 1839, twenty-nine "young ladies" founded the Centre Missionary Sewing Circle (CMSC). They too drafted a constitution, elected officers, and committed the membership to "united benevolent effort and mutual acquaintance." The women's purpose was expressly to assist foreign missionaries to "win over the unhappy subjects of the Prince of darkness." Inspired by stirring accounts of the exploits of Protestant missionaries, the women vowed to do their part for the worldwide effort through financial support and prayer.[28] Twice a month, from two o'clock in the afternoon until nine o'clock in the evening, the circle gathered in the homes of its members. The women did plain and fancy sewing and displayed the work for sale in a "show box" at the American Temperance House, a popular Worcester meeting place. The officers reinvested a portion of the profits in new materials and donated the balance to the ABCFM. Arguing that ". . . the Missionary Enterprize is soon, to become the absorbing interest of all civilized nations" and was "destined to triumph," the members considered themselves foot soldiers in an international religious campaign and looked forward to the day when they would meet "souls in Heaven, redeemed thro[ugh] our exertions." Declaring expansively that "Our 'field is the world,'" the women calculated that roughly "800,000,000 of our fellow beings" were waiting for "the bread of life" that they would help to provide. Their interest was timely, the women explained, for in the late 1830s the ABCFM faced an "embarrassed state of the treasury" as a result of the Panic of 1837. The ABCFM's distress roused the women to "new and vigorous exertions!" to support what they proprietorially referred to as "our Board."[29]

The missionary cause was also appealing because the women were convinced that Protestantism was a unique force to raise women's status worldwide. Such a faith was widely embraced by evangelicals and reflected a deeply ingrained sense of their own cultural and racial superiority. But it also testified to the aspirations of evangelical women to improve the status of their sex generally, and, by implication, their own status. The result was a powerful stimulus for reform that yielded a reflexively woman-centered perspective. Indeed, so strongly did the members identify with the central figure of Christianity that their rhetoric muddled the distinctions between Jesus and themselves: "The humble, self-denying Christian will always find some way to honor that Savior who was meek & lowly, shrinking from no fatigue or pain, who bled & died for him, tho sometimes he may be anxious & properly to have his sphere of usefulness enlarge." Was it Jesus who was anxious about enlarging "his sphere of usefulness," or was it the "humble, self-denying Christian" such as themselves? The women concluded: "We are not attempting to do great things in the eyes of the world, but if the prayer of faith attend our earnest efforts, we shall receive a large reward."[30]

The members of the CMSC were also concerned with their own intellectual and moral development. To guard against excessive chatting, the "reproach to our sex," the women resolved to sew to the accompaniment of an appropriately uplifting text. The *Missionary Herald*, the *Mis-*

sionary Offering, and reports from the ABCFM kept them up to date on the cause for which they labored. The circle also enjoyed tales of missionaries battling heathenism in exotic locales and was especially fond of narratives written by or featuring pious women triumphing over adversity through the strength of feminine virtue. The women admired the fiction of Harriet Beecher Stowe, whose father, the Reverend Lyman Beecher, had presided at the dedication of their church, as well as the fiction and advice books by their former pastor, the Reverend John S.C. Abbott. Best of all, however, were their own thoughts and opinions, for they filled the hours of labor with lively conversation, occasionally to the annoyance of the woman reading aloud.[31]

The decision to organize the CMSC was in part a response to the impersonality that increasingly characterized their community, then in the throes of economic and demographic expansion. After decades of slow growth, Worcester's population increased seventy percent between 1820 and 1830, and sixty-two percent between 1830 and 1835, largely as a result of its location at the crossroads of newly built railroad lines connecting metropolitan Boston with western Massachusetts and New York. From 1840 to 1855, the population nearly tripled; moreover, movement in and out of town was even greater than the absolute numbers suggest.[32] As new faces appeared and disappeared at services with disconcerting regularity, the congregation struggled to maintain a sense of community. As the minister remarked one Sunday, "[O]nly about one third of those whose names were given me on my coming here remain with us . . . yet the actual number of the congregation is twenty-five per cent higher." While the brethren formed Standing Committees to draw up accurate membership rosters, the sisters organized a sewing circle to bring together those "whose various callings in life seldom permit them to meet elsewhere" in "one common aim, viz. to do good," and they actively recruited new members. The sewing circle not only raised money for a cause but converted strangers into friends and colleagues, united by a shared ideology and a commitment to benevolence.[33]

The nearly one hundred married and sixty single women who formally subscribed to the antebellum circle can be broadly described as middle class. Most of the women were married and lived in homes separate from their husband's place of employment. More than half of the husbands were professionals (such as lawyers, physicians, or teachers), merchants, or manufacturers, but nearly forty percent were skilled artisans (such as carpenters, masons, or machinists). There were at least five widows, while most of the single women were the daughters of members and lived in the parental household. Within the circle the women recognized a hierarchy that combined an appreciation of moral authority with a meritocracy rewarding hard work. Nearly one-quarter of the women, usually those married to a merchant or a skilled worker, were members for more than five years. The circle's officers were drawn mostly from this group, but single women were also elected to office and sat on all of the committees. For the first few years Hannah Sweetser, the minister's wife, served as circle president. When Sweetser retired in 1844, the women elected Mary Banister, married to the city's postmaster, president and Sarah Goulding, a machinist's wife, vice president. As secretary the members chose Sarah Waldo Taylor, a schoolteacher. In the society's second and third decades, tenure in office decreased while the ratio of leadership positions increased from one officer for every five members in 1839 to one for three by 1854. The proliferation of office holding reflected a desire to reward members for their labor, but was also an acknowledgment of the increased responsibilities that came with the group's involvement in politics and poor relief. The CMSC, like other sewing circles, provided a way for women in Worcester to gain experience directing a moneymaking voluntary society.[34]

Women founded and ran the sewing circle but men were welcome. In rural areas, where a gendered division of labor was less common well into the nineteenth century, men were known to help "put in a quilt." As boys, Samuel Swett Green and his brother, sons of a local physician, were taught worsted embroidery. Others learned to knit. In 1839, Levi Lincoln Newton of Worcester, a student at Harvard College, wrote to his sister that he had attended a fair where "One of the first things sold in the morning was a pair of baby's socks, I understood, knit by a Cambridge student last vacation, while he was sick." Whether it was the skill of the knitter or the sex of the knitter that made the socks so popular is hard to say.[35]

More typically, gendered spheres of labor divided the sewing circles temporally. At the sewing circle of Maine midwife Martha Ballard, the fifteen women who sewed in the afternoon were joined in the evening by twelve men for a social gathering, and the CMSC followed this pattern. From the very beginning, men attended the convivial teas that often capped the afternoons of labor. Soon the women decided that the men would have to pay if they wanted to play. In 1843, the CMSC extended honorary membership to "those gentlemen in the habit of meeting with us" if they paid the regular annual dues of twenty-five cents. In effect, the women had created a men's auxiliary: the all-male honorary members were subordinate to the all-female full members and all-female officers. The men were not expected to work but neither were they given any say in running the circle; however, in the evening the men did raise their voices in song. Male membership was substantial, ranging from more than one quarter of the total membership to about one third. Most were husbands of members but the proportion of single men grew from thirty-four percent of all male members in 1849 to forty-four percent in 1856, perhaps because the teas offered a genteel setting for courtship. But men also savored the companionship of the circle, and although George Dresser and David Hitchcock followed their wives into the CMSC, they remained after they were widowed.[36]

The presence of so many men at the women's sewing circle is still more significant in light of the men's reluctance to form their own missionary society. In September 1839, two months before the CMSC was founded, the brethren of the Calvinist Church voted against organizing a "Gentlemen's Missionary Association, having reference only to the Gentlemen" and instead took up a collection for the ABCFM. When the women founded the sewing circle shortly thereafter they were more exclusive, and while they encouraged the men to join them for tea they did not initially welcome men as members. The sewing circle was thus an organization that subverted the prevailing gender hierarchy: in the circle, the women voted, made policy decisions, and invited the men to entertain them. The pattern was not unique to the CMSC; indeed, it seems to have been common. The Tatnuck Ladies Sewing Circle, organized in 1847 in the Tatnuck section of town, was similarly structured. Moreover, despite its name, the Ladies and Gentlemen Literary Association of East Haddam, Connecticut, also founded in 1847, was a sewing circle dedicated to raising money for books. Membership was open to both sexes but only the women worked, only the women voted, and only the women were elected to leadership positions. In 1853, the women acknowledged their centrality by changing the group's name to "The Ladies Literary Association" even though they continued to receive men as dues-paying members. As these examples suggest, in the first half of the nineteenth century the traditional sewing circle was transformed. Within the circle, as a result of her skill with a needle, the woman was a moneymaker and the man an auxiliary diversion after the work was completed.[37]

The CMSC's local prominence quickly intensified. From its original twenty-nine members in 1839, the society swelled to seventy within three years, and by 1850 one hundred and twenty women and men crowded together in the evenings. But such stellar success provoked a brief retrenchment. In part, it had become increasingly difficult to find hosts with sufficiently ample parlors and pantries. More important, however, the group's popularity precipitated worry about declension, for although the evening social hours were consistently well attended, the afternoons of labor were less so. The women interpreted the falling away as a test of the character of "true New England females" and resolved to forego the more elaborate teas in favor of simpler gatherings where they would partake of "nice bread & butter & many varieties of cake."[38]

Work was at the heart of the circle's mission and by making and selling clothes and embroidered goods, the women tentatively ventured into the antebellum market, where they learned both the problems and the pleasures of making money. The CMSC started out tailoring clothes for the family of a missionary "in a very destitute situation." Within a few weeks they had finished the task and cast about for a new project. Encouraged by their industry, the members decided to make and sell items for cash to send to the ABCFM. For a year the circle met fortnightly, manufacturing a variety of "caps, collars, dickies, aprons, needlebooks, penwipers, safeguards, &c" as well as quilts, stockings, men's shirts, and children's clothing. As the pile of assorted goods grew higher, the women contemplated with pleasure how "the mite" they earned would "ere long gladden the heart and relieve the wants of the destitute and needy." But trading their hard-won skills for cash taught them what the less fortunate knew well: that the market little valued women's labor. At the end of their first year, the women were dismayed to learn that their hundreds of hours of labor had yielded a net profit of thirteen dollars. The members had not expected to make a lot of money but apparently neither had they anticipated that "their mite" would be quite so small. The women sought comfort in falling back upon a value system that measured their work not in "*dollars & cents*" but in a more familiar moral currency. The circle's meetings, they reassured one another, encouraged worthwhile "social & friendly feelings" and stimulated a commendable interest in missionary work.[39]

Yet the women were clearly taken aback to discover that while their social talents were recognized and rewarded, witness the popularity of the evening teas, their hours of labor were not, as evidenced by the echo in their treasury. They responded in two ways. First, they reproached themselves for not working hard enough; at the root of their difficulties was "a want of *individual effort*." Shouldering the blame permitted the women to sustain their faith in their ability eventually to use the market to their own ends. Second, the circle diversified its goods, emphasizing the more laborious but more lucrative "fancy work" in lieu of plain sewing. By so doing the women hoped "to attract purchasers and thus realise the profits of our labor" that had thus far eluded them. The group also considered setting up a second show box but settled upon enlarging the one it already had. Despite these adjustments, the second year of labor was even less remunerative and the group earned but ten dollars.[40]

One obstacle to successful fundraising was that the CMSC vied with other associations for the time and energy of its members. Temperance rallies, lyceum lectures, and church meetings drew upon the same body of adherents; political contests, military musters, and civic celebrations also sapped attendance. The New England climate created further complications when winter's cold, summer's heat, and the "Equinoctial storms" of the spring and fall turned Worcester's unpaved streets into icy or muddy sloughs that posed physical barriers to a membership garbed in voluminous gowns and traveling mostly by foot, often with small children in tow. "We have been completely blocked up by the snow, & now we have a light snow covering the ice, & occasionally making people more humble than is agreeable to them," wrote circle member Lydia Stiles Foster to her sister during the winter of 1843. "Yesterday, going to church . . . I found myself compelled to sit down on the sidewalk rather quicker & harder than was at all pleasant. . . ." One year, fully one-third of the meetings were canceled and months could pass without a single gathering. Until the group established a preeminent claim upon its members, it could not reasonably expect to reach its goal.[41]

Had the women resigned themselves to a minor role in their chosen cause, they might have continued to meet intermittently, earn money almost incidentally, and enjoy their social exchange. Instead, their failure goaded them to greater ambition. Displaying an entrepreneurial flair common among Worcester's business community, the women transformed the organization in its third year by revamping their goals and tactics. The CMSC had been forwarding its meager profits to the ABCFM but the women now realized that the group's lack of commitment was linked to its invisibility. "There has been so little [money] raised by us, and so often the interest in our meetings has flagged," the secretary explained, "that we believe it advisable for *ourselves* to try some *new plan.*" In January 1842, the women made two critical decisions: to disburse the money themselves and to "work for a more *definite object.*" Insisting they meant no reflection on the ABCFM—"we *still* believe that the Secretaries of the Am. Board would devote the money quite as judiciously as ourselves"—the women justified their decision by emphasizing the insignificance of their monetary contributions. But such rhetoric obscures what was in reality a radical departure: the women had rejected their initial presumption that the profit of women's labor was properly controlled by the men of the ABCFM.[42]

But if not the ABCFM, then whom? Alarming reports in the missionary press that "the meddlesome policy of the Jesuits" was making inroads among the Armenians, "the finest body of Christians in the East," emboldened the circle to subsidize the education of a mission school student. (There was no suggestion that renaming the student influenced their decision.) In the summer of 1842, the women read the journal of the Reverend Cyrus Hamlin, excerpted in the *Missionary Herald,* and concluded that his school at Constantinople was "unusually promising." A year's tuition and board amounted to sixty-five dollars, a substantial sum, the women acknowledged, "compared with our past efforts," but one they were sure was within their reach.[43]

To accomplish this more ambitious goal the women overhauled their marketing strategy. Instead of passively waiting for customers to wander by the show box, the circle decided to sell more aggressively by holding a fair. A year's diligent labor yielded "a great variety of useful & ornamental articles" that the women arranged "in a tasteful manner" in the public rooms of the American Temperance House. The CMSC delightedly collected forty-five dollars, which, when added to its outstanding balance, was "more than sufficient." With great ceremony, the secretary forwarded the funds to the Reverend Hamlin, requesting that he bestow it upon a student "whom we may regard in the light of a 'protégé.'"[44]

The fair was a turning point. Exhilarated by their success, the women redoubled their efforts. The Reverend Hamlin was profuse in his thanks, explaining that, compared to the "pure unmitigated unblushing selfishness" of the Jesuits, the women's efforts were proof of the power of disinterested benevolence. Hamlin also informed them that he had selected Simon Bedrozen, "a pious young man," to receive their scholarship. The women had sought a "more *definite object*" for their benevolence; now they had a name and a history to attach to the fruits of their labor.

Not content with one protégé, they pondered taking on two; circle meetings were held more regularly and were better attended; the group had at last won the primary loyalty of its members. The women continued to fill the show box for incidental sales, and to send clothes to missionaries, but concentrated on producing goods for the annual fair, eventually adding a for-profit tea. To boost revenues still further, the circle began advertising the fairs, as well as scheduling them so as to take advantage of special events, such as the Cattle Show "when on account of strangers expected, [the goods] may meet with a ready sale." As a result of these adjustments, profits soared from thirteen dollars in 1842 to three hundred dollars in 1852. By 1853, when a single fair netted nearly two hundred dollars, the women deemed their efforts "*not . . . a total failure.*"[45]

Making goods to sell for cash also required the women of the circle to be reliable and disciplined workers, who arrived on schedule and labored diligently for the time allotted. It proved to be something of a struggle. Members were often laggardly in paying their dues, sometimes did not bother to participate in decision-making, and too frequently straggled in late. Provoked by what she viewed as a "growing informality," secretary Sarah Waldo Taylor rebuked the membership in her 1844 annual report. "Every one will acknowledge that some degree of system is necessary in managing the concern of any society," Taylor wrote politely but pointedly. "The rules & regulations to wh[ich] each member voluntarily subscribes may be regarded as links in the chain, wh[ich] holds that society together." To encourage the members to work in a more disciplined fashion, Taylor utilized a metaphor she hoped would appeal to their imaginations. Rules and regulations did not simply bind the circle together, Taylor wrote, they were "*the machinery by wh[ich] that Society seeks to accomplish its ends.* It is true, that in our Sewing Circles the links of the chain are *few*; the machinery extremely simple. But it is then, the more necessary that such few regulations as we *have*, should be observed, otherwise, we shall fail to accomplish our object. . . ." Taylor was then twenty-four years old, a public school and Sunday school teacher. Piety was a family tradition: her parents, Samuel and Lydia Taylor, who owned a jewelry store, were among the original subscribers of the Calvinist Church and her brother, Samuel Austin Taylor, was a missionary in Syria. The daughter of merchants and the sister of a missionary, Sarah Taylor brought the two together by encouraging within the sewing circle a businesslike approach to benevolence. Taylor's many social reform efforts were cut short when she married and moved from Worces-

ter, dying in childbirth in 1849 at the age of twenty-nine. But Sarah
Taylor's approach lived on in the growing business orientation of the
CMSC.[46]

Even as they exulted in the success of their endeavors, the women
felt twinges of guilt. The money was proof of their sober industry and
was vital to the missionary cause. But the drive to maximize profits provoked a concern that their benevolence had lost its disinterested, or selfless, dimension. In the wake of a lively debate over whom to bless with
their funds, the members paused to reflect, "do we need the reward in
prospect to incite us to benevolence and kindness? Is not the happiness
we experience . . . in doing a kind act an ample compensation, a sufficient motive for perseverance?" In fact, the women were disturbed to
realize that pride in fundraising, not happiness in doing a kind act, had
led them to persevere. And this raised the ticklish issue of gender. The
women of the circle were chary of applying allegedly "masculine" virtues
to themselves and confessed repeatedly their difficulties in overcoming
an "aversion to business" owing to their "natural delicacy & timidity."
Such self-deprecation was somewhat perfunctory, for the women were
plainly delighted by their "activity and skill." But to resume an appropriate feminine modesty they diminished their actions rhetorically, and the
result was a peculiarly bifurcated narrative. Celebrations of their profi-
ciency at fundraising alternated with descriptions of the cosmic Christian battle between good and evil in which they played a very humble
role. Thus even as they boasted that their group was a "large society,
large in the community" the women hastened to add "small in the world."
As justification for engagement in worldly concerns, religious activism
was, for these orthodox Calvinists, a double-edged sword.[47]

Yet as the women became more familiar with producing goods for
profit, their self-consciousness yielded to self-confidence. The circle's
experiences had taught the Horatio Algeresque lesson that "whatever
[we] wished & attempted, [we] could carry forward to a successful termination." The women urged one another "to take an interested part in
the necessary business transactions" and to that end made each member
responsible for a portion of the year's scholarship goal. (It is not clear
what, if anything, happened if a woman did not meet her quota.) Another sign of self-confidence was the cash value they assigned to their
labor. In 1849, the circle outfitted one of its members, Esther Howland,
who proposed to become an ABCFM missionary. When Howland's
"plans for life changed," the circle deemed it "just & proper" to accept

payment for the clothes it had made for her. Production for profit thus confronted the women of the CMSC with previously unexamined inconsistencies in their roles. The worldly competed with the spiritual; ambition with self-denial; assertiveness with passivity; pride with modesty. The women ultimately resolved these conflicts by rejecting a passive piety in favor of an entrepreneurial activity.[48]

For three years the members of the CMSC basked in their role as champions of an international Protestant crusade, believing that "while laboring more particularly for *one* portion of this vast field of the world, we are at the same time benefitting the whole." In 1846 they noted abruptly, and without explanation, that "our engagement with Mr. Hamlin is ended," and with it their attention turned closer to home. When the president proposed that the circle resume an emphasis on missionaries and their families, the members reluctantly agreed for want of an alternative "more worthy of our interest." But donating goods in kind, women's traditional form of benevolence, was evidently less satisfying than manufacturing goods for sale, women's newer form of benevolence, for attendance at the circle plummeted by seventy percent. The women's flagging enthusiasm rekindled briefly when Esther Howland thought to become a missionary; indeed, so interested were the women in sending one of their own into the field properly attired that they canceled plans to assist a Reverend Tucker in Maine, mollifying him with a box of clothing. When Howland changed her mind, the circle was left uncertain as to its next move. By the fall of 1849, the circle's tenth anniversary, the heady days of raising money for a global Christian campaign had passed, replaced by desultory efforts at crafting shirts and stockings for impoverished frontier ministers.[49]

Within months the members had hatched a new scheme. In January 1850, the women shifted their attention to a more immediate concern. "New England is indeed the glory of all lands," the secretary wrote, "but who can estimate the amount of poverty sin & suffering perpetrated & endured even here." With renewed zeal the circle announced its intention to undertake a "wise & well directed effort . . . to alleviate some small portion of human misery" in Worcester. But much to their surprise the minister, the Reverend Seth Sweetser, pronounced himself "decidedly against" diverting money and goods originally earmarked for missionaries to the city's poor. It was not that Sweetser did not support benevolent work. In his eulogy for a local philanthropist, Sweetser fully endorsed public charity, asserting "Here then is the great demand of

God upon us, *that we live to do good*," and he urged his congregation actively to cultivate benevolence for fear that "the opportunity will be gone before the good deed is perfected." Sweetser also supported women's benevolent work and characterized Dorothea Dix, a former Worcester resident, as a "benefactor of society." The Reverend Sweetser was, however, a firm believer in duty, insisting that "In whatever sphere of life God calls us to act . . . we must train ourselves to excellence in that department." It is possible that the minister considered the CMSC rightfully called to act on behalf of missionaries, not the city's poor. It is also possible that he did not consider the local poor, many of whom were Irish Catholics, sufficiently deserving. Sweetser had no veto power over the circle's decisions but its members took seriously the moral authority of their spiritual shepherd. In 1838, the women had thrown their unanimous support behind Sweetser's election to their pulpit and he and his wife Hannah, a former circle president, remained popular with them. Unsure what course to pursue in the face of their minister's unaccustomed opposition, the women retreated from their (to them) novel proposal and dutifully made clothes for a theology student at Amherst College.[50]

But an undercurrent of resentment at the minister's interference still swirled. Sweetser did not understand that the group's success required its members to feel a personal connection to a cause. Nor did he share the women's more expansive definition of missionary activity. "As a Missionary Circle," they argued somewhat inconsistently, "it is obviously our duty first to provide for our own." In 1851, noting "How much more good might we accomplish by engaging heartily in the work before us, than by wishing for other fields of labor," the women repudiated their minister and voted to "labor some for the destitute in our own city, as well as for those at a distance." To forestall further objections, they amended their constitution to include poor relief as a goal. The secretary concluded, "Some who have heretofore been anxious" to strike out in this new direction "will now have their benevolence tested." First the women had rejected the leadership of the national society they had been organized to support. Now they were rejecting their minister's advice. By the early 1850s, the women of the CMSC had come to rely upon their own judgment.[51]

The CMSC immediately committed itself to raising money for a variety of charities. For a cause to capture the women's imagination, and thus a portion of their treasury, it had to be both near enough so that results were readily visible and small enough so that the amount they contributed would have a perceptible impact. The Worcester Children's Friend Society, the Sailor's Home in Boston, and the poor of Worcester all fit the bill, and the 1850s witnessed a flowering and expansion of the circle's endeavors on their behalf. The CMSC also secured its preeminence by eclipsing, then absorbing, the greying remnants of the Worcester Female Samaritan Society, whose staid and hierarchical approach to benevolence held less appeal to the women of the 1840s and 1850s than did the CMSC's more egalitarian and activist style. The institutional church, too, benefitted from the circle's labor, for the group made new carpets for the vestry and, in 1860, contributed four hundred and fifty dollars toward new furnishings. The circle also formed committees to investigate cases of want in the parish and to render "prompt relief of those who have a claim upon our charities." While it never had the resources to engage in anything approaching systematic social welfare, the circle did offer small sums to the parish poor. Through the late 1850s the "ladies with Dorcas-like zeal" toiled vigorously to fund "deeds of *Charity*."[52]

From the outset the circle's benevolence was shaped by a postmillennialist perspective, in which history was driven by the conflict between good and evil in preparation for the second coming of Christ. In common with evangelicals of their day, these women believed that vigorous missionizing would usher in the millennium, and thus an urgency suffused their world view and fueled their activism. "*The time is short*," the women argued, for ". . . the Spirit is abroad in the world . . . . *Now* is the time to break up the fallow ground and sew [*sic*] the seeds of heavenly truth." By the early 1840s, the members insisted that the "coming and glorious change . . . was *right at hand*;" indeed, they declared, "Truly, we see signs of the latter day glory!" Not only did the women assign themselves key roles in the imminent epic struggle, they also adopted the metaphor of woman-as-soldier, who, though puny when standing alone, was formidable when standing with others. In "*union is strength*," they maintained, "A soldier standing before a fortress knows that however strong may be his arm, and bold his heart, he cannot reduce it *alone*. But rally the *army* and let their united strength draw their battering engines to thunder against its walls, and the fortress may be taken." Thus did the circle's members voice both their activist piety and their strong sense of self: "Let us never forget that the secret of power lies in the *individual units that compose the whole.* An infinite number of *ciphers* amount to nothing." They might not personally be powerful, the women seemed to be saying, but neither were they ciphers. More prosaically, the circle insisted that philanthropy was evidence of sincere Christianity.[53]

As a consequence of this perspective, the women did not assert a causal relationship between sin and misfortune. Rather, they understood poverty as yet another example of God's mystery, an inexplicable fact of life that called upon the traditional ties of community. It "is imperatively our duty to feed the hungry, to clothe the destitute," the women insisted, for the needy have "*prior* and *just* claims upon [us] in [our] associated capacity." Moreover, the poor were not necessarily strangers. They were members of the church, such as Mr. and Mrs. Gray, "elderly people in our Parish, necessitous and deserving our regard," and sometimes even members of the sewing circle, such as Susan Snow, a single woman. Mindful of the group's early troubles making money, its members recognized that a "want of profitable employment," rather than "a deficiency of effort," was too often the cause of poverty in their city. To be sure, they might condescend to the poor, declaring "it is our duty not only to relieve *physical* want and suffering, but by our sympathies, by pleasant words and kindly smiles to diffuse joy and gladness as far as our influence shall extend." But they did not necessarily intend to be patronizing. Rather, the women were affirming their spiritual power, for "a cheerful smile . . . is but the reflection of a contented mind." More to the point, a smile could be had for free and masked the reality of the group's limited resources. The women were under no illusions that they could resolve complex social problems. When the secretary of the American Seamen's Friend Society acknowledged a donation of goods with a note hinting broadly that the sailors would prefer cash to quilts, the secretary replied pointedly, "Our Treasury never overflows. . . ." Still, they felt obliged to persist, proclaiming "What we *can* do, *let us do*, with all our might."[54]

The CMSC was also a forum in which educated adults excluded by law and custom from institutional politics formed and voiced their political opinions. Because they shared the presumption that politics was a male prerogative, the women's political interests flourished in inverse proportion to the immediacy of the issues. Thus, while they felt within their rights to raise money for missionaries, the women left to the men the task of assisting those at home. Indeed, elections were initially an annoyance that forced the rescheduling of meetings "as it was feared [the elections] would prevent the attendance of the gentlemen in the evening." But the group's experiences yielded both a heightened awareness of local problems and a greater appreciation of their ability to do something about them. By the 1850s, individuals previously marginalized from American politics had taken sides in the era's most divisive issues and were actively engaged in furthering their causes. Historians have argued that the Civil War, in the manner of other national crises, politicized women's domestic labor. It was instead the culmination of a process of politicization that had occurred over decades within such organizations as the sewing circles.[55]

The roots of their politicization ran deep, for missionary work was inherently political. In antebellum America the language of politics was often moralistic, and the language of the moralist was frequently political. This was especially true in Worcester, a Whig (and later Republican) stronghold. Thus there was no single impetus for the CMSC's interest in politics. The upsurge in Irish immigration in the mid-1840s increased the number of desperately poor in Worcester, as well as the perceived threat of Catholicism. Immigration also sparked the Nativism that led the Know-Nothing party to capture the city's government in the mid-1850s. Each of these developments galvanized the circle to action. Westward expansion bred new worries. The West offered a refuge for dissident religions, which convinced the women that "now is the time to disseminate the truths of the Gospel, & support its teachers & preachers, ere Popery, or Mormonism, or any other form of false doctrine, occupy this vast country." In the West were also men "greedy with gain" who had abandoned the civilized—by which they meant more feminized—East in pursuit of "this insatiable love of Gold."[56]

To meet these threats to a Christian republic, educator and author Catharine Beecher proposed a Female Seminary at Rockford, Illinois. From its halls, an army of female teachers would sally forth to educate and to civilize the West. The CMSC offered to furnish a room at the seminary, for it considered Beecher's institution "an enterprise of no ordinary character." The women of the Worcester sewing circle would thus help to mold in their own image the expanding nation.[57]

The cause of antislavery was another rallying point. Worcester had long enjoyed a reputation as a community unsympathetic to slavery. A fast forty miles by railroad from Boston, Worcester was a regular stop on the abolitionist lecture circuit, and even a partial accounting of those giving public lectures in the city reads like a who's who of abolitionism: Frederick Douglass, Lucretia Mott, William Lloyd Garrison, Wendell

Phillips, Lucy Stone, Theodore Parker, Charles Sumner. Revealing the impact of local and national antislavery activists, and perhaps with the recent Amistad trial in mind, in 1841 the CMSC described how "... the dark slave ship continually hovers along [Africa's] coasts, waiting like a bird of prey the opportunity to snatch & bear away hundreds of wretched victims to toil & suffer in a foreign clime." Such rhetorical imaginings stimulated the women's social sympathies and may have encouraged an antislavery impulse. What is certain is that the members of the sewing circle anticipated the antislavery commitment of their church. Only months later did the Calvinist Church declare "We believe American Slavery to be a heinous sin in the sight of God, and diametrically opposed to Christianity" and resolve "we will not receive as members to this Church, those who traffic in Slaves or hold their fellow men in bondage."[58]

Neither the CMSC nor the church, however, proposed a course of action to attack the institution of slavery itself. In 1850, as the country wrestled with sectional tensions, the women of the sewing circle decided to play a more active role. Again expressing a preference for a personal connection to reform, they voted to sew clothing for fugitives passing through Worcester en route to Canada, for "We may not forget that there are those every year escaping from their native country denied their liberty by their and our own country which we who enjoy our liberty & her protection so much glory in[.] [W]e might do something to cancel their individual wrongs." In the fall of 1856, concern for the future of the West melded with antislavery when guerilla war broke out in Kansas. The citizens of Worcester followed the developments avidly as a local man, Eli Thayer, led a delegation of Free Soilers to the embattled territory in a quixotic campaign to save Kansas from the Border Ruffians. "The abused and suffering in *Kansas*" also aroused the sympathies of the circle, which committed itself "to meet the wants of those who may survive the brutal outrage daily occu[r]ring among them." So caught up were the women in the divisive politics of their era that on the eve of the Civil War, the group founded to assist missionaries was focused instead on the social, economic, and political problems of their community and their nation.[59]

Sewing for the Slave

The Center Missionary Sewing Circle was not the first in town to take up the cause of antislavery. The same year it was organized as a missionary sewing circle, seventeen other women formed the ecumenical Worcester Anti-Slavery Sewing Circle (WASSC), which was open to "any person" sharing its beliefs and "contributing to its funds." Its founders were motivated by a commitment to equality and a dedication to Garrisonian abolitionism. The preamble of the WASSC's 1841 constitution stated that "Slavery under all circumstances, is a heinous sin against God, a violation of the principles of humanity, and dramatically opposed to the religion of Jesus Christ, is ruinous to the bodies and souls of men, and ought immediately to be abolished...." In its first two years, the WASSC had neither officers nor constitution and its budget was small: four dollars to rent meeting space at the Union (orthodox Congregational) Church, one dollar for postage for *The Liberator*, and forty-five cents for postage for a letter to Boston. In February 1841, the group formalized, drew up a Constitution, and elected a president, a vice president, a secretary-treasurer, a committee of four, and four directresses to oversee the sewing. The WASSC made articles for sale locally and at the National Anti-Slavery Society Fair in Boston. Like the members of the CMSC, the women of the WASSC linked their circle to an issue of overriding local concern. But unlike the CMSC, the WASSC joined forces with other women's groups, not with a national campaign run by men.[60]

The WASSC was unusual in other ways, for it was a somewhat integrated organization. In 1840, Elizabeth "Betsy" Hemenway, a black woman, joined the circle. Married to Ebenezer, a laborer, Betsy Hemenway was the mother of seven, including little William Lloyd Garrison Hemenway. The next year Hemenway's sister-in-law, Hannah Hemenway, also joined. The women's names did not appear on subsequent membership lists, but Emily Evelith, a black teacher in Worcester's segregated public schools, joined in 1847. Still, the WASSC was dominated by white women; perhaps this was why the Hemenways did not return. However, black women and white women meeting in the sewing circle on common social ground and working together for a cause was a significant deviation from the prevailing segregation of the antebellum North.[61]

In the spring of 1848, in cooperation with the antislavery sewing circles of nearby towns, the WASSC announced the first Worcester County Anti-Slavery Bazaar to be held on April 26 and 27. A notice in the *Spy* appealed to "all the friends of Liberty" to contribute: "The products of the farm and the workshop, the dairy and the drawing room, the studio and the boudoir, in fine, the useful and the ornamental from every department of industry and ingenuity will be needed." Arguing that "we depend not on electioneering and political scrambling, but on the power of the gospel, which is might, through God, to the pulling down of strong holds," the notice was signed by thirteen WASSC members. Held in conjunction with the Massachusetts Anti-Slavery Society of Boston, the bazaar was a great success, grossing nearly nine hundred dollars.[62]

Not everyone in town shared the WASSC's beliefs. On the bazaar's opening day, the respected editor of the Democratic *Palladium*, John S.C. Knowlton, assailed the women's efforts and accused them of "Negrophilism." Under the influence of "the recent revolutionary movements in Europe," Knowlton argued contemptuously, the antislavery forces sought to demolish "all arbitrary distinctions of race, of complexion, and of condition, civil, political, or social, that have hitherto disturbed the happiness of any portion of the race." The editor suggested that the WASSC's energies would be better spent worrying about the fortunes of poor and working-class white women: "In all our large towns are slender females whom the crime of poverty has doomed to unceasing toil, with their needles and other appliances of labor, not merely for the comforts, but for the very necessities of life. It is gratifying to know that their industry has been so amply rewarded by the opulent that they are now placed in a condition of comparative independence. It must be so when benevolence no longer turns its attention to the condition of working women."[63] The women of the WASSC were unfazed by Knowlton's attack, and through the 1850s organized more fairs and teas that yielded thousands of dollars for the cause. The bazaars also served as an effective means to educate the public and to exchange ideas. In 1855, reformer Susan B. Anthony came to town to visit her cousin, Dr. Seth Rogers, a hydropathic physician who ran the Worcester Water-Cure Establishment. Anthony also took in the WASSC's bazaar, where she met many friends and colleagues. As Anthony noted in a letter to her family, "I suppose there were many beautiful things exhibited, but I was so absorbed in the conversation of Mr. [Thomas Wentworth] Higginson, Samuel May Jr., Sarah Earle, Cousin Dr. Seth Rogers, Stephen and Abby Foster, that I really forgot to take a survey of the tables." Perhaps it was just such opportunities for networking at the fairs that prompted the scorn occasionally heaped upon this type of women's activism.[64]

THE SEWING CIRCLE AS AN ORGANIZING PRINCIPLE

The belief in human rights that undergirded women's antislavery activism was extended to other reforms, both local and national. More than one in ten WASSC members, including the founding president, vice president, and secretary-treasurer, joined the first national women's rights convention that met in Worcester in 1850, although the records are so scanty that it is possible that the actual total was higher. Indeed, in 1839 Sarah H. Earle was the WASSC's first president and in 1850 the local coordinator of the women's rights convention. The WASSC also included on its roster renowned abolitionist and feminist lecturer Abby Kelley Foster. Foster initially served as a conduit to funnel the group's goods and profits to the movement's headquarters in Boston, but formally joined the WASSC after she and her husband bought a farm in the Tatnuck section of Worcester. WASSC members were also active in municipal reforms, such as the Worcester Children's Friend Society, organized in the late 1840s, and the Female Employment Society, organized in 1855.[65]

There also was significant crossover among the city's many sewing circles, and at least two members of the Center Missionary Sewing Circle played active roles in the Worcester Anti-Slavery Sewing Circle. Persis Ann Bullard Bliss was simultaneously a member of the CMSC and the WASSC; her name also appears on the newspaper advertisement announcing the first antislavery bazaar, suggesting that Bliss did not shy from expressing herself publicly. Perrin Bliss, a carpenter, supported his wife's activism, was an honorary member of both the WASSC and the CMSC, and in 1842 introduced an antislavery resolution to the Calvinist Church. Hannah S. Rice also belonged to both sewing circles. The second wife of baker Benjamin P. Rice, Hannah Rice juggled her home duties and caring for her eight stepchildren with a commitment to sewing on behalf of missionaries and fugitive slaves. So strongly did Rice feel about the causes for which she labored that she was a long-term member of the CMSC and, like Bliss, signed her name to the antislavery bazaar's newspaper announcement. Rice's husband also was an honorary member of the CMSC and the WASSC, and supported fellow congregant Perrin Bliss's 1842 antislavery resolution.[66]

The overlap among the sewing circles was likely even greater than such anecdotal evidence suggests because circle meetings were not restricted to the membership. A willing pair of hands and an open mind were the only preconditions for attending. The records of the CMSC, for example, indicate that many more women showed up at meetings than paid the annual dues. Indeed, while formal membership was preferable, nonmembers were free to drop in as they wished, and a woman might attend regularly or occasionally several of the sewing circles in her community. In 1849, Ann Jennison Barton enjoyed a gathering of a neighborhood sewing circle and two weeks later joined one associated with her church. Women also felt free to cross institutional lines. In the 1820s Mary Thaxter Wheeler was elected president of the First Church's Worcester Female Association and joined the Calvinist Church's Centre Missionary Sewing Circle in the 1840s; Rachel White Heard headed the WFA in 1835 and joined the CMSC in the 1850s; Achsah Chapin was a collector for the WFA in 1828 and its vice president in 1835, before helping to found the Worcester Anti-Slavery Sewing Circle in 1839; the list goes on. For women such as Persis Bliss, Hannah Rice, Ann Barton, Mary Wheeler, Rachel Heard, and Achsah Chapin, the local sewing circles were complementary, not competing, organizations that allowed them to act upon their concern for creating a more just and moral society. The sewing circle thus permeated the world of antebellum women more broadly than the institutional records might suggest.[67]

Some sewing circles held greater appeal than others, however, and the more controversial Worcester Anti-Slavery Sewing Circle never came close to enjoying the popularity of the more mainstream Centre Missionary Sewing Circle. Between 1839 and 1857, the last year for which there are records, the WASSC counted a total membership of at least one hundred and forty-six women and twenty men, with an annual average of twenty-five members. In comparison, in the late 1840s and the early 1850s, the only years for which its membership lists exist, the CMSC totaled at least two hundred and eighty-seven women and one hundred and twenty-seven men, with an annual average of eighty-three members. In brief, the missionary group attracted, on average, more than three times the membership of the antislavery group. Such a finding is not surprising since abolitionists were mostly reviled while missionaries were mostly esteemed. At the same time, the abolitionist group raised significantly more money per member than did the missionary sewing circle, in part because it reached out to individuals and sewing circles in the smaller towns of Worcester County. In comparison, the CMSC marshalled only its own members' labor and resources. The narrower focus of the CMSC dissolved, however, during the opening salvos of the Civil War.[68]

"April 27 [1861].... Our ladies very busy in sewing for the troops," noted an anonymous Worcester diarist just days after President Abraham Lincoln called for 75,000 volunteers in the wake of the Confederate attack on Fort Sumter, South Carolina. When the Civil War began, the women of Worcester's sewing circles moved immediately to centralize and to coordinate their organizations under a newly created women's directorate, the Worcester Soldiers' Relief Society (WSRS). The unprecedented structural shift occurred with remarkable speed and enthusiasm because what was new was not the fact of women's organizing, only its scale. Nearly one hundred and fifty women joined the WSRS as individual members while hundreds of others were affiliated through their sewing circles. Every church in Worcester—the Protestants, the Catholics, even the Spiritualists, for a total of twenty-two separate church-based sewing circles—contributed to the WSRS. But the WSRS's footprint was still greater, for the rural sewing circles forwarded their work to the urban women's organization and held teas and fairs to raise cash for the cause. In such a manner did the WSRS encompass the partisan energies of thousands of women in Worcester county. These same sewing circles also sponsored a related war relief organization, the Worcester Soldier's Rest, which provided meals, clothing, and shelter for soldiers awaiting trains at the city's busy railroad terminals.[69]

During the Civil War, the WSRS forwarded goods and supplies to, among others, Clara Barton, Dorothea Dix, the U.S. Sanitary Commission at Washington, the U.S. Sanitary Commission at Boston, the YMCA at Boston, and the Christian Commission. In 1865 the directorate estimated that over the previous four years its members had manufactured, collected, packaged, and forwarded "5851 shirts, 3578 pairs drawers, 4974 pairs socks, 8754 handkerchiefs, 5835 towels, 1038 pairs slippers, 1827 sheets, 2863 pillowcases, 1812 pairs mittens, and all other hospital supplies in proportion" as well as box after box and barrel upon barrel of preserved food and wine, "stationary, soap, combs, fans, eye shades, ring pads, compresses, books, scrapbooks, magazines," etc.[70]

As the Civil War wound down, the women channeled their energies toward the work of Reconstruction. The WASSC's own Lucy Chase went to Norfolk, Virginia, under the auspices of the Freedman's Bureau to organize a school for former slaves. From Norfolk, Chase appealed to her hometown to aid the freed people in the search for economic independence. As the Reverend Sweetser of the Calvinist Church replied to Chase, "Dear Friend, I rec'd your letter in due season. I read it to the ministers in our association, and also sent it to our Ladies to read in their sewing soc[iety]. Whether any of the ministers will do anything I do not know. The ladies thought they should be able to send you something. . . . Our ladies are at work very earnestly and accomplished a great deal. . . ."[71] Through the agency of the sewing circle, the women of antebellum Worcester built upon a tradition of individual and group sewing to become involved in local, national, and international movements for reform.

Efforts to unravel the tangled meanings and motivations of the outpouring of middle-class women's social activism in antebellum New England have tended to focus upon movements in which women played a prominent role, such as the national temperance or abolition campaigns. The often poorly documented local sewing circle, however, was both more representative of women's experience with benevolence and far more common. Sewing circles had deep roots in American culture, and as society changed, so did they—and so too did they help to change American society. It was, tellingly, as members of a missionary sewing circle, and not through their church or a secular organization, that the women of Worcester's orthodox Calvinist Church began to support fugitive slaves and a free soil crusade. Indeed, the sewing circles of antebellum Worcester illustrate the process by which women actively redefined their associated activities in an era of momentous change.

The history of the sewing circles of Worcester also finds that the long-dominant scholarly paradigm of public and private gender spheres cannot account for the ways in which these groups understood what they were doing. If, as some have suggested, by the 1850s women were pushed to the margins of national reform campaigns, such was clearly not the case in the local sewing circles, which prized women's work and relegated men to auxiliary status. As the experiences of the Centre Missionary Sewing Circle reveal, these women's groups experimented with new products, tried different methods of marketing their goods, and in general sought to make as much money as possible as quickly as possible. In so doing, the members of the sewing circles shared in the market orientation of their era. Their success led the women to take over the direct allocation of their funds, and they repeatedly rejected the assumption that social welfare was rightfully directed by men.

The sewing circle, where women reigned supreme, thus served as a forum for women's political development and for discursive analysis. Scores of sewing circles linked several generations of middle-class New England women to benevolent work, to making and selling goods for cash, and to urgent social and political questions. Through her membership in a sewing circle a woman in antebellum Worcester became educated about, and implicated in, the moral and political issues of her day. Ultimately, the links of the circle connected her not just to other women but to the fate of her community and her nation.

3

Maternal Politics

*Gender and the Formation of the
Worcester Children's Friend Society*

The most precious and comforting of titles given by our
Saviour to his disciples was that of *'little children,'*
indicating, by two words, entire dependence and the
sweetest relation earth knows. Every mother knows the
intensity of the meaning those words convey; perhaps she
best, who has early resigned her little ones to the cold
embrace of the grave.
—Worcester Children's Friend Society,
Twenty-first Annual Report

It was in the mid-1840s, Anstis Miles recalled, that her role as a city
missionary led her into "abodes of poverty and wretchedness" where
"she had witnessed the sad spectacle" of children learning from their
parents not sound household management and good citizenship but lessons in immorality and intemperance. The scenes so haunted Miles "by
night, and by day" that she felt compelled to take action. Familiar with
children's friend societies elsewhere, she proposed to form one in Worcester. Miles first appealed to local women but was rebuffed because her
proposal seemed too "visionary." Discouraged, Miles approached lawyer
and Whig politician Alfred D. Foster. When Foster gave her his wholehearted support, Miles found the courage to return to the skeptical women
and to convince them of the practicality of her venture. By the end of
1848, they had launched the Worcester Children's Friend Society (CFS),
an orphanage and child advocacy agency still in existence.[1]

Such is the nineteenth-century narrative of the founding of the
Worcester CFS, and its accuracy is dubious. According to manuscript

sources, the women were holding organizational meetings at Miles's home at the very time they were purportedly dismissing her initial entreaty.[2] The mid-nineteenth-century version of the founding of the CFS was essentially a creation myth that placed women at the center of human society. A woman embodying the maternal life force—Anstis "Mother" Miles, as she was known—sought out the support of a powerful male to legitimize her new family. Once he had performed this function, the woman relegated the male to an honorable but marginal role within the new family and turned to other women for support. Together the women fed, clothed, housed and nurtured the children until they were returned to their families of origin, placed in new families, or reached adulthood. When the founding mother grew too old to meet the demands of motherhood, the managers hired a professional to take over for her while they focused upon the social and economic responsibilities traditionally assigned to men. So successful were they at supporting the "family" that within a few years the Worcester Children's Friend Society was an established community resource for dependent women and children rendered poor by the inability of males to provide.

CLASS AND GENDER IN THE ANTEBELLUM ORPHAN ASYLUM

Studies of antebellum childsaving organizations have tended to focus upon the role of class in the founding and structuring of both large public welfare institutions and smaller private societies. The "social control" thesis of many pioneering interpretations—which argued that bourgeois reformers, worried about what they saw as rampant disorder and anxious about their own social position, attempted to control the working class by controlling their children—has come under considerable criticism. Recent interpretations tend to stress the more amorphous notion of hegemony, and have pointed to ways in which working people used, and were not just used by, institutions such as orphan asylums. Still, however defined or interpreted, class is at center stage in the history of antebellum welfare reform.[3]

Curiously, gender is not, even though the majority of antebellum orphan asylums were private societies founded and run by women. From Rochester to Boston, Worcester to Chicago, and Providence to Petersburg, women across the nation founded innovative asylums, children's friend societies, and foster family networks.[4] Historians of social welfare, however, have traditionally emphasized instead the "orphan trains" sponsored by Charles Loring Brace of the New York Children's Aid Society, and credit the Boston Children's Aid Society with developing the foster family system in 1863.[5] To some extent this is understandable, for Brace's New York CAS, founded in 1853, was arguably the most famous American childsaving organization in the nineteenth century. But the tendency for the relatively few childsaving societies founded and run by men to eclipse the far more numerous societies founded and run by women demands an explanation. In part, it points to the marked localism that characterized so many women's organizations. For example, where the men of the New York Children's Aid Society self-consciously appealed to a nationwide audience, the women of the Worcester Children's Friend Society gave priority to the problems of their immediate community and displayed no interest in developing a more widespread local network. But the antebellum separation of parenting responsibilities into paternal protection and maternal nurturance also influenced the aims and approaches of reformers operating within sex-segregated organizations. Thus, when confronted with a poor child, the men of the CAS tended to focus on the poverty while the women of the CFS tended to respond to the child. Male reformers were not uncaring nor were female reformers unaffected by economic concerns. But the managers of the Worcester CFS viewed the children in their care through the lens of their own experiences and expectations as women and mothers, leading them to emphasize the importance of meeting each child's unique needs. In contrast, in their ambition to find a national solution to what might as easily have been seen as a local problem, Brace and the New York CAS tended to lose sight, both figuratively and literally, of individual children.[6]

PATERNAL POLITICS AND CHARLES LORING BRACE

The New York Children's Aid Society (CAS) was the creation of Charles Loring Brace, a Congregational minister whose efforts on behalf of poor and vagrant children dramatically publicized the squalor of the Five Points neighborhood. In the 1850s, New York City was overwhelmed by the problem of vagrant and homeless children. Earlier that decade, a Unitarian minister had organized the Boston Children's Mission, which sent a trainload of orphaned and destitute children to families in the West. Brace dramatically expanded upon this approach and built the CAS upon two beliefs at the core of antebellum American culture: that the family was the locus of moral education and that charity should follow "the natural laws and demand for labor."[7]

To justify their societies to the public, both the CFS and the CAS cited scriptural injunctions of charity. Both also drew upon prevailing notions of gender. For the women, this meant references to their maternal feelings and to the innate benevolence of females. As a man, Brace made an appeal to reason by offering a pseudo-scientific explanation. Every needy child had "a separate moral malady," Brace argued, that required its own diagnosis and prescription. Institutions were inadequate both because they treated individuals as aggregates and because they ignored the fundamental "laws" of human nature. According to Brace, there were four such laws: small groups were preferable to large ones because small groups were more moral; virtue was necessary to a good life but "the virtues must not be drill-virtues, they must spring from the heart, and be exposed to the strain of temptation"; only a family could instill the "*sense of property*" necessary to develop "the instinct of economy"; and although the United States faced a challenge to order and prosperity from its rising industrial economy, it would not go the way of England, for America faced not an oversupply of labor, but a shortage.[8]

Brace's ambitious Emigration Plan was designed to conform to these laws of human nature by relocating urban poor children to the West, making them economic assets to farm families. Waxing Jeffersonian, Brace argued that a "peculiar *warm-heartedness*" and commitment to equality characterized America's farmers. Who better than sturdy farmers to educate and care for destitute children, who "are growing up to be citizens, and women"? Brace's plan diverted potential urban criminals into a life of usefulness building the new nation. Together, Brace exclaimed, the children composed a "little procession hastening to the land of hope in the West!" The Emigration Plan was an attractive package and it captured the American public's imagination.[9]

To find homes for the children, Brace addressed circulars to "Farmers and Mechanics and Manufacturers in the Country," advertising the child laborers. Boys, he suggested, could help on the farm or learn a trade; girls, presumptively barred by their sex from other work, could perform "the common kinds of housework." Brace later boasted that the response to the circulars was overwhelming. The CAS received "over 300 applications for our poor boys and girls, many from substantial business men, and from families of the highest character." New England took the bulk of the children during the early years, but gradually the center of demand moved farther west, to Illinois, Indiana, and Michigan. By 1856, only three years after its founding, the CAS had sent "some 2,000" children out of New York City; by 1858, this figure had reached 3,500; by 1860, 5,000. Approximately eighty percent of the children were Irish Catholics, immigrants and children of immigrants, whom Brace described as part of "the pauperism and poverty of England and Ireland . . . [that had] drained into New-York." According to Brace's statistics, one-third of the children had no parents, while two-thirds had at least one living parent.[10]

Work became the measure of the CAS child, and only children "of sound bodies" needed apply for assistance. Furthermore, Brace preferred that the sound bodies be male and was dismayed when many girls applied, for their labor was less in demand. Brace judged girls more troublesome than boys, "especially those beyond fourteen who have begun to engage in bad practices," and, he claimed, girls ran away more often. Worried about the society's "good name," Brace screened girls for good character; there was no such test for boys. As a consequence of this emphasis upon boys, the sex ratio of CAS children changed dramatically. Whereas initially there were a majority of females, 422 to 376, within two years boys outnumbered girls, 372 to 265, and by 1860, the CAS placed 617 boys but only 165 girls. Brace was not indifferent to the problems of poor girls, for he could as easily have refused to place them altogether. The CAS continued to welcome applications from "trades girls," but discouraged girls "in service," suggesting that girls armed only with traditional female skills were harder to place than boys with traditional male skills. Brace insisted that the number of girls had declined because separating girls from their families was especially difficult. "The wages of a young girl," he explained, "are much more sure to go to the pockets of the family, than those of a boy." Such reasoning does not, however, explain the large number of girls who initially applied to the CAS. Fundamentally, Brace's attack on urban poverty hinged upon employing the poor in traditional occupations. Skilled or unskilled, males were more favored.[11]

The tendency of the CAS to regard the child chiefly as a source of labor led it to neglect providing protection against abuse or exploitation. Unlike the Worcester CFS and other private women's societies, the CAS balked at accepting legal responsibility through Articles of Indenture. Indentures impeded the development of familial bonds, Brace insisted, and thus the children "will do better and stay more contentedly, than they would if bound to serve. The master too if a good man, will do as well, and even better, for the boy than if he should be bound to him for a term of years." Without indentures "the relation is much more free, and likely to be of better effect to both parties." However, indentures were not manifestly detrimental to the warmth of the master-apprentice relationship. Such rhetoric, which was more suitable to negotiating labor contracts than to arranging the custodial care of a child, suggests that the CAS hewed to traditional notions that defined children in economic, rather than in emotional, terms. But Brace really had no other choice. Articles of Indenture were pointless if they could not be enforced, and enforcement was not a simple matter even when the parties were in close proximity. The CAS dispersed children widely through the Northeast and Midwest, far from its New York City headquarters, and did not have the staff to ensure that those signing indentures lived up to them.[12]

Abstractly, a lack of indentures freed both parties to meet on equal terms. In reality, there was nothing to guarantee that families properly cared for, trained, or educated the children. In 1859, Brace boasted of a ninety-eight percent success rate among children under the age of fifteen. However, he interpreted success narrowly, using as his gauge the number of children who ended up in prison. Brace's measure is understandable in light of widely held assumptions that urban poverty bred crime; if the children grew up to be law-abiding rather than law-breaking, the CAS had obviously succeeded. Whether or not those sent west had greater economic opportunities than they would otherwise have had is unclear.[13]

But numerous documents testified to chronic problems with the Emigration Plan. *The Best Method of Disposing of Our Pauper and Vagrant Children*, which Brace published in 1859 to promote the society, reveals how little knowledge the CAS possessed of the lives of those whom it uprooted and attempted to transplant. Brace conceded that the children often lived unsettled lives, noting that "It is sometimes only after a year or two of writing that we can discover where some of the older [ones] are." He tried to view these facts positively, arguing that the reason the children were hard to find was because they moved around "with the hope of bettering themselves." Brace thus implied that the urban waifs had forgotten their bad habits and, under the wholesome influence of the West, had embraced a philosophy of self-help and upward mobility.[14]

To this end, Brace published letters from CAS field agents that sought to paint a vision of happy children in happy homes. In fact, the letters illustrate how slight was the society's information as to the whereabouts of the children, as well as the many problems the children faced in their new communities. "M.M.P.," an agent from Logansport, Indiana, was unsure how many children he had farmed out: ". . . one company of children under your society has been left in this community, that was about a year ago, and consisted of forty, more or less. A part have changed their places; the proportion I do not know. . . . Some mistakes were made at first . . . I can not say how many certainly. . . ." "J.L." from Newton, New Jersey, was even blunter: "I have entirely lost sight of the children who came to this place." The agent attempted to reassure the CAS by adding, "I feel very confident . . . that none of them have ever committed crimes. . . . If they had, my position is such that I would very likely have been made acquainted with the fact." From Hudson, Ohio, "G.D." described the selfish motives of some families who took a CAS child "to get a boy or girl who will do a good deal of work and not cost much to keep." One agent noted that children who tried the patience of their foster families might simply be allowed to leave, to face life on their own: "The one Mr. S. took, stole a horse; they followed him and on searching found he had stolen much generally. Mr. S. gave him a dollar and sent him off. I have not heard from him since."[15]

It is possible that the agents lost track of the children because they were rapidly absorbed into their new families, as Brace believed was the case. The Reverend Edward T., an agent from Kalamazoo, remarked, "One thing [that] surprises me is, *the speedy absorption of those children into the community*. Nobody seems to know where they are. They are seldom mentioned." It is hard to understand, however, how the Reverend T. could lose sight of the one hundred and twenty children that he stated "were sent to this locality." Moreover, other letters raise doubts that farm communities accepted the poor, mostly Irish Catholic children so readily. "W.W." from Ohio noted, "Many of our community think you are engaged in a glorious work, while some . . . think foreign paupers ought not to be brought here." As these letters suggest, the CAS agents had neither the time nor the resources to oversee the placement of the widely scattered children in particular homes, nor to follow up on the children once placed.[16]

An agency that did not know where its children were could not protect those who faced abuse or exploitation. Evidence of abuse is scarce, in part because the CAS had so little knowledge of the lives of the orphans in its nominal care. In at least one case, the outraged citizens of Garrettsville, Ohio, stepped in to protect a boy who had been "severely" whipped by his foster father and found him a new home. Brace was informed of the incident only by chance and only after it had been resolved. In 1857, Brace acknowledged that the CAS needed to take a more active role in watching over the children. He continued to maintain that abuse was rare; the thousands of children sent west were treated with "the most patient and generous kindness" with "only one or two exceptions." At the same time, Brace conceded that a permanent agent should be hired "to travel through many portions of the country, and personally satisfy himself of the condition of the children." Brace seemed genuinely unprepared to imagine that the New York Children's Aid Society could not rely upon the legendary "warm-heartedness" of western farm families and the gentlemen who vouched for them. "We endeavor to take the closest precautions in regard to the character of persons applying," he wrote earnestly, "but references are often given by clergymen or magistrates with too little care."[17] Ultimately, Brace's Emigration Plan better served the interests of urban reformers and rural employers than it did the interests of poor children.

MATERNAL POLITICS AND THE
WORCESTER CHILDREN'S FRIEND SOCIETY

Operating in a much smaller city and on a far more modest scale, the Worcester Children's Friend Society placed many fewer children than did Brace's New York Children's Aid Society. The distinctive profiles resulted from the fundamentally different ways their founders interpreted a common social problem and from the solutions they proposed. Brace and the CAS sought to remove the children from poverty by sending them out of the city to work on a farm; the women of the CFS sought to remove the poverty from the children by finding them an adoptive, not simply a foster, family. The two organizations shared a concern for the social and economic dilemmas confronting antebellum America, but the paternalism of the CAS and the maternalism of the CFS led their founders to sharply different strategies.

The women of the CFS concentrated exclusively on resolving the problems of their immediate community. The managers were aware of the existence of similar societies in other cities; indeed, Brace was a friend of CFS booster Edward Everett Hale and in the 1850s lectured several times in Worcester. Yet the women of the CFS did not attempt to link their society to others and expressed no interest in the possibility of a national organization. It was not that the female managers were apolitical but that they interpreted the problems of poor children in a way that, for the time being, rendered formal politics immaterial. Moreover, the women would come to learn that politicians could not be trusted. Charles Loring Brace was educated, respected, and an economically, politically, and legally independent man who hoped ultimately to reform the country, a dream made possible by his inclusion, actual or potential, in the institutions of power. The women of the Worcester CFS, although educated and well respected, were in a very different situation: they were economically, politically, and legally dependent upon others. Their power was a product of their force of will and personality, and was often quite effective on a local level. If, as their culture assured them, motherhood conferred social power, then the women of the CFS would sustain that role long after their own children had departed from the home.

"We Come in the Name of the Saviour"

By almost any measure, the women who founded and ran the Worcester Children's Friend Society were among the beneficiaries of the emerging market economy of the early nineteenth century, and their efforts were part of a more general attempt to take up social reform on behalf of others, especially children. The managers borrowed explicitly from the Providence, Rhode Island, Children's Friend Society to describe their goal as "to rescue from evil and misery, such children as are deprived of the care of their natural parents." Yet the problem of vagrant and homeless children, those most clearly "deprived of the care of their natural parents," was not their lone concern. There were not many children without families in Worcester; indeed, only a few of those brought to the CFS had been abandoned. When the managers spoke of parental deprivation, their point was not that some children did not have parents, but that some children had the wrong kind of parents.[18]

At first blush, the statements of the Worcester CFS appear to support the primacy of class motivations for reform. The judgments the women passed on the less fortunate were harsh and unyielding, rooted in ethnic and class prejudice. When they announced their creation to the public in January 1849, the managers proclaimed that their motherly hearts were cheered by the town's "multitudes of happy children."

Yet they were troubled because "hundreds of others" were not so fortunate. Experience, they insisted, refuted what instinct might command, for despite a popular faith in the innate maternalism of women "even a *mother* . . . can leave her helpless little one uncared for, and unprotected, day after day" when in the grip of alcohol or another form of immorality. They accused poor parents of being lazy and instilling in their children "a kind of professional, systematic mendacity" by sending them out to beg from strangers. In the face of such clear evidence of the abdication of parental responsibility, it was up to women such as themselves to save the children. They didn't act for themselves, the women declared, for "We come in the name of that Saviour who has said 'suffer little children to come unto me, and forbid them not'. . . ." Public-spirited citizens could do their part by contributing money, advice, sympathy, and prayer.[19]

The founding mothers listed four circumstances that justified their assuming responsibility for poor children: where the child was abandoned; in cases of "total incapacity of the parents" due to "habitual, inveterate habits of intemperance;" where it was "certain" that the child "will be sacrificed to vice" due to parental actions; or "when insanity, imbecility, or peculiar Providential dispensations" rendered the parents incapable of caring for their child. None of these measures of parental fitness was objective; even abandonment was qualified, for in the nineteenth century, a child became an orphan upon the death of its father, regardless of the health and welfare of its mother, so that an "orphaned" child could very well have a living parent, as well as other relatives. The other criteria were still more subjective, involving amorphous and culturally defined notions of vice and immorality. Indeed, their early rhetoric suggests that the women of the CFS were initially less concerned that poor children grow up in more comfortable homes than that the moral atmosphere of the homes the children already had be of a certain kind—their kind.[20]

Sentiments such as these, which were repeated by similar contemporary societies, appear to support interpretations linking middle-class social reform and social hegemony. However, if we look closely at who the women of the Worcester CFS were—their lives and deaths, their family ties and experiences—what emerges is a group portrait whose overriding theme is gendered instability, not bourgeois sanctimony. In addition, analysis of the way the managers actually ran the society— their policy decisions, their choices of whom to help and how to help them, the way they exercised power and the limits upon that power—reveals that their actions were marked not by rigidity but by flexibility, not by order but by what might be called controlled chaos. In the name of the children and in the defense of the mother, the managers repeatedly contradicted in practice their stated goal of separating poor children from wicked parents. The matriarchal family created in late 1848 became the Worcester Children's Friend Society, an anti-institutional, semi-public private "home" run by and for women.[21]

THE PROBLEM OF GENDERED INSTABILITY

In many ways the women who founded and ran the Children's Friend Society were among the more privileged in antebellum Worcester, and even, arguably, in the nation. Analysis of tax information and business relationships reveals that on average the managers enjoyed a higher level of economic prosperity than did many antebellum Americans. However, in other equally important ways, the women were much more ordinary and endured significant economic, personal and family crises over which they had little direct control. It was this combination of prosperity and instability, their intimate knowledge of both promise and failure, that is the key to understanding the women's approach to social reform and their community's welfare.

From the society's founding in late 1848 until the Civil War, seventy-three women filled the position of manager or assistant manager of the Worcester CFS. Most were mature women, whose own children were approaching or had reached adulthood. Although only in their thirties and forties, by the standards of the day most likely considered themselves to be well advanced into middle age. Nearly one-third of the managers joined while in their thirties, almost one-half joined in their forties, and fifteen percent joined in their fifties. In other words, the women of the CFS were well-established adults with considerable life experience. Nearly ninety percent were or had been married; twenty-one percent had married widowers and collected an assortment of stepchildren; twenty-two percent had buried at least one spouse, and seven of the widows had remarried. More than one out of ten, however, was unmarried; of these, only one, Hester Newton, remained on the Board after marriage. The women were also overwhelmingly daughters of New England, mostly from Massachusetts. Still, although a large portion was from Worcester itself, two-thirds had relocated there as adults, part of the influx into the city of the ambitious and the upwardly mobile that characterized the antebellum years.[22]

In their choice of marriage partners, too, the women represented the trends of their era. The largest bloc of managers, nearly sixty percent, was married to manufacturers, merchants, or professionals, those seeking to take advantage of the city's opportunities for economic growth. Some of the women came from old money. Rebecca Lincoln Newton was the daughter of Levi Lincoln I, Thomas Jefferson's Attorney General, and the sister of two governors; her husband, Rejoice Newton, was an attorney, politician, and investor who helped to bring the railroad to Worcester. Ann Buffum Earle married into a family associated with pioneer textile manufacturer Samuel Slater. Her husband, Edward Earle, manufactured card clothing equipment, machinery vital to the developing textile industry. Others began their married lives in more modest circumstances, such as Hannah Smith, a schoolteacher, who married dry goods clerk Stephen E. Temple.[23]

Many CFS women had united with men whose careers demonstrated the entrepreneurial flair upon which the citizens of Worcester increasingly prided themselves. Ethan Allen, husband of Manager Sarah Johnson Allen, started out making cutlery but became rich with his patented design for the "Allen Pepperbox," a repeating pistol that rivaled Winchester's Colt in sales and was immortalized in Mark Twain's stories of riverboat gambling. As a boy, Isana Goddard's husband, Isaac, was apprenticed to a paper maker, moved up to mill superintendent, then struck out on his own to manufacture paper making machinery. A large percentage of CFS members were married to highly skilled artisans, such as carpenters and masons, who prospered with the town's physical expansion. Maria Bigelow, for example, wed Mason H. Morse, a carpenter turned wealthy building contractor. More than one manager in five, however, was herself a head of household.[24]

The women also belonged to overlapping circles of family and friends. Five pairs of mothers and daughters joined the antebellum society, including a stepmother and stepdaughter. With just one exception, the daughters followed their mothers into surrogate parenting as they had followed them into actual parenting, seeming to assume the mantle of CFS membership as a rite of passage into womanhood. When Treasurer Rebecca Lincoln Newton died in 1855, her daughter Hester Newton stepped in and served as treasurer until her death forty-four years later. The ties among the members similarly encompassed their extended families. Sarah Parker Mason was Rebecca Newton's niece and Hester Newton's cousin, and grew up in the Newton household; Louisa Gladding Brown and Sarah Knowlton Brown were in-laws, married to brothers; Ellen Buffum married a cousin of Ann Buffum Earle's; Hannah Chamberlin Wheelock and Caroline Chamberlin Pratt were sisters; Sarah Johnson Allen and Lucinda Allen Thurber were sisters-in-law; after Thurber died in 1853, her husband Charles remarried, and Caroline Estey Bennett assumed Lucinda's role as a wife to Charles, a mother to Lucinda's two children, and a CFS manager. Such intimate ties among the women strengthened the organization by facilitating group cooperation, and underscored the society's emphasis upon communal reciprocity.[25]

Business relationships also overlay a chart of the CFS membership. Lacking the waterpower vital to large-scale manufacturing prior to the invention of the steam engine, Worcester's economic development initially relied instead upon the output of highly skilled artisans in small shops and partnerships. The organization of the economy into many small manufactories was thus an economic necessity that soon became a point of city pride. As one local newspaper bragged in 1840, "We have no *corporation* in Worcester, not one...."[26]

The business connections of CFS members reflected these familiar and often familial arrangements. Mason Morse, married to Manager Maria Bigelow Morse, built Butman's Block for Benjamin Butman, married to Manager Maria Cooley Butman. Charles Thurber, husband of Managers Lucinda Allen Thurber and then Caroline Bennett Thurber, manufactured guns in partnership with his first wife's brother, Ethan Allen, who was the husband of Manager Sarah Allen. William Brown, wed to Manager Louisa Gladding Brown, and Theophilus Brown, wed to Manager Sarah Knowlton Brown, were merchant tailors as W & A Brown and Company. Draper Ruggles, the husband of Manager Caroline Blake Ruggles, and John Mason, the husband of Manager Sarah Parker Mason, made agricultural tools as Ruggles, Nourse, Mason and Company. Thomas Drew, married to Manager Mary Shute Drew, and Edward Earle, married to Manager Ann Buffum Earle, were partners in the publishing business and went bankrupt together in 1848. Edward Earle also was a partner with Joseph Pratt, wed to Manager Caroline Chamberlin Pratt, this time in the iron business. They, too, went bankrupt, this time in 1858. The women of the CFS thus represented a combination of old money and new, established families and the recently arrived.

Their economic status was similarly diverse. Although many of the women came from wealthy families, most did not. An 1846 tax assessment indicates that thirty percent of the women belonged to families with property valued at more than $10,000; however, by 1850 this figure had dropped to twenty-five percent as a result of the economic downturn of the late 1840s. The largest group of women, more than half, were members of middle-class families who held less than $5,000 in property, while nearly one in four came from families of respectable but modest means, that is, those with less than $1,000 of real or personal property.[27]

These assessments should be considered a minimum indication of family wealth due to the peculiarities of antebellum tax assessment procedures, which assumed that the taxpayer could be relied upon to report honestly all of his or her real and personal property. Each spring, the elected tax assessors notified the Worcester public that "each of you, liable by law to be assessed" was to submit "true and perfect lists of your Polls, and all your Estates, both real and personal." The property lists of the 1846 tax assessment—which not infrequently detailed every pig, heifer, and shoat—suggest that many taxpayers complied as expected. Still, it seems likely that in the absence of revenue enforcement mechanisms, substantial amounts of wealth went unreported. Under-reporting was even more likely in the case of personal property, which composed the bulk of women's taxable wealth and was more easily concealed than real estate. Overall, however, the assessments reveal that the managers were women of comfort or privilege, although a substantial number were not.[28]

But a picture of wealth based upon tax assessments is incomplete, for if the developing economy of the nineteenth century offered unprecedented opportunities to succeed, it also held out unprecedented opportunities to fail. One history of debt and bankruptcy in the early nineteenth century found that, as a result of economic expansion and monetary instability, at least one in five householders went bankrupt, while other studies have estimated that from forty to fifty percent of businesses failed.[29] Such a high incidence of financial failure reveals that individuals worth a great deal on paper did not necessarily have sufficient reserves to ride out bad times or even to meet an unanticipated demand for payment of a debt. In the late 1820s, a wave of bankruptcy swept through western Massachusetts, engulfing both farmers and manufacturers. As Worcester lawyer Christopher Columbus Baldwin recorded in his diary, "Great distress among woollen manufacturers . . . there are failures almost daily. . . . They are mostly farmers; they average almost one a day!!" In 1834 John Davis, the governor of Massachusetts and a Worcester resident, paid taxes on property assessed at an impressive $15,000. Yet just two years earlier, his wife, Eliza Bancroft Davis, had scrambled to settle a debt of $750. As Davis wrote to her husband, ". . . you have on hand a hundred and thirty dollars—but little to meet a demand for $750 so I hope you will not have to meet the office of Gov[ernor] a Bankrupt."[30]

Although bankruptcy did not carry the degree of shame of times past, neither was it considered routine, and a good reputation remained vital to gain access to capital. Indeed, the vernacular for bankruptcy, "embarrassment in business," suggests the disapprobation visited upon those unable to pay their debts. Financial distress was made all the more devastating by a social ethic that measured a man by his economic success; economic failure implied a moral flaw.[31] In 1850, for example, an article in a Worcester newspaper cited four reasons why businesses failed: excessive ambition, laziness, greed for luxuries, and moral turpitude. In each, the fault lay with the proprietor, not with forces beyond his control, such as an unstable, unregulated economy. Imprisonment for debt, the customary punishment for bankruptcy, was rare but still occasionally enforced. Samuel Wilder had lavishly entertained the Marquis de Lafayette during the general's visit to Worcester in 1824. By 1842 Wilder's fortunes had declined, and he spent four months keeping himself entertained in debtor's prison. At mid-century a series of sketches of turn-of-the-century Worcester by Clarendon Wheelock, husband of CFS Manager Hannah Chamberlin Wheelock, vividly reminded locals of the fate of Timothy Bigelow, a Revolutionary War hero who languished and died in the town jail because he could not pay his debts.[32]

As devastating as bankruptcy was for men, it hit women with a unique force. Women seldom went bankrupt themselves if only because a woman was rarely extended credit sufficient to permit such a thing. In 1839, William Lincoln, brother of Manager Rebecca Lincoln Newton and secretary of the Worcester County Institute for Savings, flatly denied Emily Stevens's loan application "not because the security was not adequate, but upon the ground that it is inexpedient to make loans in any case where the principal is a female."[33] But if a woman found it difficult to overextend her credit by herself, it could be accomplished vicariously. Until the passage of a married women's property act in 1855, a Massachusetts woman's property was liable to seizure by creditors to pay her husband's debts. Unless she controlled an estate legally separate from her husband's, something which was usually available only to the wealthy, an antebellum woman could not be insured against impoverishment at the hands of another. The nineteenth century's assumption of female dependency, enforced by law and by custom, thus meant that for most women the power to make critical economic decisions belonged to others.[34]

Even worse, widespread gender discrimination in education and employment meant that money lost in speculative ventures or as a result of business failure was unlikely to be recouped through women's efforts.[35] Consequently, for women and girls the future was necessarily tinged with uncertainty, even fear. The recurring economic downturns of the nineteenth century—known to contemporaries as "panics," suggesting their immediate and gut-wrenching impact—could disrupt a family's hopes and plans and permanently alter lives. The Panic of 1837, which triggered numerous farm and business failures, led two Worcester girls to ponder the prospects of their schoolmates: ". . . we heard something of the Farnums. Their Father did not fail as was reported, neither are the girls working in a Factory. They expect to return to Green[field Academy] in the spring." Had their father indeed failed, the Farnum girls' preparation for middle-class womanhood would have come to an abrupt halt, replaced by a future as "factory girls." The long-term implications of financial failure were also apparent to Louisa Jane Trumbull, whose own father was the cashier of the Worcester Bank. During the Panic of 1837, fifteen-year-old Louisa recorded in her diary that the father of one of her friends "has lately failed and there are things connected with his failure which will make it impossible for him to obtain employ. This is a deathblow to the prospects of his children." Few antebellum Americans were shielded from the fallout of the developing economy's fits and starts. But the presumption of feminine legal and economic dependence rendered women uniquely vulnerable to economic instability.[36]

More than one in four members of the CFS knew first-hand the uncertainty and social embarrassment of bankruptcy. Maria Bradley Wyman was the wife of a Worcester dry goods merchant. Although his business stock was valued at $15,000 in 1846, John Wyman could not pay his debts and was forced into bankruptcy. In 1848, Osgood Bradley, a carriage manufacturer and husband of Manager Fanny Bradley, also went bankrupt. Eliza Bliss Ballard was first associated with the CFS in

1849 as an assistant manager but within a year had moved up to manager, a position she held until 1879. Her husband, Charles, followed a similar upward career path as a manufacturer of card setting equipment. Ballard's fortunes improved as he moved steadily from an independent sash and blind maker in 1845, to employment as a machinist for the firm of Ball & Rice in 1854, to buying out one of his employers and forming the partnership of Ball & Ballard in 1855. But the depression of the late 1850s forced Ballard into bankruptcy in 1860. Three years later, he was back at his old shop but reduced in status to that of an employee of a new partnership, Ball & Williams. Benjamin Butman, husband of Manager Maria Cooley Butman, was a West India goods and grocery merchant who sank much of his wealth into developing Worcester real estate. Butman's extensive properties included the Brinley Block, a row of shops and offices along Main Street, and Brinley Hall, the site of numerous lectures, parties, and exhibitions. Butman also went bankrupt three times, in 1838, 1840, and 1848, when he was unable to make good on his extensive real estate speculations. During the 1840 bankruptcy, the Butmans underwent the indignity of having their belongings sold at a public auction to satisfy his creditors, and were able to turn their fortunes around only through a timely inheritance from their nephew and adopted son.[37]

As these examples suggest, even those with considerable resources on paper could be vulnerable to the vicissitudes of antebellum America's unprecedented boom-and-bust market economy. While tax assessments indicate that many of the women of the CFS belonged to families with substantial property, the economic reality of their lives could be quite different. Economic instability as well as economic prosperity shaped their lives, and was a crucial aspect of their world over which they, as legally dependent women, had little control. A woman's class standing could thus vary significantly over time, keyed as it was to the luck and skill of her father or husband; rarely was an antebellum woman able to determine her class position through her own efforts. Or, to be more precise, rarely was an antebellum woman able to attain, through her own efforts, any class position other than poor. The era's definition of "middle class" as a sensibility rather than a distinct socioeconomic status addressed this structural and gender crisis. If a woman could not always *be* middle-class, she could at least *act* as if she were.

Fifteen percent of the women of the CFS, moreover, were self-supporting widows or single women, and most of these struggled to get by. Abigail Hunt, a single woman, juggled her responsibilities as an assistant manager with running a boarding house from rented lodgings. Eliza Cole, a young widow, had no taxable property and no home of her own. Catherine Bemis lost her three-year-old son, George, in July 1836, and her husband, John, a merchant, one month later; by the late 1840s, Bemis was supporting herself and her surviving children by running a boarding house out of her Park Street home. Charlotte Heywood Foxcroft, widowed in 1824, was more fortunate. Not only did she own a home on Park Street but she also held $600 in bank shares and had $300 in the bank earning interest, while her children awaited a paternal inheritance of $3,000. To meet her household expenses, however, Foxcroft also opened her home to those who were willing to pay her board; all the while she held the leadership position of First Directress. Not all women could balance supporting a family and the demands of the CFS. Jane Pinkham was the third wife of a dry goods clerk. When she was widowed in 1884, Pinkham needed a job and turned to the business with which she was most familiar: the CFS, which hired her as the assistant matron. Thus, while many managers enjoyed privileged lives, most did not enjoy economically secure lives, and this distinction is critical to understanding the women's motives for reform.[38]

Further evidence that instability was an essential element in the lives of the women of the CFS is provided by their high level of residential mobility. Europeans remarked with wonder upon the frequency with which Americans changed their lodgings. As Frances Trollope of England observed, "On the 1st of May the city of New York has the appearance of sending off a population flying from the plague, or of a town which had surrendered on condition of carrying away all their goods and chattel. . . . Every one I spoke to on the subject complained of this custom as most annoying, but all assured me it was unavoidable, if you inhabit a rented house."[39] Worcester was no exception. As the editor of the *Palladium* conceded wryly in 1849, the paper was "really *unfashionable*" because it was among the few in town to stay put. The women of the CFS were much more fashionable: only five of the seventy-three managers lived at the same address for the twelve years under study, and most moved every three to four years. While the less privileged tended to change residences more frequently, even the wealthiest were a migratory lot, packing up their homes and hearths in the springtime to relocate, sometimes just around the corner. For example, when Amos Brown died in 1848, he left Mary Rider Brown a substantial estate. The new widow moved with her daughters from 238 Main Street to 264 Main Street, next door to Manager Ann K. Colton. In 1850, Brown invited fellow Manager Mary Spurr and her children to move in; Spurr, widowed in 1842, had been boarding at various addresses for several years. In 1855, Brown moved again, this time south to 317 Main Street before returning to 264 Main Street in 1857, where she remained until 1865.[40]

Other CFS members moved still more often, but the circuit they followed tended to be limited to two areas: the middle-class Crown Hill neighborhood west of Main Street and the comfortable Mount Vernon and Union Hill neighborhoods northeast of the town center of Lincoln Square. First developed in the late 1840s, these neighborhoods were distinguished by their balloon-frame, two-story wood houses set on deep but narrow lots. The houses were similarly narrow, with the gable facing the street to yield a basic floor plan one room wide and three rooms deep, which facilitated heating during Worcester's long, cold winters. Sliding doors separating the parlor and the dining room could be opened to form one large room for meetings or entertaining. Relatively spacious by the standards of the day, light and airy, the houses were not especially large, often no more than six or seven rooms, and were closely packed together, a short block or two from Worcester's busy Main Street.[41]

Managers with fewer or more uncertain economic resources were even more peripatetic and tended to roam the most. Mary Ann Farwell, for example, was born in Fitchburg, Worcester county, married and moved to Big Flatts, New York, returned to Fitchburg, then relocated to Worcester, where she, her husband, and their four surviving children settled near the Blackstone Canal on Howard Street, in central Worcester. They moved across Main to Elizabeth in 1849, then two years later crossed town to the more rural Plantation Street so that Simeon Farwell, formerly a painter and a fancy box manufacturer, could take up farming. After two years, the Farwells pulled up stakes once more and moved to Michigan.

Not all managers could afford "going to house-keeping," that is, could be independent householders.[42] Women in more straitened circumstances turned to family, business relations, and each other to form extended households. The home lives of widows, such as Eliza Cole or Charlotte Foxcroft, were especially complicated. Cole boarded in the homes of others; Foxcroft took in boarders. But married managers could also find it difficult to establish their own homes. Martha Freeman Goddard's husband was an apprentice watchmaker in his father's jewelry business; the couple boarded with his parents at 14 High Street, where Martha died in childbirth in 1860, at age twenty-five. Others resided with their families out of choice. Hester Newton was economically independent, thanks to an inheritance of $12,000, but preferred to live with her widowed father in the three-story brick home her wealthy parents had built on State Street. When Newton married attorney and childhood friend John Wetherell, he joined her in the Newton family home. But whatever the particular circumstances of the women's living arrangements, they had one thing in common: in the frequent ritual of locating an acceptable new home, packing and unpacking the household, settling in children, relatives, boarders, and pets, setting their houses in order and finding just the right new place for everything, the women of the CFS experienced recurring domestic disruption, their lives characterized not by constancy but by constant change.

Taken together, the tax assessment, insolvency records, and residential data unveil a complex portrait of the women who founded and ran the CFS. The managers included women from the local (and state) political and economic elite, from the newer entrepreneurial segments of the emerging market society, and those on the financial and social margin. Some women belonged to families that were quite wealthy; most belonged to families that were financially comfortable; a significant percentage worked hard to make ends meet. Yet all were subject to the uncertainties of the emerging market, their economic security most apparent in retrospect. The lives of the managers of the CFS were directly and intimately shaped by the antebellum era's unpredictable economy, and while they might look forward to the future with hope, experience had taught that they could not do so with confidence.

Another area of life, crucial to the women's sense of purpose and of self, further illuminates the instability and the absence of control inherent in their circumstances. The founders of Worcester's Children's Friend Society also had in common the knowledge of what it meant to lose a child. All of the married women for whom data are available gave birth at least once, or adopted at least one child, for a total of one hundred and fifty children, an average of 2.8 children per woman. Yet despite their relatively privileged births, fully one-third of these children died as infants or before reaching adulthood. Stated another way, each mother in the CFS could reasonably expect to bury at least one of her children. In reality, tragedy struck unevenly. Mary Rider Brown gave birth to three daughters and buried two before they had reached their second year.

Neither of Hester Newton Wetherell's two children lived long enough to be named. Her first child, "No Name Wetherell," died five minutes after birth, while her second, also "No Name Wetherell," was born prematurely. Caroline Chamberlin Pratt gave birth to four sons: two died within the first year, one died of scarlet fever at age eleven, and the other, his father's namesake, died of a seizure at age twenty-three. Ann King Colton was more fortunate. Of five known children, she lost only one. But the loss, difficult under any circumstances, came at an especially trying time. As Colton labored to give birth to her third child, her second-born, four-year-old Mary Rodman, lay gravely ill with a fever. Two days later, little Mary succumbed. Colton, at once a new mother and a grieving mother, named the new baby after her dead daughter.[43]

In antebellum America, the first five years were the danger years and the women of the CFS knew it well. Mary Drew gave birth to five children over the course of eleven years. Her first-born, Thomas, died at four of the croup; her fourth child, Frank, also died at four, of scarlet fever. Rebecca Goddard gave birth to two girls: the first died at fifteen months, the second at twelve months; two of Mary Green's three children did not survive their first year; Abigail Rawson gave birth to twin daughters: one survived only two weeks while the other died at five months of "cholera infantum," or dehydration. But children were vulnerable at any age. Deborah Dunbar lost one son at twelve months and a second at ten years, while Dorcas Lee's son William died at five from a head wound. Harriett Russell Barry, apparently unable to have children, adopted Emma, who drowned at the age of sixteen, while Maria Cooley Butman lost two of her three adopted children, including Elizabeth Paine, who died in childbirth at the age of twenty-three. Nor did high social rank insure against disaster. Mary Pond, whose husband was a farmer with a substantial estate, gave birth at least three times: Charles died at six of scrofula, an infection of the lymph glands of the throat, and Emma died at twenty-three of tuberculosis; only Isabel, Pond's youngest, survived. The managers thus knew intimately how swiftly maternal joy could turn to sadness, for the years they spent in pregnancy and child care were too often but a prelude to a child's early death.

The managers also could not escape the constant reminders of the frailty of the body because health in general was precarious in antebellum America—and growing more so. As a contemporary and supporter of the CFS, Eliza Bancroft Davis, described to her husband in 1831, "Everybody seems to be complaining, some sick, some dying, some dead."

Family correspondence from this period reveals a preoccupation bordering on an obsession with the health of friends and loved ones, as when Rebekah Dean Salisbury, whose wealthy husband Stephen Salisbury II would become a CFS advisor, warned her sister Catherine Dean Flint, "This is not a letter but a bulletin of health." Indeed, so pervasive were health concerns that a letter writer who failed to render a timely fitness report was presumed to be hiding something. As an anxious Matilda Butterworth Chase wrote to her adult son Anthony Chase of Worcester, "My ever dear son, I have of late had many forebodings about the[e] as it has been a long time sense [*sic*] I received a letter from the[e] for fear that thou wast sick and did not wish for me to know it. . . ."[44]

Davis, Salisbury, and Chase had good reason to be anxious. The decades from 1840 to 1869 witnessed a short-term rise in mortality rates among the native-born white population and a consequent decline in life expectancy, especially for women. In antebellum Worcester, death rates exhibited a rapid upward trend: in 1828, one out of every eighty residents died; in 1838, one out of fifty-nine; in 1848, one out of forty.[45]

Although the jump in mortality is apparent, its cause is not; however, a number of factors likely contributed to diminishing life spans. While food was often plentiful and relatively inexpensive, American diets relied heavily on fatty meats, starches, and carbohydrates, and was low in fiber. Moreover, to conserve labor, busy housewives cooked large quantities at once. Farm wife Adelaide Isham Crossman of South Sutton, Worcester county, rolled up her sleeves and in one hectic afternoon baked seven meat pies, four apple pies, numerous loaves of bread and several cakes, as well as pots of soup and vats of "beens" sufficient to feed her family for the following week. Food thus prepared was stored in pie safes or cellars and subject to the depredations of rats and other vermin; moreover, a lack of refrigeration, especially in the booming urban areas, meant that food often was spoiled. The result was chronic digestive upset and the litany of bowel complaints so evident in letters and diaries of the period regardless of the economic status of the sufferer. "Mother has not been very well for the last week. She had diarrhea & tho relieved from it entirely she does not look quite right yet. . . . She is not sick only not quite well," Rebekah Salisbury informed her sister in 1841. Treatments for the recurrent bouts of dyspepsia and dysentery were imaginative if not effective. Physicians liberally prescribed emetics in cases of diarrhea, even for infants, while those who preferred tonics could sip Mrs. Kidder's delightfully named "Dysentery Cordial," which promised "an immediate and perfect cure for cholera morbus, dysentery, diarrhea, summer complaints of children, sea sickness, general debility, etc., etc." A young Stephen Salisbury, suffering from "oppression of the stomach" allegedly caused by eating cold fruit, rode horseback for two and a half miles to "shake the stomach down," but succeeded only in adding chafed legs to his digestive discomfort.[46]

Other health threats were more deadly. Tuberculosis, known colloquially as "consumption" because the disease appeared to consume its victim, was a subtle but relentless killer and the leading cause of death in the nineteenth century, accounting for approximately one out of every five deaths, and, in the 1830s, for one out of every four. In some years the death toll was still higher: in the second half of 1842, nearly forty percent of adult deaths in Worcester were attributed to consumption. Unlike epidemic diseases, which disproportionately afflicted the poor, tuberculosis was no respecter of social class or condition. It did, however, demonstrate a marked gender preference and struck women especially hard, a fact of which contemporaries were well aware.[47] A recent history of the disease points out that the consumptive's decline was not, as popular nineteenth-century images sometimes suggested, in the least bit romantic. Death from tuberculosis was often slow, in some cases taking several decades, and always involved great suffering: listlessness and fatigue, chest pain, fever, incessant coughing, labored breathing, joint pain and swelling, throat ulcers, night sweats and diarrhea, lung hemorrhages, and the dramatic weight loss that gave the sufferer the appearance of a living—but barely breathing—corpse. Medical science had no cure for tuberculosis and did not yet even understand that it was contagious; moreover, such treatments that existed were often as harsh as the symptoms.[48]

Tuberculosis also inflicted considerable emotional pain upon the victim and his or her family, for the course of the disease was highly unpredictable. Periods of apparent remission raised hopes for an eventual recovery, only to be dashed by a sudden worsening of the condition. In 1843, seventeen-year-old Maria Allen of Worcester described the consumption of her cousin, Elizabeth Allen:

> Lizzie Allen is in a consumption as you may have heard ere this. . . . She is gradually wasting away. I wish you were here to see her; I do not think that she realizes her situation in the least. Consumption is so flattering a disease that it deceives

us to the last. I suspect there is no doubt but that Lizzie is too far gone to be made better. . . .

I wonder sometimes what the sensations of so young a girl must be when she is told that she must bid adieu to all things below. I think that Lizzie will soon be calm although at first the struggle will be great. She may continue weeks but it is not at all probable; I shall miss her beyond account.[49]

Maria Allen erred somewhat in her estimation of her cousin's death; Lizzie Allen lingered for five more months before dying in February 1844, at age seventeen. (Maria Allen herself would soon learn what it meant to be young and "bid adieu to all things below" when she succumbed to scarlet fever two years later.) Bereft family and friends testified to the psychological and emotional devastation that tuberculosis wrought by repeatedly characterizing the consumptive's slow death as "sudden." Because the progress of the disease was so uncertain, the sufferer's eventual death was experienced as a shock, magnifying the blow that survivors had to absorb. Lizzie Allen's death, while clearly anticipated, was thus described by a cousin as "very sudden—she dined as usual—before tea was dead." When Albert Congdon of Worcester died of tuberculosis in 1843, a family member similarly perceived his death as "rather sudden" even though the long-consumptive Congdon "had been quite ill for a week."[50]

The women of the CFS enjoyed no greater physical immunity than did their contemporaries and experienced a representative rate of tuberculosis: of those for whom the cause of death is known, more than one in five died from the disease. In addition, four managers were widowed by tuberculosis, while five nursed children through their illnesses to their consumptive deaths. Among those hardest hit were the most privileged. Rebecca Lincoln Newton, the CFS's first treasurer and one of its initial incorporators, was born into the prominent Lincoln family, which dominated Whig and Republican politics in Massachusetts. The Lincolns were also haunted by the specter of tuberculosis. In 1845, Newton's nephew, Levi Lincoln III, died of the disease at age thirty-five; in 1846, his sister and Newton's niece, Ann Lincoln, died of tuberculosis at age twenty-eight; and 1847 found Newton traveling south with her consumptive son, Levi Lincoln Newton, in the belief that a warmer climate would ease his condition. From Virginia, Newton wrote hopefully to her husband, "Lincoln has not entirely got rid of his cough, although I think it is yielding to the influence of the warm climate." Her confidence was misplaced; Levi Lincoln Newton died not long after at twenty-seven years of age.[51]

In the consecutive deaths of her nephew, niece, and son, Rebecca Lincoln Newton glimpsed her own future for she, too, was consumptive. Even as she helped to found and run the CFS, keeping a careful accounting of its revenues and expenditures, Newton fought a painful battle against the disease. By the mid-1850s, the Newton family was running up large bills with Worcester physician Dr. John Green in the desperate search for a cure or, failing that, for some way to alleviate her suffering. In June 1854, Dr. Green was applying leeches to Newton's body, a common and useless form of treatment, and prescribing cognac and rum to control the pain. The macabre image is striking, even absurd: a cadaverous Newton, sixty-two years old, littered with leeches and sipping brandy as she struggled to breath while figuring the CFS's accounts. By January 1855, Rebecca Lincoln Newton was terminal and was eased toward death, and possibly into it, with several gallons of rum and seventy ounces of chloroform. After Newton died, the managers scrambled to finish her accounting for their *Annual Report*, for despite Newton's lengthy decline, they found they had "had no opportunity for conference with the late Treasurer" before her "sudden" death.[52]

Like Rebecca Lincoln Newton, Charlotte Heywood Foxcroft was a founding member of the CFS and a consumptive. Also like Newton, Foxcroft had to endure the death of her child from the disease they shared. Elizabeth Haskins Foxcroft, Charlotte's youngest daughter, was only eighteen when she died of tuberculosis at her widowed mother's home following a lengthy physical decline that made it difficult for the young woman to even sit up without assistance. In the spring of 1836, Elizabeth Foxcroft's "lung fever" appeared to have abated, permitting her to attend services at the Unitarian church and raising her family's hopes for a return to good health. Not long thereafter, the neighbors noticed a commotion at the Foxcroft home. Only fifteen minutes after the physician had assured her anxious mother that she was on the mend, Elizabeth gasped "I cannot breathe so much longer" and died. A stunned Charlotte Foxcroft told a neighbor that "We had time for nothing but to stand round her bed and see her die. Her death was occasioned by a sudden rush of blood upon the lungs. . . ." Elizabeth Foxcroft's hemorrhage was typical of the final moments of tuberculosis sufferers, whose deaths were announced by an outpouring of arterial blood from mouth and nose; shocked family members could do nothing but watch help-lessly as the victim choked and suffocated in the bright red pool. The following Sunday, Charlotte Foxcroft and her surviving children took what comfort they could from their minister, who used the occasion of Elizabeth's death to preach a sermon from John 14:18, "I will not leave you comfortless: I will come to you." Charlotte Foxcroft herself died of tuberculosis in 1862, at the age of sixty-nine. Witnesses to their children's deaths from consumption, Newton and Foxcroft could only wait and watch for their own slow deaths to unfold.[53]

Yet rather than impeding the women's service to the CFS, tuber-culosis may even have inspired greater dedication, for consumptives were disproportionately represented in leadership positions. Of the five women elected to office in 1849 to ensure that the society got off to a good start, three had tuberculosis: Treasurer Rebecca Newton, Second Directress Charlotte Foxcroft, and Secretary Marcia Pomeroy Knowlton. More-over, the six women known to have died of tuberculosis were distin-guished by their devotion and by their lengthy terms of service. With the exception of Foxcroft, who resigned seven years prior to her death to move to Boston to be with her daughter, all of the CFS consumptives died "in the harness." Rebecca Newton died in 1855 in her sixth year in office. Hannah Chamberlin Wheelock joined in 1849 as an assistant manager and was elected second directress in 1852; she died in office the following year, at age forty-five. Marcia Knowlton, like Newton an original incorporator, was the society's first and only secretary until shortly before she succumbed to tuberculosis in 1871. Martha Moore Wood-ward joined as an assistant manager in 1853, was elected manager three years later, and served in that capacity until her death in 1878. Finally, Sarai Wiswell Lombard served as an assistant manager for twenty-five years, from 1853 until her death in 1878. A recent study of tuberculosis has found that male consumptives were more likely than non-consump-tives to take up religious or social causes because their unusual aware-ness of death encouraged an uncompromising devotion to principle. The evidence from the CFS suggests that consumptive women responded to the hand fate had dealt them with a similar commitment to improving their community for as long as they could.[54]

Other managers endured chronic health problems that may also have encouraged their desire to be useful. Lusanna Whiting Tolman collected money for the CFS for three years despite the constant hunger and thirst from the diabetes that finally killed her in 1858. Mary Ann

Banister's red face indicated that she suffered from erysipelas, familiarly known as St. Anthony's Fire, a streptococcal infection of the skin and subcutaneous tissues marked by redness, swelling, and a general sense of malaise that also disproportionately afflicted women. In the nineteenth century erysipelas was incurable and occasionally lethal, as when it caused Banister's death at the age of sixty-three. Despite wheezing from asthma and a persistent cough, Ann King Colton worked on behalf of the children of Worcester for forty-two years. Acutely aware that life was often fleeting and inevitably involved physical and emotional pain, the women of the CFS imbued their work with a sense of urgency to accomplish what they could in whatever time they had. As the consumptive Marcia Knowlton wrote in 1855, the women's familiarity with death meant that "We would not neglect the few remaining opportunities for usefulness we may be permitted to enjoy, or waste in the pursuit of pleasure, or in indolence and inactivity, the little time given us for nobler purposes."[55]

The desire to do good, to be useful, may also have reflected a search for stability that was frequently lacking in CFS families, many of which did not resemble the domestic refuge so often described in contemporary literature. On the contrary, despite their level of material comfort, the family lives of those who joined the CFS could be tumultuous. When a widowed Sarah Murray Johnson married Ethan Allen in 1843, he was a man with a somewhat scandalous past. Allen had acrimoniously parted from his first wife, Mary, and in 1841 announced his views in the Worcester *Palladium*: "Ethan Allen finds his wife Mary Allen impossible to live with and will not be responsible for her debts in the future." Such notices were not uncommon in the years before the liberalization of divorce laws and effected a legal separation of a married couple. In his caustic public comments, however, Ethan Allen was unusually and unnecessarily vituperative.[56]

Manager Sarah Harrington Walker had an even worse scandal to live down. Her father, Jubal Harrington, was variously an attorney, the city's postmaster in the 1830s, and the editor of the *Liberty of the Press*. He was also a man of strong Jacksonian Democrat opinions. In the spring of 1850, when Sarah was only nineteen, Harrington became exercised over the temperance and antislavery campaigns then making headway in Worcester. Swearing to give Free Soil and temperance advocates "hell and scissors," Harrington lobbed a six-inch hand grenade into the office of the mayor, a temperance supporter. No one was hurt but Harrington did make an impressive mess of the mayor's office and blew a hole in the rear brick wall. Three days later, the assistant city marshall's home mysteriously exploded. All eyes apparently turned toward Harrington and, after being released on bond, he lit out for California, where his talents were better appreciated and he was elected a judge. Daughter Sarah remained in Worcester and two years later married Joseph Walker, a prosperous shoe dealer several years older than she. Whatever stability Sarah Harrington Walker found as a wife, a mother, and a CFS assistant manager was mitigated by the early deaths of two of her three children; she herself died giving birth to a fourth child in 1859.[57]

Finally, Manager Rebecca Lincoln Newton presided over a household that included her husband, her daughter Hester, and her consumptive son Levi. When her only sister, Martha Lincoln Parker, died in childbirth in 1822, Newton opened her home to her three young nieces, Martha, Elizabeth, and Sarah Parker. The girls' father, Leonard Moody Parker, was still alive, but turned over to Newton the responsibility for rearing them. When Elizabeth Parker announced her desire to marry her dead sister's fiancé in 1837, Leonard Parker gave his blessing but cautioned, "I will of course expect . . . the advice & approval of Mrs. Newton. This may be submitted to her."[58]

To this busy household was added William Lincoln, Rebecca Newton's younger brother, Rejoice Newton's law partner, an early historian of Worcester, a figure of local prominence, and an alcoholic. Lincoln boarded for a time with Eliza Bancroft Davis while her husband served in the U.S. Congress. Although the erudite and accomplished Lincoln was known for his "sparkling wit and humor," Davis found him considerably less amusing and developed an intense dislike for someone she described as "a man of impulses, not to say caprices." Davis tolerated Lincoln's drinking because she wanted the money he paid for room and board, but she did not hesitate to threaten to pack him off to his sister Rebecca's if he did not straighten up. For a while, Lincoln overcame what Davis referred to privately as the *"fling flangs,"* or delirium tremens. In January 1841, struggling with what his culture assumed to be a moral failing rather than an organic disorder, Lincoln recorded in his diary a New Year's resolution to take control of his life: ". . . the bad habits in which I may have indulged, I will attempt to reform, and I resolve that life during the coming year shall be as pure in motive and as upright in action, as it is possible for human resolution to accomplish." Lincoln joined the Washingtonian temperance society and took the pledge, even composed and delivered temperance lectures in Worcester and nearby towns, and a neighbor noted that Lincoln's relieved family and friends "were quite confident of the permanency of his reform." But instead, Lincoln turned to opium "& soon relapsed into his former habits." In February 1843 William Lincoln lost his fight. Collapsing in the law office he shared with Rejoice Newton, Lincoln was carried to his sister's house, where he died the following October, a forty-one-year-old bankrupt alcoholic. Rebecca Lincoln Newton enjoyed many advantages in life: wealth, social status, education, and a close-knit, demonstrative family. Yet her life, like those of the other women of the CFS, was also dramatically affected by circumstances beyond her control.[59]

As these examples suggest, the portrayal of the middle-class domestic circle, so ubiquitous in the literature of the period, is historically inaccurate. The antebellum American family was more amoeba-like than spherical, reaching out to embrace the ill and the orphaned, then retracting to let go of the dying and the dead. More than forty percent of the members of the CFS at one point in their adult lives opened their homes to relatives, friends, or acquaintances, or themselves boarded in the homes of others, a percentage that, once again, placed them squarely in step with their contemporaries. Rebecca Newton's family formed and reformed upon the illnesses or deaths of parents, children, siblings, and friends. In the early 1820s, the Newtons consisted of a classic nuclear family: mother, father, and two children. By the mid-1820s, the family was altered by the death of a son, the birth of a daughter, and the addition of three motherless nieces. By the early 1840s, one niece had died, a second had married, and a desperately ill brother had taken refuge under the family roof. By the mid-1840s, with the death of William Lincoln and the marriage of the third niece, the Newtons once more conformed to a nuclear family of parents plus two children. But by the mid-1850s both the mother and the son were dead, and the family was reduced to a widower and an unmarried adult daughter. Which incarnation—nuclear, extended, or reduced—can be said to best represent the Newton family experience? If instead we view the family as a dynamic but nonlinear institution, we come closer to understanding the daily lives of many nineteenth-century families, including relatively privileged families. We may also understand more fully the motives of those who founded a society whose goal was to be a friend to a child.[60]

The women who founded and ran the Worcester Children's Friend Society were more ordinary than exceptional. Their general level of prosperity and higher than average social status undeniably made some aspects of their lives more comfortable than the lives of many of their contemporaries. But no amount of privilege could protect them from the kinds of critical life experiences, such as economic uncertainty, residential instability, family disintegration, illness, suffering, and death, that much less privileged women also endured. Indeed, it was the very volatility of their personal lives that made it possible for the women of the CFS to comprehend and to empathize with the crises confronting those to whom they extended help. In brief, for the managers to identify with the poor women of their community did not require an imaginative leap across the chasm of class. Analysis of the structure and organization of the society these women founded and ran, the Worcester Children's Friend Society, demonstrates that they had mastered the primary lesson of nineteenth-century American womanhood: to innovate as well as to adapt.

4

"Rachel Weeping for Her Children"

Mothers, Children, and the Antebellum Foster Family

Society will have to pay dearly for its neglect in some way or another, if such outcasts of humanity, always to be found among us, are allowed to grow up in all the ignorance and vice, which they inherit as their only natural birthright.
—Worcester Children's Friend Society,
Eighteenth Annual Report

Organized in late 1848 by women familiar with motherhood and troubled times, the Worcester Children's Friend Society received the blessing of the state to dispense charity to the needy of their community. But when the managers actually began to deal with poor families, the society took on a life of its own. The moral indignation that characterized the managers' initial public posture ebbed when working with parents led them to unanticipated conclusions about the nature of poverty in their city. The problem, the women came to realize, was not that poor parents did not want to help themselves and their children. The problem was that they had acute economic worries. The ability and willingness of the women of the CFS to listen and to empathize led them to offer innovative social services through short-and long-term boarding, foster families, and adoption. In addition, the way the managers dealt with the nettlesome problems and humdrum details of running such a society revealed the limits upon their institution's power. Rather than breaking up poor families, a process that was more difficult to accomplish in antebellum America than is often assumed, the CFS helped to keep families together. In the process the women created a semi-official department of child protective services for a developing nineteenth-century city.

A MATRIARCHAL HOME

The first order of business at the organizational meeting of the Children's Friend Society in December 1848 was to establish an administrative framework. The corporate body the women created, and the constitution they wrote to animate it, reveal a firm grasp of management principles. They elected two "directresses," a secretary, a treasurer, and a slate of twelve managers and twelve assistant managers, two each "from nearly all the religious societies in the city." The managers were responsible for running the society and its orphan's home, locating and monitoring foster and adoptive families, investigating complaints and settling disputes, and hiring and overseeing the matron and others employed at the home. The assistant managers were charged with finding the money to pay for it all.[1]

To this structure the women added twelve male advisors to lend "character and importance to the movement." The managers did not need to look very far for suitable men; they simply scanned their church congregations, inspected neighborhood gatherings, or even glanced down the table at dinner. Forty-one percent of the first twelve advisors were related by blood or marriage to a manager; fifty percent of the second board of advisors were so connected. By 1853, more than half of the advisors had personal ties to a manager. But within this society, women reigned supreme for the male advisors played an intentionally subordinate role. The advisors convened only when the managers summoned them and served at the women's pleasure; the men had no voting rights and did not attend the regular or special call meetings of this otherwise democratic organization. When a problem arose with which the women wanted assistance, they solicited the men's advice but excused them when the business meeting began. The advisors were invited to the annual meeting, but so too was the general public.[2]

The advisors supposedly existed to lend "character and importance" to the CFS, yet clergymen were conspicuously absent from the Board, which was composed exclusively of entrepreneurs, lawyers, and politicians. Indeed, the real, albeit unstated, purpose of the advisors was to provide formally but freely their otherwise expensive expertise in business, law, and politics. The managers called upon the advisors when the home needed repairs, when there was a fire and the insurance had to be straightened out, or for legal assistance with real estate and financial transactions. The typically wealthy advisors were also a reliable source of emergency funds; however, the men offered the money not in their official capacity but as private citizens. In 1860, for example, Advisor Alexander H. Bullock pledged fifty dollars to help retire the society's debt, prompting six others to come gallantly forward, but only *after* the board meeting had been adjourned. The male board of advisors thus rendered necessary and valuable service to the CFS but had no formal power within it. The female board of managers held the reins tightly, and while the women acknowledged the men's contributions with numerous rhetorical tributes, they gave them no real power.[3]

An advisor who failed to recognize his auxiliary status and dared to speak for the society swiftly ran afoul of the managers, as Ichabod Washburn discovered to his chagrin. A classic rags-to-riches story, Washburn had arrived in Worcester in 1819 as a poor blacksmith's apprentice but within twenty years had amassed a fortune from wiremaking, a booming nineteenth-century industry thanks to the telegraph, cattle ranches, pianos, and hoopskirts. Devoted to his family, inclined toward generosity, and devoutly religious, Washburn was ideal for the board of advisors. In 1853, however, Washburn intervened in the managers' long-running dispute with a client, Mrs. Norman. Norman was dissatisfied with her son's accommodations and reclaimed him from his foster home. Apparently seeking support from a higher authority than the female managers, Norman appealed to Washburn, who was impressed with her sincerity and took it upon himself to cancel her son's indenture contract. A delegation from an irate board of managers soon descended upon Washburn, politely but firmly informing him that his presumption was greatly in error. A chastened Washburn was forced to recant his actions and never again ventured to act independently of the managers. If Norman and Washburn recognized a "natural" hierarchy of men over women, the managers of the CFS did not, and throughout the nineteenth century women remained firmly in control of the society.[4]

The women also were firmly in control of funding their society and to this end the assistant managers cultivated a variety of sources. They fanned out across the city, approaching ministers to take up church collections on their behalf, cajoling merchants and laborers into donating goods and services, knocking on doors to persuade the benevolently inclined to pledge assistance and to convince others to be benevolently inclined, then returning in due time to collect the money. Worcester's Protestant congregations were the earliest and most dependable supporters, contributing ninety-seven percent of the first year's revenues, but within four years church donations fell to slightly over half of revenues as the CFS became better known. Income from parents boarding children at the home gradually increased, and at its highest accounted for one-third of revenues. More typically, however, boarding fees accounted for less than ten percent; moreover, income from boarding fluctuated with the economic cycles and was lowest precisely when the demand for assistance was greatest. During the depression of 1857, for example, boarding fees constituted less than five percent of the year's income.[5]

Monies collected from churches or private donors, combined with the boarding fees, provided at most three-fourths of the annual budget, requiring other measures to make ends meet. One approach was to solicit in-kind donations, a highly successful tactic that significantly reduced the society's need for cash. In their annual calls for community support, the managers looked beyond the traditional cash cows of the urban middle and upper classes to embrace Worcester's many farmers and laborers. Declaring their society dependent upon the "kindness of our friends," the managers asked that "each one help . . . us in their own best way. Farmers, merchants, those with purses filled, and laborers—we look to you all for help." In response, Mr. Estey repaired a pump for the CFS, while Mr. Elsell and Mr. Healy performed routine maintenance on the home. Acknowledging such efforts, the managers proclaimed "All honor to the workingmen," published detailed accounts of the in-kind donations in the annual reports and in local newspapers, and kept a contributors' log on display at the home for visitors to peruse. Business owners also responded to the appeal. Merchants supplied the home with goods and groceries at wholesale prices. Newspaper editors sent subscriptions of the *Spy,* the *Transcript,* and the *Water-Cure Journal.* Sewing circles mended cast-off clothing and bedding, and tailored new children's garments. Hack owners conveyed people and goods about town; physicians provided care without charge; and the city sexton contributed carriages for the occasional funeral processions. The matron rode free on the railroads, as did children heading for foster families and foster families en route to the home. The CFS also benefitted from the surrounding countryside, gratefully accepting seasonal inundations of farm produce as well as steady supplies of beef, milk, eggs, and firewood. (When

Worcester's gardeners were tardy in their produce deliveries, the seldom shy managers took out a newspaper ad to remind them.)[6]

Still, cash was more flexible and the women employed various means to acquire it. The advisors were an oft-targeted source of one-time funds. When the CFS needed a new home in the mid-1860s, the managers informed the men that they should be "at liberty to consider our forthcoming appeal for a little pecuniary assistance . . . as especially intended for their consideration." The CFS got its new home, designed expressly for its needs. But the managers also drew upon the resources of the community's women's groups. In the early 1850s the women debuted the CFS Lifetime Membership, an honorific available for a twenty-five-dollar donation, and threw down the gauntlet by demanding "What societies will follow in the lead of the Union and Old South [church sewing circles], in making their pastors Life Members of our Society?" Women's groups rose to the challenge, vying to honor their ministers and their ministers' wives in a good-natured rivalry so effective that within a few years most of the local Protestant clergy had been so honored. When the roster had been exhausted, the women's groups either donated the cash or used it to honor one of their own, as when the Ladies' Benevolent Circle of the Union Church made fellow congregant Mary Rider Brown a Lifetime Member of the organization she was already helping to manage. Others took the hint as well. Levi Lincoln II, a former Whig governor of Massachusetts, the city's first mayor, and brother of Manager Rebecca Lincoln Newton, bolstered the society's treasury and social status by regularly purchasing lifetime memberships to honor his friends and political allies.[7]

Nor did the managers refrain from indicting the wealthy for not doing their share. While they had heard rumors of forthcoming endowments, the women noted bluntly, "we recollect no instances of very extravagant liberality toward the Institution among those accounted *rich*." Charity converted earthly gold into supernatural abundance, the managers suggested helpfully, and they warned that failure to assist the needy was grounds for eternal damnation. Taking another tack, the women also appealed to Worcester's rampant boosterism. Theirs was a graceful city marked by "noble structures," "luxurious homes," and commodious halls of learning, the managers pointed out; did not the Children's Home deserve similar "comforts and conveniences"? The well-to-do eventually responded to the combination of shame and flattery. Two years after the society's founding, Stephen Salisbury II donated $1,000 from the estate

of his late mother, Elizabeth Tuckerman Salisbury, who had occasionally sewn garments for the CFS. The managers used the Salisbury legacy
to purchase ten shares in the Worcester Bank and voted to invest all
future legacies, as well as the monies from lifetime memberships, in a
permanent fund, the interest from which was accessible for operating
expenses. As a result of the slow accretion of legacy money, the CFS
gradually accumulated an investment portfolio of bank shares, railroad
stocks, and government bonds. In the antebellum years, however, even
at its greatest, investment income constituted less than ten percent of
the annual budget. As late as 1863, a full fourteen years after the society's
founding, the managers were still exhorting the wealthy to do their part,
for "As yet, we have had no splendid endowments from millionaire, or
man of wealth, whereof to boast," and the CFS remained dependent
upon small donations.[8]

Also important to the society's financial health were the occasional
benefits staged on its behalf. The Chelsea Continentals, a popular band,
donated the receipts of several performances while Mr. Brewer, a "perfect stranger," exhibited his "Panorama of Mammoth Cave, Niagara Falls,
etc." and brought in $15.50. More dubious was the Spiritualist
Association's offer of the proceeds of a public lecture. The managers
politely notified the Spiritualists that while they would welcome a donation, they must decline "any part in the arrangements, or selection of
subjects." For-profit teas and fairs were a staple fundraising tactic among
antebellum women's groups but one that the managers were initially
reluctant to pursue. In their opinion, teas and fairs permitted the community to abdicate its responsibility to support the CFS directly. Moreover, the women argued that they had quite enough to do already, and
should be relieved of "the necessity of engaging in the laborious and
uncertain experiment of a Fair, or a Tea Party . . . ." However, in the late
1850s, when an economic depression dried up their usual revenue stream,
the managers changed their tune. The subsequent fairs quickly proved
why this method of fundraising was so popular: in 1859, a single fair
raised more than $650; the following year, a fair organized by the united
action of the women's benevolent societies brought in $750, surpassing
the money received that year from the church collections.[9]

A patchwork of funding sources thus kept the CFS solvent, but
financial difficulties were an annual refrain and a persistent worry. "We
must live by begging," the managers declared dramatically as they
wrapped up a decade's service still in business but several hundred dol-

Portrait of Elizabeth Tuckerman Salisbury, ca. 1840s. A woman of great wealth, Salisbury also was a religious dissenter and a supporter of local women's reform societies. (All illustrations courtesy American Antiquarian Society.)

Above, Centre Congregational (Calvinist) Church, Main Street, Worcester. *Below,* Main Street, Worcester, showing the Old South (First Congregational) Church and City Hall, 1828.

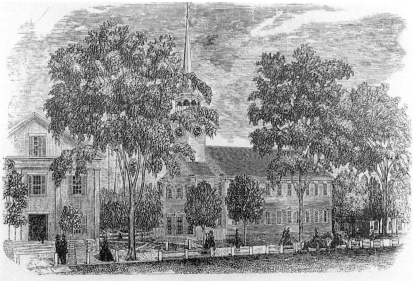

OLD SOUTH CHURCH AND CITY HALL (1828).

The Worcester Children's Friend Society Orphan's Home, ca. 1850s.

Unpublished manuscript minutes of the Worcester Children's Friend Society.

By Huffy

from a Daguerreotype

by E. Bouglier

Abby Kelley Foster, feminist and abolitionist, 1846. A resident of the Tatnuck section of the city, Foster joined the Worcester Anti-Slavery Sewing Circle and the Worcester women's rights convention.

Above, The American Temperance House, 1849, site of the Centre Missionary Sewing Circle's annual bazaars. *Below,* A panoramic view of the city of Worcester, 1858.

Ann Buffum Earle, feminist, abolitionist, and manager of the Worcester Children's Friend Society, ca. 1860s. A Quaker, Earle was active in local and national reform campaigns.

Ann K. Colton, feminist, abolitionist, and manager of the Worcester Children's Friend Society, ca. 1860s. Also a Quaker, Colton was active in numerous reform societies despite chronic poor health.

lars in debt. Confusion among the more novice assistant managers occasionally threatened the society's most reliable revenue source, the church collections, when inexperience led them to solicit contributions from some twice while overlooking others. The managers also learned the bitter lesson that those who made pledges did not always honor them, especially during hard times. The intermittent depressions that characterized the unregulated market economy of the nineteenth century forced the CFS to redouble its efforts. When contributions plunged during the Panic of 1857, for example, the managers held their annual meeting in Worcester's glittering new Mechanics Hall in the hope of arousing interest in their work. To make the society's dependence on voluntary giving even more trying, by the mid-1850s the sight of assistant managers knocking on doors to collect donations was sufficiently common to inspire fraud among the city's more enterprising female criminals. An indignant board of managers was forced to warn the public that "we have no *authorized collectors*, except those whose names are given in our Annual Report" and to furnish the assistant managers with the "necessary credentials."[10]

Conscientious and creative fundraising was vital because the society usually spent everything it collected. When the treasurer deducted expenses from receipts for 1856, for example, the CFS was left with a balance of precisely three dollars. Food, fuel, and salaries for the matron and her assistant composed the bulk of the expenses. But the managers also sought to balance economy with comfort. The women recognized that children longed for special treats and actively solicited items to please them, arguing as they did so that while "a proper attention to economy" was necessary and appropriate, an "extreme closeness in one's style of living" was not. When raising children, they explained, it was important "to provide not only for the necessities" but also "to contribute to their higher enjoyment" of life. The managers believed firmly that a home should be attractive to those who lived there and that "books, pictures, toys, and all those little treasures children so naturally love, should be placed within their reach" because "little things have much to do with the formation of character."

One year the women requested donations of plants because "some of our children manifest a native fondness for plants and flowers," and they regularly expressed appreciation for contributions of cakes and candy; for Thanksgiving, Christmas, and Fourth of July celebrations; for ribbons for the little girls' hair; for excursions to the countryside; even for a canary and a bird cage. Operating precariously close to the margin, the CFS ran into debt after a catastrophic fire at the home in the fall of 1858, allegedly sparked by the spontaneous combustion of a woolen comforter in the attic. No one was hurt but the fire badly damaged the home. Insurance paid to rebuild, but the society had to replace the items damaged or destroyed by smoke or fire and incurred the extra cost of sheltering the children until the home was repaired. As a consequence, the CFS ended its first decade with a debt of $350 and was compelled to accept the offer of several advisors to retire it.[11]

Despite the vagaries of private donations, despite their work on behalf of the welfare of the entire community, the managers consistently refused to apply for municipal or state government assistance. On several occasions the managers debated whether or not to seek public funding, but each time decided against it and concluded by reiterating their faith that "all classes of our citizens" would support the society through voluntary contributions. In part, the decision reflected a commitment to the tradition of local responsibility for welfare, which they wedded to an evangelical belief that communalism was purest, and most powerful, when composed of acts of selfless benevolence. Because "all God's children are your brothers and sisters ... the world is one great family," the managers argued, welfare was the duty of the *entire* community, not in the abstracted form of government but directly, personally, one individual to another. "All can contribute something .... There is no escaping these responsibilities," the women emphasized, and they warned that to ignore the cries of those in distress meant "incurring at every step, the displeasure of Him who is to be our final judge." Contrary to (apparently popular) local opinion, the managers announced, they were not sitting on a cache of gold nor did they wish to, for "a constant flow of charity, in small sums, from year to year, sufficient for present necessities, with faith in God and man, constitute a better fund than thousands of dollars invested in bank stock." To be sure, the women were making virtuous a necessity, since the "thousands of dollars" was hardly forthcoming. At the same time, the managers calculated rightly that their network of private donors was sufficient for their needs.[12]

Relying upon local, private resources was also a strategic choice, for it diminished the leverage of any individual or group and enabled the managers to exercise uncontested control. The danger of depending upon the government was driven home in the wake of the fire in November 1858. A decision had to be made where to house more than thirty children ranging in age from infancy to early teens, plus matron, teacher, and assistants, for the several months required to rebuild. The matron and the children took immediate refuge at Worcester's Water-Cure Establishment while the managers took stock. They declined to relocate to the State Lunatic Asylum at Worcester (an invitation that was, however, "duly appreciated"), then considered an offer from the Overseers of the Poor to take over the west wing of the almshouse for as long as necessary and "free of charge." After inspecting the premises, and mindful of the imminent onset of winter, the managers declared it acceptable and "the family" moved in until early March 1859.[13]

The following spring the managers were unpleasantly surprised when the Overseers of the Poor presented them with a bill for $126.65 for the fuel used to heat the west wing, the logic being that save for the CFS the city would not have incurred the expense. But the managers rejected this argument. To their minds it should have been obvious when the Overseers of the Poor made the offer that the west wing would have to be heated for the children. Pointing out that "free of charge" meant precisely that, and facing a revenue shortfall, the managers petitioned the mayor, the aldermen, and the common council to overrule the Overseers of the Poor and to live up to the terms of the initial offer. City officials agreed to discount the bill by twenty-five dollars but insisted upon remittance of the balance. The managers grudgingly paid.

Barred by their sex from voting, the women could not even take comfort in muttered threats to throw the bums out of office. Instead, they took advantage of the public forum of their 1860 *Annual Report* to implicitly criticize the city's duplicity, not to mention its lack of charity, toward hardworking women and poor children burned out of their home in the wintertime. Already chary of government assuming what they considered rightfully to be the duty of a community of right-minded individuals, the fire and its aftermath taught the managers that local government should not be trusted.[14]

Rendering the situation more complicated still were the ties between the managers and the officials with whom they butted heads. In 1858, the year of the fire, the mayor, Isaac Davis, was also a former advisor, as was Alderman William B. Fox; Alderman Draper Ruggles was married to Manager Caroline Ruggles; and Alderman D. Waldo Lincoln was the brother of the CFS's late treasurer, Rebecca Lincoln Newton, and uncle to its new treasurer, Hester Newton Wetherell. These men had approved the offer of assistance immediately following the fire.

In 1859, the officials to whom the managers directed their petition for redress included Overseer of the Poor Thomas Earle, a cousin by marriage of Manager Ann Buffum Earle; Mayor Alexander H. Bullock, an advisor and longtime supporter; Alderman D. Waldo Lincoln; and the president of the common council, John W. Wetherell, husband of Treasurer Hester Newton Wetherell. Despite these connections to the men who governed the city, the women were unable to prevail in something as simple as interpreting "free of charge" to mean truly gratis.

The danger of relying upon officials over whom they had no electoral power could not have been made clearer: it meant ceding control to often well intentioned men who nonetheless did not see all issues as the women did, yet who commanded the public institutions of money and power. Able to make ends meet through their own efforts and those of their female peers in Worcester—or to rely upon the generosity of the handpicked advisors in a pinch—the managers of the CFS remained financially independent of both men and male-controlled institutions throughout the nineteenth century. The worst they usually had to deal with was the occasional jealousy exhibited by donors eager to have their own contributions recognized but suspicious of the generosity of others.[15]

A HOME IS NOT AN ASYLUM

By the end of its first year, the CFS had grown from an informal organization run out of its founder's house into an actual institution with its own residence, the "Home." But the CFS was not an asylum in the contemporary sense of the word. Rather, it was one of a growing number of organizations that rejected institutionalization as a means to rear children and to impart desirable values. The managers acknowledged that institutions had their place and did not hesitate to pack off troublesome boys to the state reform school in nearby Westboro, Worcester county. Indeed, they were heard wishing for a similar school for girls. But if one sought to rescue children from immorality, "the dead, barrack-like asylum" simply would not do. Asylums were "to be commended—if we can get nothing better," the women argued, but it was a very poor way to raise a child. The managers openly scorned organizations such as the Boston Female Asylum because "They attempt simply to train them as house servants, or to the simplest trades . . . though they rescue these children from the very depths of poverty, they do not lift them very far above it." Indeed, asylums were inherently flawed because although they provided for a child's physical wants, "there are yearnings and desires in [children's] bosoms, which no corporate body, but only the single answering heart can supply." Meeting a child's emotional needs was something only a parent, especially a mother, could do.[16]

Ironically, the institutionalization of children had become so common that the women of the CFS sometimes had difficulty convincing the public that they were *not* running an asylum. The managers repeatedly attempted to correct the apparently common impression that "when children are received at the Home, they are to remain there, until able to take care of themselves. But this is not the plan. . . ." Instead, the plan was to find the children new homes with new families. The women conjured with pleasure the unions of bereft parents and desperate children that they would make possible, perhaps remembering as they did so the deaths of so many of their own children. It was their role to care for the children "until, some day, another who is in want too, shall come to the same door. And this time it is not a child who wants a mother. It is the other sufferer, yearning with a want as bitter; it is the mother who must have her child. Rachel weeping for her children."[17]

That the CFS's approach was a radical departure from traditional child welfare arrangements is highlighted by the fact that not only was adoption a circuitous process but it did not, technically, even exist. English common law recognized only marital and blood ties for purposes of inheritance and thus parental rights were inalienable and adoption a legal absurdity. Since adoption did not exist under English common law, it could not exist under Massachusetts colonial law. Those wishing to effectively adopt a child were required to petition the colonial legislature for an act to change the child's name to accord with the adoptive family's and to include the child explicitly in wills; otherwise, an adopted child had no right of inheritance. After the American Revolution, adoption remained largely informal, most often within extended families, and for those seeking to establish a legal tie the colonial procedure held sway. As a result, between 1781 and 1851 the Massachusetts legislature enacted more than one hundred bills—consisting of dozens upon dozens of individual requests—to change the names of petitioners. Finally, in 1851, two years after the CFS's founding, Massachusetts passed the first U.S. adoption law and turned the whole procedure over to the local judges of probate.[18]

Adoption remained a moot point, however, unless the managers could acquire legal custody of children at risk. But their position was tenuous at best. In the early nineteenth century, there were few laws to provide for abandoned children and none for the children of living parents. The legal mechanism that did exist was the Articles of Indenture, a contract for the exchange of services with a long history in English and American common law. Indenture contracts spelled out the mutual rights and obligations of the parties and was adapted to a variety of purposes, as when Manager Rebecca Lincoln Newton's attorney husband signed an indenture agreement with three men "to lay out and open a new street to be called Chandler Street." Parents also signed Articles of Indenture to "bind out" a child, ceding legal control to another adult, usually for an apprenticeship. The child's master was to act *in loco parentis* and teach, in addition to a trade, good morals and basic reading and writing skills. Indentures were as well the traditional means by which Overseers of the Poor acquired responsibility for dependent children, who were also typically bound out.[19]

When organizations such as the Worcester CFS took up the work of assisting needy and destitute children in the antebellum era, they too relied upon Articles of Indenture as the basis of their jurisdiction over the children in their care. Shortly after the CFS commenced operation, Judge Thomas Kinnicutt, a member of the board of advisors, drew up a boilerplate indenture contract and the women voted to print "one or two hundred copies . . . as soon as possible." On March 24, 1849, just four days before his death at age forty-four, John Mixter became one of the first to formally indenture his child to the care of the CFS by signing a document that read, "Finding myself wholly unable to support myself & family, I hereby ask you to take charge of, & provide for, my daughter Mary Mixter, aged three years, & eleven months, fourteen days. And I hereby relinquish all claim to her person or services during the term of her minority."[20]

To be a party to indentures for children such as little Mary Mixter, the CFS had to be formally recognized by the state. Incorporation would not only give the managers, as a group, rights that they did not possess as individual women, it would also enable them to lobby more effectively for support within the community. Thus in February 1849 the managers petitioned the state for an act of incorporation. The move was hardly unprecedented; by mid-century, the commonwealth was well versed in incorporating women's charitable societies. The petition was presented to the legislature with the wholehearted and confident support of Worcester's state senator, Alexander H. Bullock, a lawyer and savvy Whig politician, as well as a future advisor, mayor of the city, and governor of Massachusetts.[21]

Bullock immediately ran into problems. The senators complained that the women of the CFS sought "unusual powers" that threatened a "restraint of private [read: paternal] rights." What seems to have bothered the politicians most was that the managers sought to support children "who, for want of paternal care, are in a suffering and dangerous condition" by entering into legally binding Articles of Indenture with the father or, if the father were dead, with the mother. Men had always had the right to reassign their claim upon their children (with or without the mother's permission); what was novel about the CFS's petition was that one of the parties to the contract would be a private association of women. To a legislature already agitated that a proposed married women's property act would weaken the privileges of patriarchy, the suggestion that a women's group be authorized to interpose between individual members of families was cause for concern.[22]

Surprised and "mortified" by the senate's reaction, Bullock moved quickly to make it more palatable by asserting that the CFS was "founded . . . upon the highest considerations of public policy." Bullock appealed to their Christian consciences, arguing that the managers asked and answered an appropriate question, "Am I my brother's keeper?" The petitioners, Bullock insisted, were women of unassailable reputations, true Protestant daughters of New England, who were acting upon their womanly instincts to better the lot of their community's needy children. Bullock's approach was reassuringly familiar and persuaded the senate to incorporate the CFS on the original terms. In April 1849, Massachusetts formally empowered the Worcester Children's Friend Society to care for "indigent children, who have no parents or guardians, within the Commonwealth," to hold up to fifty thousand dollars in property, to instruct the children in "moral and religious duties," to arrange for the employment of the children when deemed appropriate, and to "place such children in the families of virtuous and respectable citizens, to be brought up in such families as adopted children and members thereof." The CFS was finally in business.[23]

The managers were now free to enter into indenture contracts with parents, but acquiring a legally binding signature proved much more difficult than anyone had anticipated. The common law principle of *feme covert*, which rendered a married woman "civilly dead," meant that she could not sign a legal contract without her husband's expressed permission. Thus the CFS technically had responsibility only for those children brought to the society by their father, or for those few whose fathers were dead. Shortly after the society was incorporated, Mrs. Lyles brought her three children to the CFS, which agreed to take over their care "if the Father's signature . . . can be obtained." Even though the burden of child support had fallen to Mrs. Lyles, her signature conveyed no more authority than an unsigned contract. The legal inequality of antebellum married women created endless complications for the CFS, and the minutes of board meetings reflect the numerous discussions about how to acquire a father's signature.[24]

To corral fathers and convince them to sign the indentures, the managers created the Visiting Committee, two women elected for a one-month tour of duty. The assignment was onerous and tended to fall upon the shoulders of a handful of women, presumably those least intimidated by face-to-face encounters with men from Worcester's lower classes. Unfortunately, the women did not record their experiences in seeking out the fathers, nor do the society's minutes provide clues to the arguments the women advanced to persuade the men to sign. In light of the reluctance with which the women volunteered for the Visiting Committee, however, it seems clear that tracking down and confronting men who, to their minds, were manifestly inadequate fathers, was distasteful, perhaps even frightening, to many of the managers. During the society's first year, Ann B. Earle and Ellen K. Buffum, devout Quakers and distantly related, served together as the Visiting Committee for three of the first twelve months; similarly, Louisa G. Brown, a Unitarian who for twenty years was by far the best fundraiser, sat on the Visiting Committee twice, although with different partners. As Hicksite Quakers active in a variety of social reforms, it is likely that Earle and Buffum were more comfortable speaking their minds than were the other managers, while Brown apparently had a gift for persuading others to do as she wished. The next year, the managers amended the bylaws "requiring the members of the Board to act as Visiting Com. regularly by rotation." Still, the same names kept reappearing, with Quakers serving out of proportion to their numbers. Yet even more perplexing than hostile or recalcitrant fathers were living but absent fathers. *Feme covert* assumed that a woman's husband was somewhere in the vicinity, but this assumption was increasingly without foundation in the highly mobile nineteenth century. What, for example, was the CFS to do about children such as Delora Center, whose mother was dead and whose father's last known whereabouts placed him somewhere in western New York?[25]

The ongoing and often frustrating attempts to secure valid signatures for the Articles of Indenture led the managers to petition the state once more. In 1851 the legislature tacitly acknowledged the problem of absentee fathers by significantly expanding the CFS's role as an instrument of welfare. The revised charter empowered the Overseers of the Poor to indenture children to the CFS; previously, only the parents or guardians of a child could do so. More to the point, the state authorized the mother of a child "when the mother and child have been deserted by the father of the child, and no provision has been made by him for their support" to sign indenture contracts with the Worcester CFS. In effect, the revised charter expanded the legal authority of women over their minor children for the state had declared the mother's signature on this particular contract to be equally binding as the father's. The legislature did not intend to advance the legal rights of women, nor did it; after all, what the mothers of Worcester had gained was the power to sign away their claim to their own children. Even then, there were stipulations: a mother's signature was binding *only* when the father deserted the family *and* left them unprovided for; moreover, the mother's action had to be approved by the Overseers of the Poor or the judge of probate. In agreeing to assist the CFS, the legislators made certain that responsible men were in a position to place a check on potentially irresponsible women. In contrast, fathers wishing to indenture their children operated under no such restrictions.[26]

Still, the new law did affirm the principle that mothers had a legal interest in their children separate from that of their husbands, and it made the CFS an official adjunct to the city by authorizing the Overseers of the Poor to hand off the community's responsibility to care for destitute children. Moreover, while the stipulation that mothers obtain the consent of the Overseers of the Poor or the judge of probate sounded restrictive, in practice it was no check at all. The Overseers of the Poor were only too happy to wash their hands of the city's needy children while the judge of probate for Worcester county conveniently sat on the CFS Board of Advisors. Neither was likely to question the managers' assumption of control over the children of poor women; if they did not necessarily trust the poor mothers, they did trust the middle-class managers. The managers recognized that their revised charter represented an advance for their organization and signaled their approval by a unanimous vote.[27]

Armed with the state's dispensation to attack poverty and immorality in their community, the women of the CFS set to work. They quickly discovered the limits of their understanding of the nature of poverty in their city. Within a few months, a society that had intended to separate poor children from immoral parents became instead a resource by which families in need, especially those headed by women, could stay together.

MOTHERS IN CHARGE OF THE ASYLUM

The women of the CFS probably would have denied it had anyone suggested such a thing, but they were an ambitious lot. Their goal was nothing less than the elimination of poverty in their city by the next generation. Therefore, the CFS managed a relatively large number of children and did not erect rigid age, gender, or ethnic policies. Due to haphazard record keeping, it cannot be determined precisely how many children were in the society's care from 1849 through 1860. A conservative estimate would be slightly more than two hundred, although anecdotal evidence suggests that the actual total was much higher. The children were young, a majority female, most brought to the home by their mothers, most propelled by poverty. Nearly seventy percent were between the ages of three and nine, while fully eighty percent were between the ages of one and nine, reflecting the society's disinclination to accept the very young or the nearly grown. Infants and babies were time-consuming and strained the society's budget, while homes for older children were harder to find. Still, more than one-fifth of the children fell under or over the age limits. When the managers sat down to make their decisions on a case-by-case basis, they frequently persuaded themselves to ignore their own policy.[28]

Also unlike many contemporary organizations, the Worcester CFS did not favor one sex over the other, although a slight majority of the children the female managers accepted into their care also were female. Compared to its counterparts in very large cities, such as Boston or New York, the Worcester CFS confronted poverty that, while grave, still appeared to be manageable. The managers thus were not compelled by the enormity of the problem, or by the meagerness of their resources, to establish priorities based on gender. Furthermore, unlike societies that aimed to find poor children employment, the CFS sought to place children as members of adoptive families. Receiving families welcomed both girls and boys, and may even have preferred little girls.[29]

A large percentage of the first children to enter the care of the CFS were Irish immigrants or the children of Irish immigrants. The Irish first arrived in the city in 1826 to build the Blackstone Canal, and their numbers increased with the building of the railroads in the 1830s. These early immigrants were highly skilled and comparatively few in number, and as late as 1845 the Irish constituted a mere 5 percent of Worcester's population. But in the late 1840s, a second wave of Irish immigration began, and by 1850 20 percent of the city's population was foreign-born. The terrible famine in Ireland brought to the United States a different kind of immigrant: poorer, more desperate, less educated, with fewer skills to offer an industrializing economy, and often disproportionately female.[30]

Word of the starvation in Ireland initially elicited an outpouring of sympathy from the citizens of Worcester. One local paper urged its readers to contribute generously to relief funds, declaring "We are blessed with abundance. Let us freely share it with those who are perishing with want." The editorial emphasized that a common Anglo-Saxon heritage demanded that Americans respond: "[Ireland's] strong arm, now paralyzed and broken, has helped to build up our strength and advance our national growth, culture and comfort. She is a part of our fatherland. Her children are with us and of us. *They* are our *brethren* that cry to us for help." The townspeople responded by forming a relief committee to raise and channel funds to Ireland; among its members were several who would shortly sit on the CFS's Board of Advisors.[31]

But the willingness to share American abundance and to claim kinship with the victims of the famine rapidly receded as the Irish emigration swelled. Within three years, the public mood in Worcester, only forty miles by railroad from the port of Boston, had grown considerably less sympathetic to the plight of the new immigrants and Nativist sentiment grew. For their part, the women of the CFS argued that it would be inhuman to "close our hearts in icy selfishness" against the "starving, friendless young creatures" standing before them in their "ragged wretchedness." The desperation of many of the new immigrants was reflected in the statistics of the home: in its first year, forty-four percent of the children were described as Irish, thirty-five percent as American, and nineteen percent as English. The managers accepted so many Irish children because they were among the city's poorest, but also because they believed that these children needed an education in American ways: "The inquiry is often stated, 'What is to be done with our foreign population?' We have heard only one satisfactory answer, and that is, 'Educate them, particularly the children.'" A dose of practicality also weighed in, for as the managers pointed out, "It is worse than useless to say we do not wish the Irish to come among us—for come they must, however coldly they may be received," and thus the problem could neither be ignored nor wished away.[32]

The presence of so many Irish Catholic children at the home was not, however, an intentional design on the part of the often self-consciously Protestant managers. An analysis of a contemporary Rochester, New York, orphan asylum finds that its founders were motivated by a belief in Finneyite perfectionism, which led them either to discriminate against Catholic children or to try to convert them. It is likely that the women of the Worcester CFS assumed that Irish Catholic children would be converted when placed in Protestant homes. But unlike the directors of the Rochester Orphan Asylum, the members of the Worcester society do not seem to have been dogmatic; indeed, the managers themselves were much more heterodox. Although exclusively Protestant, they embraced disparate sects, ranging from the orthodox Calvinists to the liberal Unitarians and Universalists, and from the liturgical Episcopalians to the pietistic Friends. Moreover, the women were flattered by comparisons of their society with the charitable Catholic Sisters of the Sacred Heart, and imagined themselves to be "an order of Protestant Sisters of Charity."[33]

However, the women did describe the CFS as a "mission" and maintained that just as Christians supported the efforts of missionaries abroad so too was there "missionary labor to be done at home." Precisely what this involved was not specified but such statements were typically linked to appeals for money. The missionary function of the CFS was echoed in the sentiments of the Reverend Edward Everett Hale, a local Unitarian minister, a well-known author and social commentator, and a staunch CFS supporter. In his 1852 *Letter on Irish Emigration*, Hale proposed that the nation employ a scheme comparable to what the CFS had created and urged that Irish immigrants be scattered across the country rather than permitted to cluster together in the cities. Dispersion would "Stimulate the Absorbents" of the Irish, Hale argued, thereby weakening Catholicism and "clannishness" and promoting Americanization. Hale concluded that "every benevolent person who adopts an Irish orphan from a poor house, assists it," a method of ethnic dilution that mimicked the efforts of the CFS.[34]

If the women of the CFS shared Hale's zeal to "Stimulate the Absorbents" of this new ethnic group, their intentions were frustrated by a rapid change in the demographics of the home. From a high of forty-four percent in 1850, the number of Irish children plunged to fifteen percent by 1857, while the proportion of children described as "American" simultaneously increased, from thirty-six percent in 1850 to seventy-eight percent in 1857. Thus in less than ten years, the home functioned primarily as a refuge for the children of the native born, not for immigrant children or the children of immigrants. Since the women of the CFS did not define their ethnic categories, it is possible that children born of Irish parents in the United States were classified as American, while "Irish" designated only those born in Ireland or en route to the United States. If so, with the passage of time more children from Irish families would have been described as American and the change in the percentage of Irish children would be more apparent than real. However, since the percentage of Irish declined so abruptly, this explanation could account for only the youngest children.[35]

It is more likely that the numbers indicate a genuine shift in the ethnic origins of the children. As early as 1834, Irish Catholics had established Christ Church in Worcester; by 1846, St. John's arose to accommodate 1,300 worshipers; by 1856, the community was large enough to require a second parish, St. Anne's. With the organization of Worcester's Irish Catholics into regular parishes came additional benefits, for the community endeavored to care for its own through parochial education, health care, and mutual benefit societies. In 1842, the Catholic Church organized a seminary, the College of the Holy Cross, in south Worcester; in 1847, the Irish community asserted its cultural pride with the first in a series of St. Patrick's Day parades; in 1849, the Irish organized a chapter of the Father Mathew Mutual Benevolent Total Abstinence Society.

The anti-immigrant, anti-Catholic Nativist movement of the 1850s, known as the "Know-Nothings," captured the city's mayoralty in 1856 but, in the process, ironically strengthened Worcester's Irish community by uniting the pre-famine immigrants with the more recent arrivals. By the mid-1850s, despite the pooling of the Irish into the least-skilled, lowest-paid occupations, despite ongoing discrimination from many native-born Protestants, the Irish of Worcester were better able to care for their own. As a consequence, the decline in the number of Irish children at the CFS reflected, at least in part, the development of a stronger, more stable Irish community.[36]

Yet because the number of Irish children at the home declined rapidly even while the number of poor Irish families in the city rose dramatically, we should look further for the causes of the change in the ethnic composition of the children at the CFS. The answer is to be found in the economic crises of the 1850s. From 1849 through 1857, unemployment spread to those whose jobs had seemed secure and poverty increased. In 1849, the year the CFS was founded, the Overseers of the Poor reported 793 paupers in Worcester, an increase of 244 percent from four years earlier. By 1853, 900 people were designated paupers, while in the depression year of 1857, nearly one thousand received public assistance out of a total population of less than 20,000. However, the situation was even grimmer than these figures suggest, for the Overseers of the Poor included in their count only those wholly dependent upon the city for their support. The officials did not bother tallying those "receiving occasional and temporary relief, a detail of which would occupy many pages and be of little interest." As a consequence, the number of those who teetered on the edge of destitution and needed some measure of public or private welfare was much greater than even one in twenty.[37]

Such widespread suffering prompted repeated calls in the local press for organized private relief to supplement public welfare. The perception of deprivation was particularly acute in 1857 because this recession struck hard among the native-born, white working class. Referring specifically to this group, one newspaper warned that "A hard winter is before a vast many persons who have not heretofore been the recipients of charity . . . strictly speaking, they are not poor, yet they will find it impossible to live without some help from others. . . . *Charity must be organized*." As native-born townspeople experienced increasing economic hardship in the late 1850s, their children crowded out the Irish at the home. The shift in the ethnic origins of the CFS children in the 1850s thus was not an expression of Nativism but a reflection of a parallel development: the strengthening of the Irish and the weakening of the native-born.[38]

The hard times of the 1850s cemented the reliance of Worcester's poorer parents, especially the mothers, upon the services of the CFS. In slightly under half the cases, the data indicate the person who brought the child to the home; of these, nearly two-thirds were mothers while twenty-two percent were fathers. Mothers composed the largest group to avail themselves of the services of the CFS because women were uniquely vulnerable to economic crises. Barred by gender conventions from the better-paying, skilled occupations that might afford men a measure of security and independence, women who had to support themselves or their families clustered in low-paying jobs and were especially prone to unemployment. The rigors of housekeeping, childbearing, and childrearing severely limited the opportunities of even the educated; married women, for example, were rarely hired to teach, one of the few skilled occupations open to women. Once married, a woman did not have the right to her own wages, and an intemperate or spendthrift husband could squander with impunity a woman's wealth, however modest, whether earned or inherited. Even a woman with a dependable, sober, and hardworking husband could not be insured against catastrophe. A woman who lost her husband also lost her economic support and confronted an uncertain future for herself and her children. As one historian of antebellum New York has noted succinctly, "Widowhood was virtually synonymous with impoverishment."[39]

Confronted by the harsh realities of being poor and female, the women of the CFS cautiously came to recognize the unregulated economy as the cause of much of the distress in their community, especially the peculiar vulnerabilities of their sex. The attack on immorality in their public discourse dimmed, to be replaced by criticisms of gendered economic and legal inequality. Unsure how to resolve these larger issues, the managers focused on the poverty they could do something about and committed themselves to rendering parents, especially other mothers, immediate and practical assistance.[40]

A HOME AWAY FROM HOME

Among the CFS's contributions to their community was the boarding of children at the home temporarily, an uncommon social service in antebellum America. In at least one case out of five, parents, usually the mothers, boarded their children to tide them over particularly tough times. Often the immediate problem was the departure of the father from the family through death or desertion, forcing a woman to reassess her family's future. In such a crisis, the boarding service of the CFS could be pivotal, for it permitted a woman to maintain her legal rights to her children until she found a solution to her problems. The home was also a refuge for children whose mothers were ill and needed someone to look after their offspring while they recovered. Mary Ann Hill's mother was looking for "a situation" and intended to remove Mary as soon as she found one. Mrs. Emery brought her son to the home because "his father has disappeared [and] his mother [is] unable to provide for all her children." A few months later, Emery arranged to board her daughter to "enable [Emery] to attend to some profitable employment." The Macier boys boarded briefly because "their father left his home about two years since & has never been heard from . . . it is feared he has been murdered." The willingness of the managers to care for children temporarily, rather than insist upon placing them permanently, eased the often agonizing alternatives confronting a woman with too many children and not enough money. Mrs. Benchley turned to the CFS for help because "She has two and can only support one." The managers were on the verge of asking Mrs. Gerry to retrieve her son when she became pregnant; under the circumstances, they agreed to continue to care for the boy. Trying to plan ahead, Mrs. Gerry applied "for an infant child of hers to be taken into the Society's care, wishing she says, to give it up (*as soon as born*) to our control." Walter Kimball's mother brought him to the CFS when his father was incarcerated in the county jail. Although uncomfortable with the situation, the managers agreed to board Walter on the condition that Kimball take his family and leave town as soon as he was released.[41]

The CFS had not been founded to provide short-term and emergency child care, but the service was desperately needed by the working parents of Worcester and the managers found it difficult to refuse. Within a month of founding the CFS, the managers set the boarding rate at seven shillings a week, the equivalent of about one dollar, which they later lowered. The women were also willing to adjust the boarding fee when parents could not pay. Louisa Jane Buck's mother agreed to pay fifty cents a week to board her child at the home, but after three months retrieved Louisa Jane and settled her account with three dollars, half the agreed-upon amount. Even this nominal charge might be waived, as in the case of the Gates children, whom the managers agreed to board "free of expense to their mother, who is sick and unable to take care of them." The children remained at the home until their mother recuperated. The managers expected those who could afford it to reimburse the society, but made their decisions on a case-by-case basis. In July 1853, the CFS took in three-year-old Daniel Moly, an "uncommonly bright" child who suffered from curvature of the spine. Although Daniel's mother would neither pay his board nor indenture him, the managers decided against taking "strenuous measures" with her, apparently believing she had enough troubles, and eventually canceled her debt. The managers' willingness to board children temporarily, often without the expectation of reimbursement, gave women such as Mrs. Gates and Mrs. Moly options that antebellum women elsewhere did not have. In times of family crisis, they did not have to confront the alternatives of losing custodial care of their children or of leaving them to the untender mercies of the city almshouse.[42]

Not all mothers who brought their children to the home were anxious to retrieve them. When Hannah Ratican's year-old daughter died suddenly at the home, the managers were unable to find Ratican to inform her of the death, leading them to conclude that she "cares very little for the child." Similarly, Mary Jane Fitzpatrick's mother abandoned her at the home and "left for parts unknown." The "earnest solicitation" of George Clark's grandmother persuaded the hesitant managers to board the boy "long enough to learn to read, or till April next." Six months later, George was still at the home despite determined attempts by the exasperated managers to convince the grandmother to take him back. Even unmarried mothers—women or girls whose condition violated emerging notions of feminine purity and domesticity—found an ally in the CFS. A mother at fifteen, Miss Chilson of nearby East Douglas relinquished her infant daughter for adoption. The CFS offered Chilson a chance for future respectability and her daughter the possibility of greater economic security and social acceptance. The CFS therefore also provided services to women for whom the maternal role was not feasible.[43]

The men of Worcester also turned to the CFS when in need, and nearly one quarter of the children were brought to the home by their fathers. Although gender discrimination advantaged men as a class, it did not necessarily benefit them as individuals, and many confronted misfortune, low wages, and chronic unemployment. Thus John Mixter indentured his daughter because he was "wholly unable to support self & family." The three Wheeler girls, possibly the children of a second marriage, arrived at the home because "their father is an old man, unable to provide for them." Men unwilling to part with their children, but sometimes unable to support them, also turned to the CFS for immediate and temporary assistance. A man without a wife was less imperiled economically than a woman without a husband, but he still needed someone to care for the children while he worked to support them. After his wife died, Mr. Hall boarded their three children at the home until he could arrange for his mother to take over their care. Mr. Campbell, a widower, first boarded his children with the CFS in 1850. Over the course of the next few years, the Campbell children were in and out of the home while their father faithfully paid their board. For men disinclined or unable to remarry, but loathe to part with their children, boarding them at the CFS was a welcome alternative.[44]

In some cases, indifference underlay a father's desire to find new homes for his dependent children. Moses Center, a minor himself, brought his younger sister to the home when their father abandoned them. Mr. O'Haran asked the CFS to assume the care of his teenaged son John, but after a visit to the family the managers refused, stating flatly that they did not "see that the Father's request for care [is] necessary." When O'Haran persisted, the managers relented and used their contacts to apprentice John to a carpenter. For five years the CFS maintained an interest in John O'Haran, ending its oversight only when he reached adulthood. The managers tended to be less overtly judgmental of men who renounced their parental responsibilities than they were of non-maternal women. Whether or not this was because they expected less from fathers is unclear, but the women voiced their strong disapproval of Hannah Ratican's abandonment of her infant daughter, yet accepted Mr. O'Haran's surrender of his son.[45] For both the mothers and the fathers of Worcester, the Children's Friend Society provided a resource that was often flexible and responsive to their situations.

GENDER, CHILD CUSTODY, AND SOCIAL CONFLICT IN THE INDENTURE CONTRACT

Whether offering vital social services to help parents navigate short-term crises, or arranging long-term placement through foster families and adoptions, the managers of the CFS sought to gain legal custody of the children through Articles of Indenture. Historians have viewed with some suspicion the use of indentures by nineteenth-century charitable societies, for the contract seems to imply the triumph of bourgeois calculation over communitarian empathy. The history of the Worcester CFS, however, offers a different interpretation. Despite their public statements, the managers did not require indentures. Nor did the managers usually apprentice children. Moreover, when they did hold indentures, the women frequently did not exercise them, and when they did seek to exercise them they learned that doing so was much harder in practice than in principle. Indentures were less legal contracts than negotiated social contracts, because the same maternalist arguments the managers advanced to defend their activism proved equally powerful when wielded by a poor mother to defend her interests.[46]

The managers did not require indentures for the many children sheltered on a temporary or emergency basis, or for those for whom the issue of long-term or short-term care had yet to be resolved. In 1854, the Overseers of the Poor of nearby Blackstone sent Oriana Taft to board at the home. Five years later Taft was still there, still without indentures, when the managers voted "to retain her and give her every possible advantage to obtain an education the same as if she were bound to the Board of Managers." The managers clearly preferred that the children be indentured, but were motivated less by aspirations for social control than by a first-hand knowledge of the complications the lack of indentures could cause. In 1853, the managers learned that Ellen Lee had disappeared from her foster home, apparently spirited away by her mother. They concluded, "as we have no legal claim upon her there seems to be nothing that we can do in the case." Nor did the managers necessarily accept children with indentures. In 1855, the Overseers of the Poor indentured William Clovey to the CFS. Two months later, fearful that the boy's mother would "cause a good deal of trouble if her child is at the home," the board of managers reversed itself and declined to be a party to the indenture contract.[47]

The managers had good reason to tread cautiously. Experience had taught them that, regardless of the law, their power over the relationship between parent and child was limited. An aggrieved parent, especially a mother, could appeal to the public's belief in the sacredness of the parental bond to exert considerable extralegal leverage. In their *Fourth Annual Report*, the CFS addressed the issue bluntly:

> It sometimes happens ... that the *mother*, retracting her own voluntary act in surrendering [her child], and unable or unwilling to understand the terms of the indenture ... appears to renew and assert her former claims. ... If these claims are disallowed ... she complains of being cruelly and unjustly

treated.... Through the agency of such discontented spirits, prejudices are excited in some minds, and grave charges are preferred against a company of women, who are supposed to set at naught the maternal relation, and take upon themselves the unauthorized responsibility of separating children from their parents.[48]

One such "discontented spirit" was Rosannah Kelly, whose clash with the CFS early in its history clarified the actual limits to the theoretical power of the law. In January 1851, Kelly indentured her five-year-old daughter, Annie, to the CFS. She then changed her mind and insisted upon reestablishing contact with Annie. Before long "her importunities became so urgent and troublesome" that, after considerable debate, the managers agreed to void the contract. The Board reported that Annie was soon spied on the streets of Worcester "dirty and ill-clad."[49]

The following July, Rosannah Kelly was arrested for being drunk and disorderly and was jailed for six months on assault charges. A neighbor brought Annie to the almshouse because there was no one to care for her and because Kelly had refused to send her back to the CFS. But Kelly's inability to support her daughter while in jail meant that Annie was "thrown upon the city," which permitted the Overseers of the Poor to indenture her to the CFS. In September, Annie Kelly returned to the home and was placed with a family that wanted to adopt her.[50]

Two months later, Rosannah Kelly was released from jail, irate at finding her child gone. She "soon renewed her former annoyances in regard to the child," the CFS reported, "claiming the right to know where it was, to see it at its place of residence, and to remove it if not agreeable." Worried that Kelly might simply take Annie away, the managers refused. They did agree to a visit between mother and daughter but only on the condition that Kelly promise to leave her daughter alone. In response, Kelly shrewdly appealed to the public, declaring "that she has been cruelly treated, in having her child removed from her maternal care...." Kelly's allegations stung, for although the law was on their side custom was not, and the managers found themselves on the defensive, accused of a misappropriation of maternal authority.[51]

Uncertain what their next move should be the managers summoned the advisors. If they returned Annie to her mother, the women explained, they would "disregard their obligations to the child" as required by the indenture contract. But if Kelly's charges damaged their reputation, then "some of the important objects for which the Society was instituted, are incapable of accomplishment." The advisors recommended that the managers remain firm in principle but accept a practical compromise, proposing "that the mother be permitted to have reasonable intercourse with [Annie], under the direction and supervision of the managers" and trusting to the future to determine what other arrangements might be necessary. With considerable trepidation, the managers scheduled a meeting between Annie and her mother, but Kelly stood them up. One year later, the "so much dreaded meeting" took place, to the apparent satisfaction of the parties. Thus did a poor Irish immigrant with a criminal record contest the power of a group of established and well-connected reformers. Kelly's weapons were her maternal claim and her willingness to take her case to the Worcester public, and as an arsenal it was sufficient. The resolution of the case was due more to Kelly's willingness to let the matter lie as it was to any power inherent in the indenture contract.[52]

Other women did not have the daring to challenge the managers as directly as Rosannah Kelly did, but many just as effectively subverted their legal authority. The society's records reveal numerous instances of mothers taking matters into their own hands and reclaiming their indentured children. Mrs. Fairbanks retrieved her son Richard from his foster home without the society's knowledge or consent. Eliza Barry's mother ignored the indenture agreement and "carried [Eliza away] to her miserable home in Clintonville" leaving the managers to wonder "what shall be done."[53] There was little they could do. There were no civil authorities to turn to; indeed, for much of the nineteenth century, the CFS *was* Worcester's de facto child welfare agency. In any event, abrogating an indenture contract was not a crime but a civil dispute, and dragging a poor mother into court to repossess her child was clearly not an acceptable option. The power of the managers of the CFS stemmed from their ability to persuade, cajole, or intimidate others in face-to-face encounters. Such power is not inconsequential and on the whole the women appear to have been rather good at it. However, those parents who were neither persuaded nor intimidated, and who resolved situations to their own satisfaction, had little reason to fear any consequences. As the case of Rosannah and Annie Kelly had demonstrated, there were practical as well as ideological limits to the lengths the managers could or would go in challenging the rights of even an indigent mother.[54]

The managers themselves limited the society's power, for they frequently voided a child's indentures when it was clear that a family crisis had passed. Sarah McMann's parents indentured her to the CFS before moving to Dorchester in search of economic opportunities. Apparently they found some, for several months later the managers returned Sarah to her parents. In the summer of 1857, Mrs. Reed indentured her son William to the society. When Reed's fortunes took a turn for the better in the late fall, the managers agreed to "let Mrs. Reed keep her little boy for the winter." In the spring the managers noted that Reed was "in a situation to take proper care of the child" and voided the indentures. The CFS canceled these legal contracts out of the belief that, whenever possible, a child's best interests lay with the birth parent, especially with the mother.[55]

Returning a child to its family was not automatic, however. Morality, not economics, was the litmus test of maternal fitness because to the managers' minds morality, unlike economics, was within a woman's control. The managers were therefore more apt to cooperate with a poor but "respectable" mother than one in better circumstances but whose character was more suspect. In 1857, Mrs. Macier indentured her two sons after their father disappeared. When Macier wanted one son back, the managers consented because "she seems respectable." The society also agreed to return Ellen Ashton when her mother remarried but "reserv[ed] the right of taking her again to our charge if the place proves unsatisfactory." A year later, they did just that. The managers voided the indentures of Macier's child but exercised the indentures of Ashton's child. Flexibility, not rigidity, marked the use of indentures and the Board's decisions depended upon the circumstances of each case.[56]

The CFS also was willing to turn over the care of a child to its relatives if assured that they could provide a good home. Sisters seem to have been particularly interested in the welfare of their younger siblings. In 1854, the secretary reported that Charlotte Wright had returned to the home "on account of the death of the gentleman in whose family she has been for several years (the wife having no home for herself)." The managers agreed to send Charlotte to live with an adult sister "who promises to send her to school and take care of her, and who is very desirous to have her with her" so long as the Board remained satisfied "with the place and treatment." When Sarah Mixter's sister offered her a home in the neighboring town of West Boylston, the managers dispatched the matron to appraise the situation before agreeing. Not all sisters could pass the matron's muster. Eliza Leachlin was one of three siblings orphaned en route from Ireland in 1850. An older sister, herself a minor, persuaded Eliza to run away from her foster home "with a view to go to Lowell" to work in a factory. The girls were spotted at the train station and an indignant matron charged to the rescue. The managers had never bound a child out to work in a factory and were apparently reluctant to permit such a thing under any condition. Grandparents, aunts, and other close relatives could assert a special interest in a child but not an overriding claim. In the winter of 1854, Ozilla Earle's mother indentured her to the CFS. When a grandmother offered the child a home, the managers sent Ozilla "to stay a while on a visit" but later moved her to a foster home. Similarly, the women permitted one of Mrs. Dickey's two children to live with an aunt but rejected a grandmother's request for the other. Emily Budding's grandfather brought her to the CFS to be placed in a foster home, but when he wanted her back a few weeks later, the managers honored his request. When he returned Emily after one month, the managers insisted upon indentures and Emily was adopted.[57]

The often complicated case histories of CFS children and their families demonstrate how difficult it is to characterize simply the relationship among the children, the parents, and the women of the CFS. The indenture contract does not, by itself, tell us much about the nature of the guardianship the managers exercised, or indeed, whether they exercised guardianship at all. If instead we look at particular cases, we see a flexible approach to defining a child's best interests. Mothers and fathers boarded their children at the home in times of momentary crisis and indentured their children when the future looked bleak. Both actions were voluntary and, most importantly, neither was irrevocable. Worcester's parents, most often the mothers, appear to have believed that the women of the CFS could be relied upon—or convinced, one way or another—to respond to their needs. According to the law, Articles of Indenture signaled the end of direct parental influence over a child. According to the parents of Worcester, Articles of Indenture signaled the redefinition of the parental relationship and the opening of negotiations with the women of the CFS.[58]

"CHILDREN OF THE PROMISE" AND THE FOSTER FAMILY

Meeting the society's goal of long-term child care led the managers to develop a new approach: the foster family. The managers experimented with their own families first. In March 1849, Ann Buffum Earle, a life-long member of the board of managers, a mother, and the wife of a wealthy manufacturer, opened her home to six-year-old John Tyler and arranged for her sister to take nine-year-old Emma Tyler. Even after the CFS acquired its home, the managers occasionally still served as foster mothers, as when Manager Mary Rider Brown took home with her five-year-old Josephine Wright, who had expressed "a strong feeling against being placed at the Home."[59]

A more permanent solution meant recruiting likely homes from the city and county of Worcester. Foster families were hard to come by, given the society's aim to have the children accepted as integral family members, not as servants or laborers. Moreover, it was not sufficient that families be willing; applicants had to meet the board's criteria, loose and ill-defined though they initially were. To evaluate a potential home, the managers asked, "Is it a good family? Are they suitable persons to be entrusted with the care of a child? Making a liberal allowance for the absence of parental affection, will it be a desirable home?" The ideal family was one in which "the glad voice of childhood has been forever hushed...." The managers knew from personal experience that the death of a birth child might create a void for an adopted child to fill, and so in uncharacteristically blunt terms they invited "bereaved parents" to visit the home and "transfer their affections from the dead, to a living child."[60]

The managers expected that the children would be fully integrated into their new families, resoldering, as it were, the broken family chain. The women conceded that this could take time, but were often sorely disappointed at the lukewarm welcome some children received: "the remark so often heard at the home, from persons applying for a child, [is] 'I do not expect to love or treat this boy or this girl as I do my own children.' We sometimes wish that the expression of this feeling might be withheld until the question of the necessity of indulging it could be fairly settled by time and experience."[61] The managers recognized that the role of foster parent was a demanding one and they warned families to expect to exercise "a patient and forbearing spirit" with the children. "Perfect children are very desirable," the CFS intoned drolly, "but nowhere, we venture to say, are they in greater demand than at our Orphan's Home." The women repeatedly reminded foster families of "the importance of [taking children] with a fixed determination of allowing them, if possible, to remain, and to do the best they can to correct their numerous faults." Given time, they hoped, a loving bond would develop. The managers knew that some of the children, scarred by their experiences, manifested emotional and behavioral problems. In the five years that Sarah Brigham was under their care, the women found it necessary to place her with five different foster families. But they did not blame the child and continued to hope that the right family and the right amount of time would be the solution. Be patient just a little longer, the managers counseled those disillusioned by the behavior of some children, and they wondered "is it too much to ask, that persons proposing to adopt children . . . take them just as they are, and resolve to do their best to train them for a life of usefulness?"[62]

Such statements reveal the CFS's bedrock assumption that families were formed not by blood but by sentiment. By the 1850s, several generations of Americans, and especially those of the educated middle class, had been exposed to the idea that affective bonds were central to republican family values. As American law drifted further away from its English common law origins, with its historic emphasis upon patrilineal descent of property, American society slowly shifted the balance of power within the family away from a reflexive patriarchy and toward a philosophy of individual rights, which included an expansion of the rights of mothers and children. Increasingly, emotional and not strictly dynastic attachments defined the middle-class family. Reflecting this assumption, the women of the CFS sought not to find poor children more comfortable homes but more loving homes, and to create new families from the remnants of those torn apart by death, poverty, and immorality.[63]

Extending the parental bond from a birth child to an adoptive child was, however, an idea still ahead of its time. Not only was the legal status of adopted children ambiguous—as late as the 1880s Massachusetts courts were still ruling on their right of inheritance—but prejudice against equating birth children and adopted children remained strong. Indeed, CFS foster parents often proved less interested in completing their families than in acquiring cheap labor. Indentured servants had traditionally supplied New England families with domestic, field, and shop labor and many foster families apparently had this arrangement in mind when they applied for a child. The managers, however, instructed the matron to reject applications from those whom she suspected of "mercenary" intentions. It was partly for this reason that the managers preferred to accept young children, who were less likely to contribute significantly to a family economy. The CFS thus asked foster families to assume considerable economic and psychological burdens with little immediate compensation, much as parents did for their birth children.[64]

Since the managers would not promote the children through their value as laborers, and discouraged families from thinking of them in such terms, they attempted to attract foster families with the spiritual dividends to be accrued through caring for a needy child. They reminded the public that "it will surely be something worth living for, to be made the means of rescuing even one immortal being from misery and vice." God had so arranged the world to provide for all: "And as God's world is ordered, there are enough, who can take home these orphans. Is it you? Is it you? who shall make them children of the promise,—children of adoption; and bring them up to blessedness,—to Him!" Worcester families could take part in God's design by making room for a foster child.[65]

The shortage of acceptable foster homes, combined with their faith in the essential orderliness of the universe, meant that the managers were careful not to overlook a potential match. If a home did not prove suitable for one child, perhaps it would fit another. Since they yielded the Articles of Indenture only when the child reached adulthood or was adopted, there was a myriad of possible combinations of children and foster homes. In 1858, for example, the managers reported thirty-two children residing at the home and one hundred and fifty in foster homes, all under their legal control.[66]

Bringing up these "children of the promise" could be challenging, the managers acknowledged, but they often thought foster families gave up too soon. Seeking to exonerate the well-intentioned for the "summary dismissals" of children, the women conceded that "it is impossible to know how much sickness, or unexpected changes" could befall a family and force it to renege upon its agreement to care for a child. "Still," they asserted in the *Fourth Annual Report,* "we have sometimes thought that a little longer trial, a little more faith and patience and persevering effort, might, with the blessing of God, produce a marked change in the character of these neglected ones...." The measured tones of the society's published remarks stand in sharp contrast to the clipped anger expressed within the pages of the secretary's private notes. Foster families, the managers lamented among themselves, heartlessly summoned and dismissed the children, not seeming to recognize that they were, after all, only children. "*Helen Charlotte Sparks* returned to the home from Sturbridge," the secretary recorded in 1858, "not for any fault of hers, but a son had come home to them, so they dismissed the little girl." The CFS placed Ednah Louisa Handy with the Phipps family in the hope that she would "be adopted if liked they have no child." But Ednah was not liked and the Phippses returned her, the secretary wrote, "with various trivial excuses which we have reason to believe were any thing but the right one." Occasionally a foster parent was quite candid, as when Mrs. Goodale returned George Tyler "with the old excuse of being too small. . . ." Disgusted, the secretary noted that George had "the character of a good boy" and added, in a rare moment of sarcasm, "We would advise that the next place to which he shall go shall be one where size shall not be the test."[67]

The CFS's experiences with foster families were not unrelievedly grim. By modern standards, the society's record keeping was casual, even slapdash, with children appearing and disappearing without explanation. Moreover, since Board meetings dwelled upon problems, not happy endings, its minutes were skewed toward the contentious. Still, in 1854 the CFS reported that in the five years since its founding, sixty-two, or nearly forty percent, of the one hundred and fifty-seven children admitted for placement "have reasonable prospects of a permanent home." But adoption was not the sole marker of success and it seems likely that many placements resulted in stable families. William Griffin took the name of his foster father, the traditional symbol of acceptance into a family. Esther Kircup lived with the family of George Dryden, a manufacturer of hay cutting machinery. At one point the Drydens had returned Esther "but after a few days, it was found that she had so strongly engaged their affections, that they were unhappy without her & came to beg her return to them. . . ." Years before public foster and adoption programs were developed, private women's organizations such as the Worcester CFS were already experimenting with and refining the means for creating new families.[68]

THE MATRON AND MATERNAL OVERSIGHT

Before children were placed in foster families or with relatives, they lived at the CFS home in the care of the matron. The matron was critical to the smooth functioning of the CFS in light of its desire that the home be as much like a real home as possible. For five years founder Anstis Miles served in this role, but when she left the city in 1854 the managers promoted forty-year-old Tamerson White, then the home's schoolteacher, to matron and superintendent. White held the position for thirty-one years, until she died "in the harness" in 1885. After death, White remained a symbolic presence for she was buried in Worcester's Hope Cemetery alongside the children who had died at the home.[69] White had received no training to be the matron of such an institution but she had taught school for many years. Women teachers became commonplace after 1830 when the northern public school system expanded. Confronted with a shortage of qualified male applicants, and mindful of the much lower salaries women were forced to accept, school boards justified the hiring of women by stressing the maternal nature of teaching. The managers agreed, arguing that schoolteaching had taught White to be "quick to discern, and careful to correct whatever is wrong in the dispositions or habits of her youthful charges." Like those of a good mother's, the matron's duties were all-encompassing: she was to "execute and receive all indentures of children bound to the society," to regulate and manage the "family," and to "provide for the intellectual, religious and physical education and well being of the children." The matron was also an incipient social worker who located, investigated, and evaluated foster families, and oversaw the children after placement.[70]

To carry out these daunting maternal responsibilities the managers hired a childless, never-married woman. White's position as matron suggests that if a commitment to maternalism could make professionals of mothers, it could also make mothers of professionals. Gender roles were being transformed in the face of economic development, and a deluge of advice books sought to teach women the skills their foremothers had mastered through years of apprenticeship. The managers also found religious justification for delegating maternal authority to the matron. Just as motherhood was a divinely ordained role for married women, so too, they argued, did God sanction surrogate motherhood for single women. Indeed, the managers asserted that White had been "called . . . by an over-ruling Providence" to her labors. Motherhood, the managers seemed to say, was both a profession capable of being mastered by women who were not biological mothers and a religious duty, a "calling" to which single women could respond.[71]

The managers considered White a great success in her calling. She threw herself into the job, they reported, "with a self-sacrificing devotion, which it is almost painful to witness." Year after year they praised White's dedication and skill in the performance of her duties as surrogate parent and housekeeper, commending the "quiet dignity" with which she "commanded respect and obedience." To an extent that few men of their day could, the women appreciated the difficulties involved in run-

ning a large and busy household, and they empathized with the intermittent depression the matron's ceaseless labor kindled. Betraying an
ambivalence about the role that shaped their own lives so profoundly,
the managers spoke frankly of the occasional cracks in White's maternal
facade: "We have not been surprised or alarmed, to hear her speak in
some moment of unallowed despondency, of her failures in duty—and
now and then . . . confess to a feeling of discouragement in view of her
multiplied cares and responsibilities. Is there here a single sensible judi-
cious Christian mother, who cannot properly appreciate and sympathize
with her in feelings like these?"[72] Still, the managers argued, despite the
incessant demands, White "probably experience[s] more real enjoyment
than will ever be attained by those engaged in the pursuit of exciting
pleasures or frivolous amusements." In part, such rhetoric was common
among reformers, who insisted, sometimes strenuously, that duty gave
more pleasure than frivolity. At the same time, it is possible that the
managers sought to reassure themselves that the trials of motherhood
brought ample compensation. If anyone would know, surely it would be
a woman who was surrogate mother to thirty children. By the same
token, the managers jokingly asserted that the matron's perseverance
was not entirely natural, indeed, was almost eerie. White was "an exor-
cist," the secretary wrote playfully, who drove away the "unclean spirits"
of profanity, vulgarity, and deceit. Successful mothering, the women of
the CFS seemed to say, required a lot of hard work and more than a
touch of magic.[73]

Very early into White's tenure the managers ceded her complete
control of the home's daily economy. In light of the need to live within
their tight budget, this was an important vote of confidence. Under
White's stewardship, they explained, "the wonder is often expressed how
so many children can be clothed, fed, and made very comfortable on so
scanty an allowance. . . . The secret is, [White and her assistant] understand their business." White had not been hired on the basis of her business acumen; by what gauge, after all, would this have been measured?
Surrogate mother, social worker, and household manager, White helped
to expand professional women's waged work beyond the parameters of
teaching.[74]

The adult managers were thus well pleased with White. Less clear
were the opinions of those whom she most directly affected, the CFS
children. It is entirely possible that the qualities that pleased a board of
managers would not be the standards of a group of children. However,

the evidence suggests that White was popular with at least some of those whose lives she directed daily. In the 1860s, women who had come to the CFS as children pitched in to furnish White's room in the new home, while other women voted with their feet—in this case by marching them down the aisle—and chose to be married from the home. In 1874, a group of former CFS children returned to the home to celebrate White's twenty-fifth anniversary with the society and to unveil a portrait of her that they had commissioned. That their time at the CFS conveyed some good memories may have been because White identified with her charges, asserting "My children are just as good as anybody's children." The thought became the deed when White adopted a little girl as her own. To a foster family in search of "a very good boy," White retorted, "I haven't any such good boys; my boys are full of life and mischief. I wish you wanted one not quite so good." White knew whereof she spoke; she lived with the children, ate the same food as they, and shared their table. White also was sensitive to the status of the children in their own eyes and in the eyes of others. Aware of the importance of clothing in determining social rank, White "was scrupulously careful that there should be nothing in their dress or general appearance that should suggest any unpleasant comparisons between themselves and the children with whom they associated." The children, for example, did not wear uniforms but clothing that had been altered or sewn for them by the matron and the community's many sewing circles. "We have no misfits," the managers wrote, "If the garment fails to fit the child, there is always a child to fit the garment."[75]

After they were placed with foster families, CFS children remained in contact with White, writing letters "expressing great affection for her and in every respect very gratifying," visiting the home on occasion, and sending the matron periodic updates. Lucy Parkhurst stopped by on a visit to tell the matron that she was living nearby "where she has a very pleasant home." After the CFS found Oliver Hooker a foster home, he corresponded regularly with the matron. Hooker was one of fifteen former CFS boys to enlist in the Union army during the Civil War, and when he was killed in battle in 1863, the managers reported that "Miss White . . . had received a letter but a short time before . . . informing her of his enlistment."[76]

The ongoing communication testifies not only to some of the children's affection for White but also to the conscientiousness of the CFS. White maintained contact with the children in part to ease their transition to a new life but also to learn whether their situations were suitable. As she had with Oliver Hooker, White wrote periodically to the children and their new families "so that we are thus made acquainted with the circumstances and progress of each individual," and she routinely visited them in their new homes. If White suspected that a child was not being well treated, she notified the managers, who decided whether to exercise the indentures and remove the child. When the managers heard "unfavorable reports" from Laura Jane Watson, who had been placed with a family in nearby Templeton, they dispatched White to investigate; Laura Jane returned to the home the following month. Sometimes the matron acted unilaterally. In 1859, the managers noted simply that a child was back at the home because "Miss White did not find his place suitable for him."[77]

The women exercised such caution because they were worried about the children and the possibility of abuse. The plight of the "friendless" orphan in the clutches of a lascivious or wicked protector was a staple of romantic literature from Hansel and Gretel through Cinderella, and antebellum newspapers printed numerous variations on this theme. But the problems confronting such children were not purely fictional. Only one month after the CFS was founded, an eleven-year-old orphan, Prudence Arnold, was brutally murdered by a man who worked on the farm where she resided in Uxbridge, Worcester county. The local papers covered the girl's "most horrid and unnatural murder" in bloody detail, attributing the crime to intemperance. The murderer's brain, one editor reported, had "been set on fire by some *three quarts* of cider...." A year later, the trial of Prudence Arnold's murderer held the city's rapt attention.[78]

Prudence Arnold was not a child from the newly founded Worcester Children's Friend Society, but the tragedy likely reminded the managers of the vulnerability of their own charges. The possibility of the abuse or neglect of the children under their care was profoundly disturbing, yet it placed the women in a potentially awkward position. On the one hand, the CFS existed to rescue children from evil. To cause them subsequently to be exposed to abuse or worse not only violated their mission but made them complicitous in sin. On the other hand, excessive vigilance would alienate the foster families, whom the society needed in order to function, as well as offend the public. Yet the murder of Prudence Arnold vividly demonstrated that foster families could not always be relied upon to protect children. The managers therefore sought to avoid acrimonious confrontations by anticipating and resolving problems early and quietly.

One way to preempt accusations of meddling in domestic affairs was for the managers to broach the issue publicly. In its *Tenth Annual Report*, the CFS described the matron's efforts to screen foster families and acknowledged occasional reports of "ill-treatment" of the children. The women flatly denied having "the smallest desire to organize an inquisition . . . or to keep a strict surveillance over any family," but insisted that neither could they ignore reports of neglect or improper treatment from "intelligent, unprejudiced persons." Their goal was to help the children, the managers stressed, adding pointedly that "if we cannot accomplish this object, or in some good degree improve their condition, we might as well leave them to grow up in ignorance, or perish in the streets of our city, as place them in the hands of strangers to be improperly trained, neglected or abused." It was therefore in the community's best interests for allegations of abuse to be investigated.[79]

For both humanitarian and political reasons, however, it was far better to prevent child abuse than to expose it. Because the indenture contracts conveyed guardianship to the CFS, not to the foster family, the women had the authority to visit foster homes, which White and the Visiting Committee did. Moreover, the children seem to have been told that they could return to the home if they were unhappy. As early as February 1849, the managers took up the case of Thomas Wright, aged eleven. The CFS had placed him with one of Worcester's leading citizens but within a month he was complaining of "ill usage." The situation posed a dilemma for the fledgling society: how to remove the child, for whose benefit the CFS existed, without giving offense to a solid citizen, whose support it needed? The managers decided to remove Wright on the grounds that he did not "give satisfaction" and found him another family. When the Visiting Committee checked on "Tommy" in his new home a month later, they found him more contented. A child's complaints were heeded and a potential conflict between the CFS and a foster mother had been quietly defused. Through letters, visits, and discreet inquiries, the women of the CFS apprised themselves of the children's situations, hoping to make certain that the children in their care would not meet the fate of the tragic Prudence Arnold.[80]

THE LIMITS OF MATERNALISM

The women were not, however, concerned equally with the situations of all the children of Worcester and would not agree to care for certain categories of children. Their approach to the care and treatment of infant and sickly children, of African American children, and of unmanageable children demonstrate the limits of the women's commitment to the community's progeny. Sometimes the limits grew out of pragmatic concerns, sometimes they were the result of racial prejudice. The women did, however, evince considerable dedication to a number of children whose behavior might have tried the most deeply devoted guardian. Unlike many other antebellum societies, the Worcester CFS assisted difficult children before and after placement.[81]

Infants and babies were among those whom the managers explicitly refused to accept into their care. The managers' own experiences had taught that the labor-intensive, specialized care demanded by the very young was unavoidable and, because they respected women's work, a substitute mother's labor was expensive. In 1854, the secretary noted, "The babe that Mrs. Hood is taking care of is very troublesome requiring all the time of the person to attend to it, we think she ought to have more compensation than she now receives." Nursing this one infant consumed nearly four percent of the entire year's budget. Babies placed too great a drain on the society's limited resources and thus were not routinely accepted at the home.[82]

Nonetheless, the appeal of infants was such that, while the women were reluctant to accept legal responsibility for them, "sometimes our sympathies overleap all rules." If a formal subsidy was out of the question, a private one might be arranged. At a special meeting in 1849, the managers "Voted to raise thirty dollars, by subscription, to be given to Mrs. Chickering [a wetnurse] as a present; without any reference to the child now in her care, which has not yet been admitted by indenture into the Society." The records reveal that the managers made numerous other exceptions to their age policy when experience proved that homes for babies often were quickly found. The managers accepted Mary Smith, "a sweet little infant," because they had a foster family lined up "and we are in hopes of soon finding a more permanent home for her." During her tenure as superintendent Anstis Miles resorted to something approaching guerrilla tactics to find homes for infants. She allegedly had no compunctions about dropping in unannounced on prospective homes, infant in arms, thrusting the child at the startled family and commanding: "Take this child and nurse it for God, and he will give thee wages." The direct approach apparently often worked, and Miles's success, the managers intoned as they described such scenes with relish, was evidence that "an argument so authoritative, in connection with an appeal so tender, were not to be resisted." When it came to infants and babies, the women of the CFS repeatedly subverted an unpalatable rule they had adopted by necessity.[83]

The managers advanced a similar argument against accepting children in poor health and thus, like infants, in need of special care. In 1849, a Worcester minister brought to the home James Hyde, eighteen months old, whose father was dead and whose mother was destitute. Sadly, James was frail and Miles returned him to his mother. The managers reassured her that the decision was "justifiable" since "the funds of our society will not enable us suitably to provide for weak & sickly children, who demand extra attention." When a boy "belonging to the cook at Mrs. Bean's" arrived at the home, the matron noticed something was wrong with the child and summoned the physician, who "thinks one side partially parylized [sic], extending to the brain & recommends the asylum in South Boston as the best place for him—he will soon be removed." Children in poor health also posed a non-financial threat. There were no vaccines against childhood afflictions and the introduction of contagious disease into a household of thirty children was no small matter. In the spring of 1853, fourteen of the children at the home contracted measles; a year later, the malady returned and of the nine children infected "eight . . . were sick at one time." In the summer of 1860, half of the children came down with measles while six months later scarlatina, measles and varioloid struck in rapid succession and the home was placed under quarantine. The quarantine was an extreme situation but, in general, until sickness passed the managers would neither accept nor place children and all activities ground to a halt.[84]

The women also had a more sentimental reason to avoid the sick and the frail. These children could fatally infect others or die themselves. The children at the home enjoyed a generally high level of health, a fact that the society's annual reports regularly announced with a mixture of pride and relief. "There has been no uncommon sickness in the family during the year, and no death has occurred," the women boasted in 1859, "which, considering the number of inmates, is a noticeable fact." The managers described the children as "Bright, active, vigorous, and promising," adding dryly, "they are not suffering from any weakness of the vocal organs."[85]

But even the most conscientious care could not protect some children from death. When a child at the home died, the women of the CFS took it hard, none more so than the matron whose task it was to nurse the sick back to health. In 1853 the managers reported that "little Addison Barnes" was "attacked violently" by illness and quickly died. The reassurances of the child's mother that they had done all they could helped console the managers. Joseph Carter's sudden death at twenty months was all the more shocking because "for a few days previous Miss White had flattered herself that he was improving." Little Jenny Valentine, "a special favorite," had been found abandoned "with an icy tear upon her cheek." A few months after the child's February 14 arrival, the managers reported, "neither medical skill, faithful nursing, or Miss White's affection could detain her longer from her home in Heaven." Jenny Valentine was one of but four children who died at the home that year. Sick and frail children strained the society's resources, endangered the health of the other children, and even shut down the home altogether. Their responses to the children's deaths suggest that the women of the CFS had an emotional investment in the well-being of their charges. The managers as well as the matron knew many of the children personally, describing one as "a perfect gem of humanity" and another as "a good boy." The policy against accepting sick children into the society's care was a protection both for the home and for themselves.[86]

Other children posed problems that reflected not concerns with money, health, or sentiment, but with accepted notions of racial equality. The city's African American population was not large but it had deep roots. After serving in the Revolutionary army, Jeffrey Hemenway, for example, moved from Framingham to Worcester, bought a home, and raised a family; his wife, Hannah Hemenway, was a founding member of Worcester's mostly white First Baptist church. The city's black population also played a role in community rituals. An antebellum wedding was simply not fashionable unless Hepsy Hemenway baked the cake and Widow Powers was an attendant. There were as well personal and business ties among blacks and whites, and several managers—Maria Butman, Ann Colton, and Sarah Walker—stood as references for William Brown, an upholsterer and carpet maker. The city provided segregated public education for its children and segregated cemetery plots for its dead. African Americans were thus accepted into the community as long as they remained in a subordinate status.[87]

Antislavery sentiment was, moreover, traditionally strong in Worcester. The city took pride in noting that it was a local lawyer, Levi Lincoln I, the father of Manager Rebecca Lincoln Newton, who defended Quark Walker of Barre, Worcester county, in the case of *Jennison v. Caldwell*, which resulted in the 1781 Massachusetts Superior Court decision declaring slavery contrary to the new state constitution. As early as 1828, Benjamin Lundy of the National Anti-Slavery Society and editor of the Baltimore *Genius of Universal Emancipation* came to Worcester to organize a local chapter and invited "Persons of both sexes" to attend his lecture. In the 1830s, a convention of ministers opposed to slavery met in Worcester; shortly thereafter, abolitionist William Lloyd Garrison came to town and declared, in a reference to Worcester's motto, "The heart of the commonwealth is sound." By the late 1850s, antislavery fervor was so strong that a riot broke out upon the arrival of a federal marshal rumored to be in pursuit of longtime Worcester resident William Jankins, a former slave. The marshal narrowly avoided being lynched by an outraged community, thanks to the intervention of local abolitionists, including Manager Mary Drew's husband, Thomas.[88]

Many of the managers were personally committed to abolitionism or antislavery. Sarah Brown, Maria Butman, Mary Drew, Mary Hadwen, and Ann Earle belonged to the Worcester Anti-Slavery Sewing Circle. Ann Earle also hosted William Lloyd Garrison and Lucretia Mott on their frequent visits to Worcester, and was reputed to have harbored fugitive slaves. Earle's husband, Edward, was the secretary of the Worcester County South Division of the American Antislavery Society, formed in 1838; Ann Colton's husband, Samuel, was its treasurer; Louisa Brown's husband William and Sarah Brown's husband Theophilus both signed its constitution. Mary Drew's husband, Thomas, served as the chair of the Ladies' Fugitive Tea Party in 1851, which protested the recently passed Fugitive Slave Act and raised money to assist those fleeing slavery. Thomas Drew also gave numerous antislavery lectures as part of the Worcester Lyceum. When the Union victory in the Civil War signaled the collapse of America's peculiar institution, the managers paused for a moment to declare "Thank God, we have seen an end of one institution, as a system of legalized oppression, so long our country's sin and shame. Old things are passing away, and the spirit of Freedom, released from the bondage of centuries, is going forth to make all things new. It is the Lord's doings, and marvellous in our eyes."[89]

The Lord's doings had not come without personal cost. Manager Mary Ann Spurr's only son, Thomas Jefferson Spurr, was a lieutenant in the Fifteenth Massachusetts Volunteers. At the Battle of Antietam in September 1862, Spurr was shot in the upper thigh by a minnie ball, shattering the bone. He fell behind enemy lines but was carried into the shade of a tree by several Confederates who were former classmates from Harvard. There he lay for two days until the lines shifted and he was found by Union soldiers. Upon hearing the news, Mary Ann Spurr raced to Hagerstown. Mother and son were close; Thomas was only four when his father died, and Spurr had raised him and his sister Mary by herself. Spurr made it to her son's bedside in time to pray with him, and then she watched him die: "He fixed his eyes in one last gaze upon a familiar countenance; he spoke in tones of cheer; he uttered the word, 'Mother!' he crossed his hands upon his bosom, and fell asleep." As she accompanied her child's body on the long trip back to Worcester, Spurr had time to reflect upon what Thomas had told her as he lay dying: "He was fully aware, he said, when he gave himself to the cause of the Union . . . that many must fall; that he had no right to claim exemption; and that he might as well be the victim of sacrifice as any."[90] The willingness to sacrifice for freedom was shared by others and, in the years after the Civil War, Mary Spurr's fellow managers Ann Earle, Sarah Brown, Ann Colton, Dorcas Lee, and Nancy Moody labored for the Freedmen's Relief Society; Ann and Edmund Earle, whose family motto was "substance and not form," also worked for the Freedman's Administration.[91]

Opposing slavery and dying for freedom was one thing, supporting social equality at the home was quite another.[92] The CFS had no stated racial policy and did board African American children at the home temporarily. In so doing, the managers assisted the children's parents in their search for jobs and better situations. In 1851 the secretary's notes referred to a "little colored girl" who would be permitted to remain at the home "as long as her board is paid weekly." A year later, another little girl was taken in on the recommendation of Manager Ann Colton, an abolitionist. In deference to Colton, the society agreed to board the child "at the rate of twenty five cts. a week," approximately half the usual boarding fee. Six months later, the girl was still at the home, at which point the managers sent her "to the Shelter in Providence," presumably a refuge for black children. However, on at least one occasion the managers contemplated assuming permanent responsibility for a black child. In the spring of 1857, a little girl was "left at the home . . . without note or comment. . . . The man who brought her did not wait to see Miss White." The managers voted to receive her if they could get indentures for her from the city, the usual procedure when a parent's signature was not available.[93]

Despite their willingness to accept custodial care of some African American children, it is clear the managers did so reluctantly. The cases involving black children were disproportionately few: only three of the more than two hundred children cared for during this period. Furthermore, it is telling that the managers did not record the names of black children or their parents, referring instead to "a colored girl" or "the colored woman"—their race being, in the women's minds, sufficient identification. This manner of designation stands in stark contrast to the way the managers addressed white children and their parents, referring to them by name and, in some cases, by nicknames, and always bestowing upon white parents a title, "Mr." or "Mrs." Even the unwed mothers merited "Miss." This was simply not the case for African Americans. Black children also posed a challenge to the society's goal of placing children as full members of foster or adoptive families. It is unlikely that the managers were prepared to ask white families to accept black children as their own. Unless the women recruited adoptive and foster families from the city's African Americans—a course of action they do not seem to have considered—the CFS's mission made no place for black children.[94]

If the managers were ambivalent about accepting African American children into the home, they minced no words when it came to tolerating the delinquent behavior of those children they did accept, particularly that of boys. Although the women refused to model their society after an asylum, preferring the structure and ambience of a "home," they agreed that institutions had a place in the management of recalcitrant or troublesome children, those for whom family-style discipline was insufficient. The managers thus did not hesitate to send boys to the state reform school at Westboro, Worcester county. In June 1849, thirteen-year-old Hugh Conaldson arrived at the home from Vermont, but the managers found him "perverse & refractory in disposition & so vicious in habits" that they turned him over to the police court, which shipped him straight off to Westboro. Similarly, when John Wright stole money from his foster family and ran away, the CFS passed him on to the reform school. The managers also thought that there should be a similar institution for girls and cheered when the state announced plans for a school "for juvenile delinquents of our own sex." When the school opened, Manager Ann Buffum Earle and her husband attended the ceremony.[95]

The Westboro boys' school did not, however, represent a solution of last resort but was a permeable institution, with boys moving back and forth between it and the home. Henry Hooper's foster family returned him to the home with "a poor report" that his mother blamed on the foster family. Once back at the home, willful Henry's conduct was as bad as ever and, with "great regret," the managers packed him off to Westboro. Several years later, however, Henry Hooper was once more living at the home. Similarly, although the managers sent Joseph Williams to Westboro a few months after his arrival at the home, they maintained their interest in him and five years later were still corresponding with the superintendent of Westboro about him. Nor did the managers necessarily wash their hands of troublesome boys, as the case of sixteen-year-old Charles Tyler indicates. Sixteen was well beyond the age limit for acceptance into their charge; Charles was nearly grown and not likely to be adopted. Nevertheless, the managers found him a home and must have been frustrated when he ran away, complaining that he wanted to work on a farm. Within a month, they had arranged it.[96]

The women demonstrated even greater patience with the girls under their control. Particularly in the cases of Cynthia Pige and Helen Gaylord, the managers refused to give up despite the considerable aggravation the girls caused. Their forbearance symbolizes their commitment to the children under their care, but also suggests a lack of practical alternatives. Cynthia Pige came to the home in 1849 and rapidly passed through a series of foster homes. She seldom lasted longer than a few months with any family, leading the society's otherwise staid secretary to dub her "our wandering Cynthia." Time and again the managers allowed themselves to hope that Cynthia had settled into a family, only to find her back at the home within a few months. In 1855, Cynthia Pige disappears from the records. Perhaps she at last found an agreeable home, or possibly she became an adult. For six years the managers sustained their interest in her well-being, accepting with relatively good humor her difficulties at adjusting to foster families.[97]

Helen Gaylord's behavior also was a trial. In the fall of 1853, her mother brought fourteen-year-old Helen to the CFS, which quickly placed her. Helen was returned to the home within a month, the first in a series of rejections by foster families who "complain sadly of her behavior." The matron intervened to chat with Helen and suggested to the managers "the propriety of some of the ladies calling occasionally to see her as a word in season might have a good effect and enable her to retain a good home." But the pep talks did not work and, against the society's wishes, Helen returned to her mother in 1855. When Helen's stepfather threw her out of the house three months later, the managers welcomed Helen back and again placed her. This time she lasted longer, but in 1857, "after an absence of two years," Helen once more returned to the home. Now eighteen, Helen was a legal adult, beyond the age of residential care. The managers, however, hoped to arrange a position for her, "where she may receive small wages & attend school, all or part of the time." The managers persisted in their support of Cynthia Pige and Helen Gaylord, visiting them in their homes, repeatedly unearthing new families, eventually finding at least one of the girls a job.[98]

One source of the women's patience may have been a lack of practical alternatives. The managers would not send a child back to its parents unless both the parents and the child so desired, and until 1856 there was no equivalent for girls of the Westboro reform school for boys. The women of the CFS were, in essence, stuck with the girls in their custody who manifested undesirable behavior. Perhaps it was their experiences with Cynthia Pige and Helen Gaylord that lay behind the managers' enthusiastic support for a reform school for girls. However, a lack of options does not alone account for the women's dedication to their sometimes vexatious charges. It is not clear whether or not the CFS was legally responsible for Cynthia, but it certainly was not responsible for Helen. The managers had accepted Helen with the understanding that her mother would sign Articles of Indenture, but the mother rebuffed their attempts to secure her signature. The managers therefore did not sustain their interest in Helen Gaylord because they had to but because they felt obliged to assist her despite, or perhaps because of, her troubled history.[99]

A deeper source of the women's tolerance was likely more personal. Cynthia Pige and Helen Gaylord were not delinquents, after all; they had committed no crime and were apparently in no danger of doing so. Rather, they were unsettled young women without supportive families. An antebellum American woman acquired her sense of self, her social and economic security, even her name, from her relationship with others: her mother, her father, her husband, or children. A girl on the verge of womanhood without such ties, with no family to assist her socially and economically, was in an alarmingly vulnerable position. The popular literature of the period replayed endlessly the dangers, real and imagined, of a woman alone. In the course of their work of welfare, the managers had seen enough to be unusually well acquainted with the hardships and the pitfalls that awaited single, uprooted women. Furthermore, as women themselves, and as the mothers of daughters, it is possible that they empathized with the obstacles Cynthia and Helen were facing as they headed into adulthood. The legal and economic disabilities of women were daunting enough for those from stable and supportive families, but for those without families the challenges could be overwhelming. And so they exhibited great patience with the older girls in their care; the older boys could better fend for themselves. Although the language detailing the girls' cases reveals the managers' thinning patience, the women remained nonjudgmental. In their eyes, the rootless and demanding Cynthia was "wandering," she was not "perverse & refractory," as they had considered Hugh Conaldson to be. In their own society, as in society at large, gender made a difference.

Comparisons of cases within a category, as in the disparate treatment of Henry Hooper and Charles Tyler, or between categories, as in the different levels of tolerance of the behavior of girls and boys, yield few hard and fast rules by which the managers ran the Worcester Children's Friend Society. Rather, the women determined their courses of action on a case-by-case basis, preferring not to make sweeping policy decisions and rigidly adhering to them. Moreover, they persistently violated the policies they did make. The women had considerable authority over the children in their care and the potential to structure and to stratify the children's lives was great. But they ran the society in a manner comparable to the institution with which they were most familiar, the family. CFS children were not groomed to depart as servants or apprenticed laborers but as integral members of a new family. In so doing, the managers rejected the conventional wisdom and trusted in their own experience.

 Their emphasis upon the familial nature of the society also helped to keep it in the hands of its founders. The Worcester CFS did not go the way of the orphan asylum of Petersburg, Virginia, whose founding mothers lost control to a male board of trustees. By adamantly denying men power within the institution, and by shrewdly linking the success of the home to a more general commitment to maternalism, the managers of the Worcester Children's Friend Society guaranteed their society's influence and autonomy, and to a great extent their own, in a culture generally threatened by female independence.[100]

5

From Feminism to Female Employment

Organized Women in Worcester in the 1850s

Great men make mistakes as well as little ones. This was illustrated the other day by Mr. Calhoun, who took the position that "all men are NOT created free and equal." Said he, "only two men were created, and one of these was a *woman*."

—*National Aegis*, April 3, 1850

In 1848, more than one hundred women and men gathered in Seneca Falls, New York, to hold the first American convention dedicated to the advancement of the legal, political, and economic equality of women. Until the outbreak of the Civil War a dozen years later, women's rights advocates assembled at least annually to analyze women's position in society, rally the faithful, and debate the movement's goals and tactics. In 1850, feminists met in Worcester for the movement's first national convention and they returned to the city the following year. Although only a relative handful of the women of Worcester appear to have openly supported the women's rights movement, others were not immune to its message. An examination of some of the organized activities of the women of the city in the 1850s suggests that their voluntary societies implicitly, and at times explicitly, supported the demands the feminists articulated. For the women of Worcester, the critical decade of the 1850s, a period of intense politicization in the face of mounting sectional conflict, was also an era of organizational growth and expansion.[1]

A heady sense of optimism permeated the Worcester women's rights conventions, for recent events suggested that the "reign of might," which favored men, was ending and that a "reign of right," which favored women, was dawning. In this new era, feminists believed, the possibilities for social improvement were immense and women would figure prominently because they were the more moral. The antebellum feminists tempered an emerging cultural belief that the common good stemmed from competition among individuals—a perspective that would reach its apogee only in the postbellum era—with an awareness that the competition as staged was inherently unfair and ultimately detrimental to society. Although the development of the economy had brought a growing association of morality with femininity and a partial exclusion of women from a recognized economic and political role, women did not allow this to pass unchallenged. Indeed, a commitment to providing economic opportunity for all, as well as to expanding the body politic, was the point at which feminists and more conventional local reformers converged. In the mid-1850s, on the heels of the rights conventions and with the backing of Worcester's established women's organizations, activists sought to expand women's opportunities and to further institutionalize the value of social cooperation by founding a Female Employment Society dedicated to empowering poor women to support their families. Thus in the 1850s Worcester witnessed the maturation, rather than the repudiation, of many years of women's independent social activism.[2]

FEMINISM COMES TO TOWN

The decision to hold the first national women's rights convention in Worcester, and to return the following year, was likely influenced less by the political climate of the city than by its geography. Centrally located in the Northeast, Worcester was the hub of numerous railroad and stage lines, making it relatively easy to get to, and could accommodate large groups at its many hotels, meeting halls, saloons, and restaurants. Indeed, the antebellum city was the site of numerous conventions, which delighted local business owners but exasperated the locals who preferred quiet. "Another Convention at Worcester!" Christopher Columbus Baldwin, a lawyer and the librarian of the American Antiquarian Society, recorded grumpily in his diary in 1833. "This is the third grand State Convention at this place since the first of September; each assembly of from three to five hundred delegates." Many of the groups holding their meetings in Worcester were dedicated to political reform. The People's Convention of Massachusetts convened there in 1848 to form the state's Free Soil Party, while in 1854 a second People's Convention met and renamed itself the Republican Party. Others focused on social issues. Temperance supporters convened in Worcester in 1832 and, diarist Baldwin noted disdainfully, made spectacles of themselves after imbibing "very freely of Cyder; and that which was of the very worst and most unpalatable sort."[3]

By the early 1850s a steady stream of conferences flooded Worcester during the fall convention season. A local paper commented wryly that "The Whigs, Democrats, Free-Democrats, Land Reformers, Come-Outers, Disunionists and Thusologists" had already held "their respective Conventions for the season, and most of them in this city." The "only remaining organization" yet to meet, the paper noted, was that which argued the woman question. Indeed, so popular was Worcester as a host city that when the women's rights convention finally did meet there, Brinley Hall still echoed with the speeches of the Anti-Hanging Convention that had just concluded. Several of those who sought an end to capital punishment in Massachusetts remained to discuss women's rights.[4]

Through the summer and fall of 1850, repeated newspaper notices prepared locals for the upcoming convention, and when the advocates of women's rights arrived in late October, the Worcester public greeted them with a mixture of curiosity, ridicule, and encouragement. Merchants were pleased with the approximately one thousand people from eleven states who descended upon their city, and stocked their shop windows with lacy goods calculated to appeal to female conventioneers. The proprietor of a clothing store seized upon the theme of dress reform to advertise jovially that "One of the Convention Resolutions found floating around town strikes us as being to the point: Resolved, that when we get our rights, we will to the man buy our breeches of A. Maccular and Co." The Worcester *Palladium*, a Democratic paper, praised the eloquent oratory of convention speakers Lucretia Mott, Ernestine Rose, and Abby Kelley Foster, but dismissed the women's movement generally as a thinly disguised *"form of anti-slavery agitation"* with which it had no sympathy. Still others were much less respectful, and those speaking at Brinley Hall had to make themselves heard above the strains of "Oh Susannah" wafting up from a side show exhibition of an obese sixteen-year-old in the hall downstairs. (Critics of women's rights sneered that the 400–pound "American fat girl" was an example of "what woman would be if she had her rights.") But others took the convention more seriously. Asaph Rice, eighty-two, of Northboro, Worcester county, arose early and walked eleven miles "before breakfast" to ensure a good seat at the meeting. Rice's strategy was well advised, for on a "glorious Indian summer" day, Brinley Hall filled to capacity and organizers had to turn away eager crowds. The following year, when the second national women's rights convention returned to Worcester, organizers arranged for the use of a larger hall to accommodate the throng that turned out for the popular evening sessions. Part of the draw was undoubtedly the presence of so many feminists, abolitionists, and social reformers with national and even international reputations, including Frederick Douglass, Lucretia Mott, Lucy Stone, Charles C. Burleigh, Ernestine Rose, William H. Channing, William Lloyd Garrison, Abby Kelley Foster and Stephen S. Foster.[5]

Unlike the *Palladium*, the Whiggish local press was friendly, even enthusiastic. The *Spy* wrote up the convention's proceedings in laudatory detail, praising the meeting's "decorum," the intelligence of the extemporaneous speeches, and the "great interest" manifested by all who attended. The *Spy*'s editor, John Milton Earle, a Quaker, an abolitionist, and a Republican, denounced the "exceedingly scurrilous" reports from the hostile out-of-town press, especially the Boston *Daily Mail* and James Gordon Bennett's *New York Herald*, which ridiculed the women's convention as, among other things, a "motley organization" with "horrible, fanatical, absurd, and infidel" ideas. Preferring to dwell upon the women's appearance, the *Herald* noted with approval that Abby Kelley Foster of Worcester was "a very striking personage" and that Ernestine Rose, a Polish immigrant from New York, had "black eyes, delicate features, [and] black hair, let down in ringlets over her ears," but dismissed Lucretia Mott of Philadelphia as "all bone, gristle, and resolution." "No man with the feelings of a gentleman" would have written such things, an indignant John M. Earle retorted, nor would a "paper with any regard to its character with respectable people" have published them. Earle's staunch support of the convention was, no doubt, influenced by the fact that he was married to Sarah H. Earle, the convention's organizer. The *Spy*'s chief rival in town, the *National Aegis*, also covered the conventions. While cool to the cause of women's rights—the *Aegis* editor facetiously proposed a "compromise" whereby women received the suffrage but their husbands exercised it for them—the subtly mocking tone that suffused the paper's discussion of the 1850 convention disappeared in 1851, when it wrote a mostly favorable account.[6]

Those who wished to attend the Worcester women's rights conventions thus enjoyed some local support. Approximately one thousand people at the 1850 convention met in morning, afternoon, and evening sessions to debate the issues and consider strategies; of these, two hundred and sixty-eight declared themselves members, which entitled them to vote. Nearly one-third of the declared members were from Worcester, and of those whose sex can be determined, seventy percent were women. Of those for whom family occupational data are available, more than half were self-supporting, including four proprietors of boarding houses, three schoolteachers, two nurses, two dressmakers, two female physicians, one who was variably a laundress and a wetnurse, and a future assistant matron at the orphan asylum. Among married women for whom data are available, two were married to farmers, two to merchants, one to the treasurer of Worcester county, one to a newspaper publisher, and one each to a bootmaker, a dentist, a carpenter, and a carder at a mill.[7]

It is a testament to the movement's goals that it found support among economically independent women and those who worked outside the home. "Dispute our rights, envy us our claim as mothers, but leave us our privilege to *labor*," exhorted one convention speaker, "Give us our just remuneration." Many of the convention members from Worcester knew first-hand both the privilege of laboring and the desire for a just remuneration. In the late 1840s, Abigail H. Metcalf, a single woman, learned how to run a boarding house from her widowed mother; by 1852, Metcalf was running the business herself while her sister, Mary Metcalf, worked as a dressmaker. Abigail and Mary Metcalf lived together and together became members of the 1850 women's rights convention. Anna Goulding and Frances A. Pierce were "female physicians," their medical education and practice artificially limited by the gender discrimination repeatedly indicted at the convention. Elizabeth Stamp and Caroline Farnum were married to machinists; both also were nurses, a job that required the women to leave their own families to live and work in other people's homes. When Farnum's husband died in 1852, she gave up nursing to start a boarding house, which enabled her to be at home with her children while she supported them. Sybil Worcester, a widow, ran a boarding house with the assistance of her adult daughters. Phebe and Adeline Worcester worked alongside their mother and sat side-by-side at the 1850 convention. Anna Ruggles, also widowed, also ran a boarding house; Mrs. Chickering took in laundry to supplement what her husband, John, could earn as a laborer; Emily Prentice, who became a member of the convention along with her sister, Sarah Prentice, was a dressmaker. The feminist demand for greater employment opportunities and improved pay held particular meaning for these women in Worcester, who supported themselves and their families through their own earnings.[8]

A second significant occupational group at the convention was the public schoolteachers. Teaching emerged in the antebellum era as one of the few professions open to educated women, and by 1850 more than ninety percent of the teachers in Worcester's rapidly expanding public school system were women. What the male schoolteachers lacked in numbers, however, they made up for in salaries: on average, the full-time male teachers earned more than one thousand dollars a year, while the full-time female teachers earned two hundred dollars a year, or twenty percent of the salary of their male colleagues. Over time the women's pay slowly increased while the men's held stable, so that by 1860 the city's female public schoolteachers earned an average of $288 annually. However, this sum was still barely more than one-quarter of the men's average annual salary of $1,050. In Worcester, as elsewhere in America, blatant gender discrimination meant that female schoolteachers were grossly underpaid.[9]

The glaring disparity between the salaries of male and female schoolteachers—a fact regularly made public in the city's published annual reports—may have encouraged Adeliza Perry, Lydia Wilmarth, and Martha B. Earle to join the 1850 women's rights convention meeting in their city. In 1849, Perry was an assistant principal (one of three teachers) at Worcester's Summer Street Boys' Primary, where she earned $156. Perry was also an aspiring writer; although she taught briefly in 1850, earning $18, she spent most of the year composing *The Cinderella Frock*, a children's book that appeared in 1851. Also in 1851 she resumed teaching, becoming the principal, in the sense of the only, teacher at the Front Street Grammar School, where she earned $275. Five years later, Perry's annual salary had increased to $350. Lydia Wilmarth's pay rose more slowly. In 1849, Wilmarth was the principal (of two teachers) at the Pleasant Street Infant School, earning $208; in 1850, her pay was increased to $225, and in 1853 to $250. By 1860, after a full ten years as the lead teacher at the same school, Wilmarth was earning only $300 a year. Wilmarth's interest in the 1850 women's rights convention might also have been piqued by the woman with whom she taught all day at the Pleasant Street School, Martha B. Earle, daughter of the convention's organizer, Sarah H. Earle. Presumably Earle was influenced in her beliefs by her mother; but even had she not been, her concern for a fair salary might have been sparked by her own situation: as an assistant teacher in the city's public schools, Earle earned only $150 a year.

Professional educators such as Perry, Wilmarth, and Earle, paid less than one-third of the wages of their male counterparts, likely responded positively to the feminist demand that "women ought to have equal opportunities, privileges, and *securities* with men for rendering themselves *pecuniarily independent.*" As important as the right to vote was—and speaker after speaker at the Worcester conventions demanded the suffrage—property rights and access to education and the "industrial avocations" were just as vital. Feminists asserted confidently that when women had obtained equal employment opportunities, "all other opportunities, privileges, and securities of law, custom, and usage [will] follow."[10]

The middle of the nineteenth century seemed an auspicious time to inaugurate such far-reaching change. The feminists at Worcester pointed to an "upward tending spirit of the age" that to their minds heralded the advent of an era of unprecedented respect for human rights and equality. Indeed, they appeared confident that public sentiment was "undergoing rapid change for the better." Americans were discussing the rights of women as never before, many noted, and the "uprising of womanhood" in conventions such as theirs constituted proof that "the age of war is drawing towards a close, and that of peace . . . is dawning." Evidence of a renewed interest in pacifism, combined with the invention of the steam engine, signaled to the Worcester conventioneers the onset of a social order in which economic productivity and prosperity were less correlated with human muscle power. As the market value of men's physical advantage vis-à-vis women waned, those speaking argued, so too would men's claim to patriarchal privileges as well as society's justification for women's legal and economic dependence upon men. These very same forces, moreover, threw women's allegedly superior morality into greater relief. As a consequence, the feminists at the Worcester conventions stressed, centuries of inequality would soon pass away and the sexes would stand on equal footing, for "ours is an *epochal* movement."[11]

Equal footing, but still separate. Indeed, as historians have frequently noted, the antebellum women's rights movement did not repudiate but rather embraced their culture's essentialist assumption that traits associated with masculinity and femininity were rooted in biology. Speaker upon speaker at the Worcester conventions expressed a commitment to the immutability and the desirability of allegedly sex-linked character traits. Paulina Wright Davis, who presided over the conventions, stood before the assembled and stated flatly, "I will not accept the concession of any equality which means identity or resemblance of faculty and function [between women and men]. I do not base [women's] claims upon any such parallelism of constitution or attainment." Where women's rights advocates and their antifeminist opponents parted company, however, was in their interpretations of this common theory. Feminists argued at Worcester that precisely because the sexes were so different, no man was qualified to judge what was best for a woman and thus women had a compelling need for legal and economic autonomy. Moreover, their faith in innate gender differences led feminists to insist that cooperation, not competition, was the true nature of human social relations. The fates of women and men were irrevocably linked by an "absolute unity of interest and destiny which nature has established between them . . . [and thus] there can be no real antagonism of position and action." Just as the security and the prosperity of an individual family was the product of the cooperation between husband and wife, so too was the stability and the morality of the human family dependent upon the fundamental cooperation between women and men. "Man cannot fulfill his duty alone—he cannot redeem his race unaided . . ." wrote a pregnant Elizabeth Cady Stanton to the 1850 convention, for "there are deep and tender chords of sympathy and love that woman can touch more skillfully than man."[12]

To the extent that feminists supported the primacy of woman's maternal role, they sounded quite conventional. Women have a "conceded superiority in the family affections," Paulina Wright Davis declared, and thus should "be entitled to exclusive control in the domestic function." Indeed, domesticity and feminism were not only compatible, they were inextricable. The Worcester feminists argued that it was because mothers exerted "a most potent influence" that the nation's future required that women no longer live a "dwarfed humanity." Davis acknowledged that women were the "gentler sex . . . the loveliest of the two," but concluded that respecting women only for their physical attributes was "*selfish* and *savage*" because it denied "the integral development of the whole being." Such rhetoric built upon and appealed to the ideologies and the activism of several generations of women's religious and secular organizations, and reveals the extent to which antebellum feminists were very much in step with their times.[13]

But the feminists at Worcester did not stop there. Rather, they proceeded to so broaden the definition of "woman's sphere" as to rob the concept of its potentially insidious implications. The conviction that women and men were endowed with distinct yet complementary physical and moral traits did not mean that a woman's place was in the home, they argued. To the contrary, by virtue of woman's virtue, woman's sphere logically included the worlds of politics, law, economics, and social reform. Indeed, feminists rhetorically linked their movement to the postmillennialism of many contemporary women's organizations when they argued that the reformation of the world—which the "signs of the time" portended was imminent—would not occur unless and until women achieved "FREE EQUAL RIGHTS." Elizur Wright, insurance reformer and editor of the Boston *Chronotype*, dismissed as an instance of men's "palpable puppyhood" the argument that respectable women should not participate in politics because their genteel sensibilities would reel at the uncouth behavior of male voters and politicians. Such rowdiness was simply proof, said another, that "men ... are continually doing what *they ought to be ashamed of*" and in need of woman's civilizing discipline at the polls. For the sake of their families, their nation, the world, and the coming Christian millennium, women must have an active social and political role, balancing "wrong-headed" men with "right-hearted" women.[14]

Acknowledging that "what '*woman's sphere*' is is the very matter of the dispute," the convention speakers asserted that "woman's sphere differs immensely" over time and space. These feminists agreed that gendered spheres encompassed "the orbits of circuits of employment and action" but argued that the contours of those spheres had yet to be determined. What's more, they insisted, a definitive notion of woman's sphere was ultimately impossible because it was ever evolving and always for the better. Antoinette Brown, a theology student at Ohio's Oberlin College, illustrated how subversive education can be when she argued that history demonstrated that "Woman's sphere is not fixed. . . . No, it is rising." For antebellum feminists, history proved, and current developments upheld, women's claims to formal civic incorporation.[15]

To the extent that it could be defined, woman's sphere was woman's work, and the Worcester conventions focused upon the need to expand the numbers and kinds of occupations available to women. Abby H. Price of Hopedale, Worcester county, educated the assembly on the economic hardships confronting women who thought to support themselves and their families through traditional "women's work." The trades open to women, such as sewing, Price explained, paid so poorly—"about 30 cents a day"—that sheer necessity drove some into prostitution, a sordid fact from which a moral community must recoil. Harriet K. Hunt, a pioneer physician, argued that theirs was an "age of transition" in which "the minds of the community are asking the why and the wherefore of all things." Hunt proclaimed motherhood "the highest law of [woman's] nature" and took for granted women's distinctive religiosity. But from these premises, Hunt argued that women were especially well suited to the medical profession, for "what could be more delicately feminine, more truly womanly, than to take the hand of a sister, afflicted in body and mind, and to show her the cause of her diseases? . . ." Thus although the antebellum feminists trafficked in the rhetoric of separate spheres, and argued that separate spheres were entirely congruent with economic and political equality, they effectively deflated its customary meaning.[16]

In 1851, the second national women's rights convention met once again in Worcester and featured many of the same faces.[17] The convention revisited the issues addressed the previous year but reflected a shift in mood, for the cause appeared to be gaining momentum, endorsing the efficacy of the nascent movement's beliefs and tactics. A few medical schools and design schools had opened their doors to women and a number of state legislatures were considering married women's property acts. Traditional barriers were evidently crumbling, leading Paulina Wright Davis to wonder "if a year or two of our history registers such advancements as these, what will not the quick-coming future bring with it?" The women's movement also took heart from its growing international influence. Writer Harriet Martineau sent an encouraging letter from England describing the impact the American conventions were having abroad. Unitarian minister William H. Channing, excoriated in the New York press as, among other things, an "abolitionist demagogue," read a letter from two women imprisoned for their activism during the French revolution of 1848. From their Parisian jail, socialists Jeanne Deroine and Pauline Roland urged the Worcester convention to bear in mind that their own revolution had failed because it "forgot to break the chain of the most oppressed of all—of Woman, the Pariah of humanity."

When women's rights were sacrificed, the French feminists soberly reminded their American counterparts, all human rights were threatened.[18] Emboldened by the apparent pace of change and by the sacrifices women at home and abroad were making for the cause of human rights, the 1851 convention speakers assumed a more militant tone, exhorting women to seize the moment and demand equal rights. Feminist orator and Worcester county native Lucy Stone brought a roar of approval from the crowd when she declared "Friends, we are our own helper. . . . Instead of asking, 'Give us this, or give us that,' let us just get up and take it." Wendell Phillips, a leader of the abolitionist movement, beseeched women to "*take* your rights! . . . It is for you but to speak." Ernestine Rose urged those assembled to enlist in the feminist cause, which she characterized as a "crusade . . . far holier and more righteous than [that which] led warriors to Palestine." In an address shot through with irony, editor Clarissa I. Howard Nichols of Vermont eloquently skewered the common law principle of *feme covert*, which conferred upon the husband all property belonging to a married couple regardless of its source. Nichols described a scenario that every woman present could imagine herself confronting one day: "if [a woman's] husband should be taken from her by death . . . [her] home must be divided, and a corner in the kitchen, a corner in the garret, and a '*privilege*' in the cellar, be set off to her *use*, as if she were a *rat!*" Nichols's words created a "great sensation."[19]

Abby Kelley Foster, a Worcester resident, a feminist, and an abolitionist known for her passionate oratory, had been mostly silent during the 1851 proceedings. The previous year, with characteristic forthrightness, Foster had declared, "I do not talk of women's rights, but of human rights, the rights of human beings. I do not come to ask [for] them, but to demand them; not to get down on my knees and beg for them, but to claim them." Foster urged women to seize the most basic right of the oppressed, "the right to rise up and cut the tyrants' throats." The next day, a more peaceable Lucretia Mott attempted to cool Foster's fiery words by emphasizing the spiritual nature of the women's rights movement.[20] In the last minutes of the 1851 convention, Foster rose to announce that women themselves were the greatest impediment to equality for "the reason why woman is not found in the highest position which she is qualified to fill, is because she has not more than half the will." Only when women accepted "the full weight of [their] responsibilities," she maintained, would they achieve their rights. In a soon-to-be-famous autobiographical statement, Foster indicted women for their complacency and reminded them that "bloody feet, sisters, have worn smooth the path by which you have come up hither." "Action, action is eloquence!" Foster declared, and was vigorously cheered when she challenged women to earn their rights through "toil—earnest, self-sacrificing toil." In these and other statements at the conventions, Foster placed the responsibility for attaining equality squarely upon women's shoulders, strengthening the contemporary belief that the movement's goals could be realized within the status quo. The second Worcester convention closed with an address by Emma Coe of Ohio, who noted presciently that "Injustice knows no peace."[21]

The first and second national women's rights conventions held in Worcester in 1850 and 1851 were early explorations of gender roles in American society. Optimism permeated the gatherings despite the chorus of choleric jeers, for it seemed that in an era of unprecedented change, the wrongs facing women needed only to be pointed out to be speedily remedied. Even feminists as radical as Abby Kelley Foster insisted that women could bring about reform if they willed themselves to action. In retrospect it is clear that antebellum feminists underestimated the structural and ideological impediments facing the movement, and may have precluded, at least for a time, a more thoroughgoing critique of gender relations in America. At the same time, a willingness to sacrifice to bring about change, and an abiding faith that such change was possible, was critical to the success of the early movement, which was buffeted by criticism and ridicule.

FEMINISM AND SOCIAL ACTIVISM IN 1850S WORCESTER

The confidence the feminists displayed at the conventions at Worcester also may have stemmed in part from the evidence of change within their own communities. Several Worcester reform societies shared the critique and the commitment of the feminists at the women's rights conventions; indeed, an interest in feminism seems to have spurred an interest in local reform. At least five members of the 1850 women's rights convention, or almost 8 percent of the known membership from Worcester, had close ties to the city's Children's Friend Society. For two members of the 1850 convention, the CFS provided economic opportunities. Louisa Gleason, who grew up in a boarding house run by her widowed mother, Sarah, signed her name to the convention's list of members; shortly thereafter, Gleason became the assistant matron at the CFS, a position she held for six years. Mrs. Chickering, also a member of the 1850 convention, regularly hired out her services to the CFS as a wetnurse and for infant child care. Seth Rogers, a hydropathic physician, a cousin of Susan B. Anthony, and the director of Worcester's Water-Cure Institute, joined the 1850 convention and offered to house the matron and the children of the CFS when the society's home burnt in 1858. Mary R. Hadwen, married to a retired manufacturer, and Abigail P.B. Rawson, married to a merchant, also subscribed to the 1850 convention; two years later, both sat on the CFS Board of Managers. Thus, while scholars have tended to see participation in the feminist movement as the culmination of antebellum women's politicization, typically through their participation in local voluntary societies, the evidence from Worcester indicates that interest in women's rights also spurred interest in local reform.[22]

From advocating women's rights to working on behalf of children and mostly female-headed families was a logical progression, for an affinity of interests connected the CFS to the goals of antebellum feminism. The women who ran the CFS had always considered theirs to be a private society operating for the public good. As the CFS prospered, and as the managers' experience with social problems grew, they began to speak out on related social issues. Three months after the 1851 convention, perhaps influenced by Abby Kelley Foster's eloquent call to action, the CFS for the first time openly endorsed the goals of the women's movement. In their 1852 *Annual Report*, in phrases similar to those expressed at the recent convention, the managers asserted that "the precise boundaries of woman's sphere of action and of duty, in this eminently progressive age" were yet to be determined, as was women's fitness for "positions of higher honor and more extensive usefulness." The women of the CFS decided that they would leave these questions to the "more skilful hands, wiser heads, and abler advocates" in the women's movement and would devote their energies to defending and advancing the "inalienable rights" of mothers, a reform agreeable to antebellum feminism. Women's organizations such as the Worcester Children's Friend Society could thus find common cause with the national women's rights movement because both endorsed the legal and economic rights of women.[23]

Further supporting the association of feminism and women's social activism in Worcester in the decade before the Civil War was a society organized in 1855 in response to the perception that poverty in their city was increasingly feminized. The Worcester Female Employment Society began as an offshoot of the Relief of the Poor (ROP), a men's society formed in 1847 to "protect the community from the frauds of vagrants and professional beggars; and to relieve the deserving poor" during Worcester's freezing winter months. Each fall the ROP commenced its annual campaign by soliciting donations to fund "systematic action in the relief of the poor." The men divided the city neatly into twenty-two districts, distributed fliers in poor neighborhoods advertising its charity, assigned three of their members to each district as "Visitors," and hired a male agent to coordinate the undertaking. The ROP doled out clothing, food, fuel, and coupons that could be exchanged for goods at designated stores; the poor were never to receive cash. The ROP also urged "any person who can give any sort of work to men or women in want of employ" to apply at its agent's office.[24]

The ROP's aim was to tide over the rough winter months those who did not otherwise receive public assistance. To qualify for aid under antebellum Massachusetts's strict settlement laws, it was necessary to be a citizen, to have resided in one town continually for ten years, and to have paid taxes at least half that time. In a rapidly growing city such as Worcester, many native-born Americans, and virtually all immigrants, could not meet these requirements, and thus fell into the category of state paupers. But because Massachusetts reimbursed towns for supporting state paupers at the miserly rate of forty-nine cents a week, local authorities were encouraged to warehouse the poor in the city almshouse, a fate those in need avoided if at all possible. Complicating the problem of poor relief were the economic crises of the late 1850s, which threw out of work many who had been self-supporting but who now needed some assistance until the economy improved. The suffering was particularly acute during the depression of 1857, when one local paper reported that "worthy young men who would gladly earn their own support" had nothing to do. Confronting New England's long, bitter winters without sufficient resources, they came to the ROP for emergency aid.[25]

Yet the majority of those assisted needed more than the short-term charity the Relief of the Poor was designed to provide. Families headed by widows, or chiefly dependent upon a woman for economic support, accounted for nearly two-thirds of the ROP's applicants. Their lot was not likely to improve significantly come spring because their economic problems were not weather-related. Uncertain how to redress the chronic poverty of female-headed households, the men of the ROP turned to the women of Worcester, who in 1855 founded the Worcester Female Employment Society.[26]

The history of the Female Employment Society (FES) confirms the potential for an ideological link between organized antebellum feminism and local women's reform societies. Of the forty-seven women who joined the nonprofit society in the late 1850s, eight, or seventeen percent, also belonged to the Children's Friend Society. More significantly, eighty percent of the women had moved from the CFS to the FES; that is, they turned from wrestling with the disintegrating effects of poverty upon mostly female-headed families to preventing poverty by finding women adequate employment. Furthermore, at least some women in Worcester viewed the FES as a way to address the economic concerns analyzed at the recent rights conventions. Julia T. Harris joined the women's rights convention in 1850 and put her beliefs into practice by helping to found the FES five years later. In 1857, Ann Buffum Earle was simultaneously the Second Directress of the Children's Friend Society and the president of the Female Employment Society; she was also the sister-in-law of the 1850 women's rights convention organizer, Sarah H. Earle. Nor were Ann Earle's ambitions restricted to social reform: in 1869, she ran for and won a seat on the Worcester school board, and later served as vice-president of a suffrage convention. Julia Harris's and Ann Earle's several allegiances highlight the ways in which a shared feminist sensibility could undergird a variety of strategies to attack the effects of gender inequality in antebellum America.[27]

The women of the FES stood on common ground with feminists in their analysis of the economic handicaps of antebellum gender roles. The men of the Relief of the Poor had bid poor women to get out of the house and to find work, but offered no help to make it possible for working women to simultaneously care for their children. The women of the FES understood the dilemma working mothers faced and argued that "the weight of poverty is felt by woman" because she, unlike a man, could not leave the children to "seek employment which will bring their daily bread." But in attempting to find a solution that would permit women to earn money at home, the FES ran full tilt into the customs that excluded women from employment that could provide self-sufficiency. As the futility of their approach became clear, the women of the FES increasingly voiced a feminist critique of antebellum economic and gender relations.[28]

Because taking in sewing was a traditional female occupation that allowed women to work at home, the women of the FES decided to pay poor women to sew garments which the society would sell to the public. Private and church donations subsidized the start-up costs, and with the assistance of a hired agent, Persis Davenport, the women of the FES cut up and distributed cloth and staffed a downtown store opened with great expectations in January 1856. By one measure, the undertaking was an immediate success: in the society's first year, one hundred and thirty women sewed more than thirteen hundred garments, confirming the need for employment that could be combined with child care. Yet by another measure, the effort was a dismal failure: by the end of the year, the FES had paid its workers a total of slightly more than four hundred dollars, or approximately thirty cents per item. As these figures suggest, no woman could depend upon the Female Employment Society for even subsistence wages. The society did guarantee immediate payment for the work, so it was at least a reliable source of supplemental income, offering to some the small comforts of tea or sugar on their tables. Sweetening poor women's tea was not, however, the goal the organizers of the FES had set for themselves. Still worse, most working women lacked the skills of professional seamstresses and none could compete with the new sewing machines. Moved by the eagerness with which women "seize the prepared work affording relief" to their families, the FES found itself buying garments crafted by women with more tenacity than talent.

But what else might one expect, the women of the FES asked compassionately as they eyed the shoddy quality of many of the garments they bought, since "most of this sewing is done by women who have all kinds of labor to perform, and, usually, a good deal of it, and who must sew at night in rooms not well warmed, and with the least possible light (for these rooms are not lighted with gas) and with 'fingers weary and worn.'" Due to its policy of guaranteed payment, the FES quickly accumulated a pile of unsold and unwanted "coarse garments," leading it at the end of its first year to suggest hopefully that the city's benevolent take them off its hands.[29]

Newly sobered by the "fearful uncertainty as to what our duties are, and how we shall answer them," the FES commenced its second year in a thoughtful mood. Telling the poor to work when there were no jobs to be had was pointless, the women acknowledged, but they insisted that those willing to labor "had a right to demand work, and a fair compensation for it" for "it is not enough to relieve the suffering, we must labor to remove the cause." Yet removing the cause of poverty was much harder than they had anticipated, even while the demand for relief continued unabated. By the end of its second year, the FES reported that 159 women had sewn more than twenty-three hundred garments—"some well, some indifferently, some badly"—to earn six hundred dollars, or an average of twenty-five cents per item. Cognizant of just how paltry such wages were, the women of the FES were troubled by their inability to provide working women with decent compensation. They recalled how "In one instance, last winter, a woman was found to have lived solely on the earnings of the sewing given her by your society—and, as this was at a time of great pressure [i.e., economic depression], it had been very little; your agent computed it to be about thirty-seven cents a week, for seven weeks."

The whole point of their organization was to insure that "no woman, *here* and *now*, should plead in vain for work to gain a livelihood," yet within a year the women of the FES had learned how few were the options available to working women. Frustrated because so many women lacked marketable skills, and because so many occupations providing a competence were closed to them in any event, the women of the FES decided to emphasize fancy sewing, hoping it would be more remunerative than plain sewing. In the meantime, they spent hours trying to teach the rudiments of plain sewing to women whose long-term economic prospects, they had come to realize, were decidedly bleak.[30]

The poverty of their peers led the women of the FES to extend their analysis of women's economic handicaps to their own, more privileged class. They reported uneasily to the Worcester public that while there were indeed those who were poor because they were lazy, it was their experience that "an ever-increasing class" of the poor consisted of "women, whose husbands are shiftless, intemperate or unfortunate—widows with children to provide for—young girls in delicate health—refined women, nurtured in competence, perhaps wealth, and deprived of it, who have no resource but their needle." Women, in other words, such as themselves. Indeed, the managers of the FES made numerous comparisons between themselves and their clients, revealing their awareness of how little separated them from their poorer contemporaries. In one breath they told of a woman whose family subsisted entirely on cornmeal, while in the next they noted that "We . . . fare sumptuously every day." And, perhaps unconsciously projecting their deepest fears of falling into poverty and out of respectability, they suggested that by assisting poor women, women of their own class "may have saved some from the degradation, perhaps infamy, into which the temptation of poverty hurries many, whose own souls cry out against the desecration." The psychological connection with poor women was further highlighted by the FES fairs, through which privileged women's sewing subsidized poor women's sewing.[31]

Abby Kelley Foster had exhorted feminists at the 1851 women's rights convention to "inculcate upon our daughters, that they should be able to provide for the wants of a family . . . . That is the duty we owe our daughters to-day; that is the duty each one owes to herself to-day." The problems the women of the FES were encountering, and their understanding of the tenuous economic position of women of their own class, lent Foster's words particular credence and the women of the FES soon were expressing similar sentiments. Educate your daughters, they warned Worcester's parents—and each other—not to make them better wives and mothers but to give them a skill "instrumental in gaining a livelihood." In America's developing economy "fortunes are as easily won and lost," the women of the FES conceded, and they advised *all* women to master "some one thing" to arm themselves against becoming "that most pitiable of all human beings, a helpless dependent upon the bounties of others." Well tutored in the realities of poverty and economic discrimination, the women of the FES explicitly rejected feminine passivity in favor of feminine activity. Indeed, helplessness and dependency—two of the central tenets of the alleged "cult of true womanhood"—were neither attractive nor desirable in the face of economic need, they stated bluntly. Rather, dependency was an affront to "the talents God has given [woman], or the acquirements she has attained." To their minds, a woman had a God-given right and duty to protect herself by cultivating herself for herself.[32]

The organizers of the FES therefore spoke out for economic equality and economic opportunity for all women. Woman's sphere "of labor and usefulness is gradually enlarging," they noted approvingly, once more echoing the ideas and the rhetoric of the recent women's rights conventions. They, too, expressed confidence that "honor and honesty" would shortly force American society to embrace a philosophy of equal pay for equal work, for "when [a woman] does a specified work as well, or better, through her quicker perceptions and more delicate sensibilities, than the other sex," she deserved "an equal compensation." Labor is "an ordinance of God," they insisted, for women as well as for men. The dictates of a just God and a just economy thus commanded that women's work merit its full market value.[33]

Working women in antebellum Worcester did not, of course, receive a fair day's wage for a fair day's work, and the FES's strategy of supporting women through hand sewing proved to be outmoded before it had even begun. If, during its brief tenure, antebellum Worcester's Female Employment Society failed to find a solution to the problem of gendered unemployment and economic exploitation in their city, or to effect adequate compensation for working women, its members did at least educate themselves on the nature of American women's economic problems at mid-century. In this endeavor, they joined common cause with the Worcester's Children's Friend Society and the spirit of antebellum feminism. On the eve of the Civil War, the organized women of Worcester had accepted the analysis of, and reached the same conclusions as, the organized feminist movement.

Conclusion

The Civil War changed Worcester forever. A booming wartime economy drew thousands of eager workers and, by 1870, Worcester was a major manufacturing center and the second-largest city in Massachusetts. By 1880, Worcester ranked twenty-eighth in the nation. The mature industrial city of the late nineteenth century was a distant cousin of the prewar city, sharing a vague resemblance but with markedly different temperaments. Whereas antebellum Worcesterites described their city metaphorically as the "Heart of the Commonwealth," the postbellum generation embraced the less lyrical "City of Diversified Industries."[1]

The years of bloody internecine warfare, the unleashing of rampant greed and materialism, and the onslaught of new scientific theories such as Darwinian evolution, led, in the words of one scholar, to the "twilight of humanitarianism" in Gilded Age America, and pessimism characterized the efforts of the postbellum reformers.[2] In comparison, a hopeful, inclusive, democratic humanitarianism was the touchstone of the disparate women's organizations of antebellum Worcester. Whether as members of a church or of a sewing circle, mothering their own broods or the children of others, concerned with their own situations or the fortunes of others, the women of the antebellum city shared a more general ambition to improve, even to perfect, an increasingly fractious American society, and were especially committed to expanding their own social and political roles.

At least two generations of academic historians have convincingly demonstrated the richness of the history of women and of a related category, the history of gender. Yet there remains considerable disagreement as to the character or boundaries of past women's many social roles. Pathbreaking analyses in the late 1960s and early 1970s described the creation in the early nineteenth century of new and more separate gender spheres. A separate spheres ideology, it was argued, exalted some aspects of women's social roles and contributed to the development of a sense of "sisterhood" that could, and sometimes did, cross boundaries of race, ethnicity, religion, and class. At the same time, however, separate spheres bound women more tightly to the ideals of dependency and domesticity. Thus, to be a woman in antebellum America meant to live one's life within artificial restraints, and even the most privileged could expect to incur the disdain of society should they dare to venture beyond their sphere.

These early works triggered an avalanche of interest in American women's history and a second generation of scholars began to put the separate spheres ideology to the test. Without denying the limits of gender roles, many of these studies pointed out that women, like men, had other social identities and loyalties. Working-class, African American, and immigrant women and men, for example, developed their own standards of femininity and masculinity which blurred or even rejected the separation of spheres. If separate spheres existed anywhere, it seemed, it was in the antebellum white, native-born, middle class. Yet even here, historians argued, the need to assert one's place in a rapidly changing world meant that women might have more in common with the men of their class than with the women of their larger community. Ironically, the ideology of separate gender spheres thus functioned not as a bridge across the classes but as a bridge across the spheres, uniting men and women in defense of their shared interests. Scholarly discussion of the potentially radical implications of cross-class gender solidarity, along with interest in the antebellum feminist movement, has consequently faded.

This study has drawn different conclusions. It does not deny the strength of abstract gender ideologies to shape lives and to influence individual choices. But it does deny their unbridled effects. Women and men spent their lives in the concrete present, their daily reality conditioned as much by the pedestrian details and demands of family and community as by grander social forces, and this had special meaning for women. Being unilaterally barred from formal positions of power was a clear disadvantage, but less so in the early nineteenth century than it would be for later generations because "the state" was still in its infancy. Far more influential over nineteenth-century lives were local power structures. But here disenfranchised women were able to exert themselves and enforce their will upon a rapidly changing community. Antebellum Worcester, for example, was a city where people still knew each other, and informal face-to-face encounters remained the norm. Unlike the increasingly impersonal urban behemoths of New York City, Boston, or Philadelphia, Worcester was like other antebellum cities: small, compact, and surprisingly intimate. In such an environment, social boundaries were neither rigid nor restricted and there was yet considerable room to maneuver.

And maneuver they did. An in-depth investigation of this antebellum city puts women in their proper historical place, namely, at center stage in community productions. In an age of religious awakening and church formation, women in Worcester composed the majority of church members and fought to institute their beliefs. In an age of market revolution and class formation, women in Worcester experienced considerable economic instability. This forced them to recognize that their current reality and future prospects hinged upon their gender, for the simple reason that while a woman's class status could change abruptly, her gender status changed more slowly. In an age of an expansive political culture, disenfranchised women in Worcester insisted upon being heard, and their seemingly "private" organizations, such as sewing circles, served an expressly "public" and political function. In an age of geographic mobility, family dissolution and reformation, and increasing poverty, women in Worcester built upon a tradition of benevolence to offer innovative social services to meet new social problems. Finally, in an age of seemingly endless change, women in Worcester combined reform with feminism so as to take advantage of the manifestly "upward tending spirit of the age," with the hope of tending to their own issues and concerns.

Such efforts were not always successful; indeed, they often were not very well defined nor their implications well understood. A melange of gender, class, and idiosyncratic experiences and loyalties, women's social activism in antebellum Worcester was nonlinear, multifaceted and constantly evolving. Like the varying images of a kaleidoscope, it represented no single viewpoint or meaning. Their goals and tactics do illustrate that many women, conventional and feminist alike, continually dealt themselves into the game of community politics and sought to draft new, more equitable rules. As echoed by Worcester jeweller Joseph Boyden, whose exasperated comment introduced this study, gender prescription was not social description, and "the mother at home" often wasn't. The organized activities of the middle-class women of Worcester, Massachusetts, reveal that in antebellum America the barriers separating women and men, the secular and the sacred, public and private, work and domesticity, were as porous in fact as they were often pronounced in fiction.

Appendix

Statistical Data

1 Age at Joining of CFS Members
N = 36 (50% of Total)

Years	%	N
21–29	8	3
30–39	30	11
40–49	47	17
50+	14	5

2 Place of Birth of CFS Members
N = 61 (84% of Total)

Place	%	N
Worcester	36	22
Worcester County	13	8
Other Massachusetts	18	11
Total Massachusetts	67	41
Other New England	15	9
Total New England	81	50
Other:		
New York	1.6	1
Pennsylvania	1.6	1
Ohio	1.6	1
Unknown	14	12

3 Family Occupations of CFS Members
N = 73 (100% of Total)

Occupation	%	N
Merchant	29	21
Artisan/Skilled Labor	15	18
Manufacturer	16	12
White Collar/Professional	14	10
Farmer	4	3
Widowed	12	9
Single	11	8
Boarding House	1	1

4 Assessed Valuation of CFS Members, 1846
N = 54 (74% of Total)

Value of Property	%	N
More than $20,000	6	3
$15,000–20,000	9	5
$10,000–15,000	7	4
$5,000–10,000	20	11
$1,000–5,000	33	18
Less than $1,000	24	13

5 Residential Mobility of CFS Members, 1848-1860
N = 67 (92% of Total)

# Moves	%	N
1	15	10
2	30	20
3	16	11
4	22	15
5	7	5
6	4	3
7	3	2
8	1	1

6   Age Distribution of CFS Children
    N = 45 (22% of Total)

Age in Years	%	N
Less than 1	9	4
1–2	11	5
3–5	31	14
6–9	38	17
10–14	7	3
15 and older	5	2

7   Sex of CFS Children
    N = 165 (81% of Total)

Sex	%	N
Females	54.5	90
Males	45.5	75

8   Religious Affiliation of CFS Members
    N = 43 (67% of Total)

Affiliation	%	N
Congregational	36.7	18
Unitarian	20.4	10
Baptist	16.3	8
Friends	8	4
Methodist	6	3
Episcopal	6	3
Universalist	2	1
2nd Adventist	2	1
Free Church	2	1

9 Sources of CFS Children
N = 95 (46.5% of Total)

Source	%	N
Mother	61	65
Father	21	22
Overseers of Poor	4	4
Grandparent	3	3
Clergyman	2	2
Sibling	1	1
Police	1	1
CFS Manager	1	1
Other	1	1

Notes

INTRODUCTION

1. The literature on separate spheres and domesticity is voluminous; see, for example, Barbara Welter, "The Cult of True Womanhood: 1820–1860," *American Quarterly* 18 (summer 1966): 151–74; Nancy F. Cott, *The Bonds of Womanhood: Woman's Sphere in New England, 1780–1835* (New Haven: Yale University Press, 1977); Nancy F. Cott, "Passionlessness: An Interpretation of Victorian Sexual ideology, 1790–1850," *Signs* 3 (fall 1975): 15–29; Ann Douglas, *The Feminization of American Culture* (New York: Alfred A. Knopf, 1977); Barbara L. Epstein, *The Politics of Domesticity: Women, Evangelism, and Temperance in Nineteenth-Century America* (Middletown, Conn.: Wesleyan University Press, 1981).

In his massive *The Market Revolution: Jacksonian America, 1815–1846* (New York: Oxford University Press, 1991), Charles Sellers argues that middle-class women were "market-dislocated" and "relegated to the reproductive roles—uncompensated and altruistic" where they were "religious avatars of embattled altruism" (pp. 205, 226, 227). Pushed to the margins of productive economic life, women fought a losing battle against the (male) egotism of the market. Despite attempts at holding the antinomian line through their benevolent organizations, Sellers states, women eventually "meekly" allowed themselves to be eclipsed both by men and by the market (231). For a different perspective on women's relation to the market, see Jeanne Boydston, *Home and Work: Housework, Wages, and the Ideology of Labor in the Early Republic* (New York: Oxford University Press, 1990).

2. Three examples from work not directly concerned with domesticity suggest the pervasiveness of the separate spheres paradigm. A study of infant death rates characterizes the middle-class household as "secluded," where women were "alone at home with children," left to deal with their "private agonies" in "their increasingly separate sphere at home." Nancy Schrom Dye and Daniel Blake Smith, "Mother Love and Infant Death, 1750–1920," *Journal of American History* 73 (September 1986): 329–53, especially 339, 345. Similarly, Rowland Berthoff argues that "the walls of the modern household had closed tightly around the respectable middle-class wife" in "Conventional Mentality: Free Blacks, Women, and Business Corporations as Unequal Persons, 1820–1870," *Journal of American History* 76 (December 1989): 753–84, quotation from p. 773. Finally, Michael Grossberg refers repeatedly to "the newly isolated home,"

the "worldly male and homebound woman," and "the rigid segregation of worldly males and home-bound females" in his study of nineteenth-century law, *Governing the Hearth: Law and Family in Nineteenth-Century America* (Chapel Hill: University of North Carolina Press, 1985), 7, 9, 300.

Other studies, especially those dealing with politics, ignore women altogether. In an otherwise thoughtful and thorough study of Worcester county, *The Heart of the Commonwealth: Society and Political Culture in Worcester County, Massachusetts, 1713–1861* (New York: Cambridge University Press, 1989), John L. Brooke largely omits any discussion of women's activities even though the concept of political culture might seem to include women's activism.   '

3. Cott, *Bonds of Womanhood*; Carroll Smith-Rosenberg, "The Female World of Love and Ritual: Relations between Women in Nineteenth-Century America," *Signs* 1 (autumn 1975): 1–30; Keith E. Melder, *The Beginnings of Sisterhood: The American Women's Rights Movement, 1800–1850* (New York: Schocken Books, 1967); Barbara Berg, *The Remembered Gate: Origins of American Feminism* (New York: Oxford University Press, 1978); Mary P. Ryan, *Cradle of the Middle Class: The Family in Oneida County, New York, 1790–1865* (New York: Cambridge University Press, 1981), 217; Nancy A. Hewitt, *Women's Activism and Social Change: Rochester, New York, 1822–1827* (Ithaca: Cornell University Press, 1984), 22–23, 219–23; Suzanne Lebsock, *The Free Women of Petersburg: Status and Culture in A Southern Town, 1784–1860* (New York: Norton, 1984), 224–36.

4. For women and politics see, for example, Mary P. Ryan, *Women in Public: Between Banners and Ballots, 1825–1880* (Baltimore: Johns Hopkins University Press, 1990); Elizabeth R. Varon, *We Mean to Be Counted: White Women and Politics in Antebellum Virginia* (Chapel Hill: University of North Carolina Press, 1998); Norma Basch, "Marriage, Morals, and Politics in the Election of 1828," *Journal of American History* 80 (December 1993): 890–918; Ronald J. Zboray and Mary Saracino Zboray, "Whig Women, Politics, and Culture in the Campaign of 1840: Three Perspectives from Massachusetts," *Journal of the Early Republic* 17 (summer 1997): 277–315; Rebecca Edwards, *Angels in the Machinery: Gender in American Party Politics from the Civil War to the Progressive Era* (New York: Oxford University Press, 1997). For women and national reform movements, see, for example, Lori D. Ginzberg, *Women and the Work of Benevolence: Morality, Politics, and Class in the Nineteenth-Century United States* (New Haven: Yale University Press, 1990); Ellen DuBois, *Feminism and Suffrage: The Emergence of an Independent Women's Movement in America, 1848–1869* (Ithaca: Cornell University Press, 1978); Sylvia D. Hoffert, *When Hens Crow: The Woman's Rights Movement in Antebellum America* (Bloomington: Indiana University Press, 1995); Suzanne Marilley, *Woman Suffrage and the Origins of Liberal Feminism in the United States, 1820–1920* (Cambridge, Mass.: Harvard University Press, 1996); Judith Wellman, "The Seneca Falls Women's Rights Convention: A Study of Social Networks," *Journal of Women's History* 3 (spring 1991): 9–37.

5. A recent study of women in New England seaport communities concludes that historians have overstated women's agency, which "lets patriarchy off the hook." Elaine Forman Crane, *Ebb Tide in New England: Women, Sea-*

ports, and Social Change, 1630–1800 (Boston: Northeastern University Press, 1998), quote from p. 3. I do not share this perspective. Similarly, recent studies of rural women have emphasized that separate spheres was an urban phenomenon and that rural communities and small towns did not operate this way; see Karen V. Hansen, *A Very Social Time: Crafting Community in Antebellum New England* (Berkeley: University of California Press, 1994) and Nancy Gray Osterud, *Bonds of Community: The Lives of Farm Women in Nineteenth-Century New York* (Ithaca: Cornell University Press, 1991). My study suggests that if separate spheres existed anywhere, it was in the major urban centers, not small urban centers.

1. KEEPING THE FAITH

1. Elizabeth Tuckerman Salisbury (Worcester) to Stephen Salisbury I (Boston), April 7, 1818, Salisbury Family Papers, box 18, folder 3, Manuscript Collection, American Antiquarian Society, Worcester, Massachusetts (hereafter cited AAS); Susan M. Meyer, *The Salisbury Family Mansion: A Plan for Furnishings* (Worcester, Mass.: Worcester Historical Museum, 1986).

2. Elizabeth Tuckerman Salisbury (Worcester) to Stephen Salisbury I (Boston), April 7, 1818; Salisbury Family Papers, box 18, folder 3.

3. Elizabeth Tuckerman Salisbury (Worcester) to Stephen Salisbury (Boston), April 7, 1818, Salisbury Family Papers, box 18, folder 3; see also entry for April 6, 1818, in *Diary of Isaiah Thomas* (Worcester, Mass.: American Antiquarian Society, 1909), 1:383.

The raid on his foliage was a personal affront to Daniel Waldo, a patron of the Massachusetts Agricultural Society, an early promoter of the Worcester Agricultural Society, and a supporter of local cemetery beautification. See the letter from J.N. Lorrell of the Massachusetts Agricultural Society to Daniel Waldo, February 2, 1818, Waldo Family Papers, box 2, folder 3, Manuscript Collection, AAS; William Lincoln, *History of Worcester, Massachusetts* (Worcester, Mass.: Moses D. Phillips & Co., 1837), 325–26; Levi Lincoln's Memorial to Daniel Waldo, July 9, 1845, Waldo Family Papers, box 2, folder 5. Waldo, an ardent Federalist, was elected to the Massachusetts State Senate in 1816 and served three consecutive one-year terms. According to the family, he declined renomination in 1819. Less sympathetic sources insisted Waldo knew he would not be renominated. Lincoln Memorial, Waldo Family Papers; Worcester *National Aegis*, March 10, 1819; April 8, 1818; Worcester *Spy*, April 8, 1818.

4. Elizabeth Tuckerman Salisbury to the First Church, undated but January, 1819, in *Origin & Progress of the Late Difficulties in the First Church in Worcester, Mass.* (Worcester, Mass.: Manning and Trumbull, 1820), hereafter cited as *Origin*. Written by Charles Goodrich, *Origin* recounted the First Church's version of events.

The history of the Worcester schism occurs at the intersection of scholarly debates over the feminization and democratization of American religion. The "feminization" of Protestantism has become virtually axiomatic among scholars, who argue that in the era of the Second Great Awakening women were so numerous and so active that they made the churches more reflective of, and responsive to, their needs and interests. See, for example, Barbara Welter, "The Feminization of Religion in Nineteenth-Century America," in Mary Hartman and Lois Banner, eds., *Clio's Consciousness Raised: New Perspectives on the History of Women* (New York: Harper Torchbooks, 1973), 137–57; Nancy F. Cott, "Young Women in the Second Great Awakening in New England," *Feminist Studies* 3 (fall 1975): 15–29; Cott, *Bonds of Womanhood;* Lonna M. Malmsheimer, "Daughters of Zion: New England Roots of American Feminism," *New England Quarterly* 50 (September 1977): 484–504; Richard D. Shiels, "The Feminization of American Congregationalism, 1730–1835," *American Quarterly* 33 (spring 1981): 46–62; Mary P. Ryan, "A Woman's Awakening: Evangelical Religion and the Families of Utica, New York, 1800–1840," *American Quarterly* 30 (winter 1978): 602–23; Ryan, *Cradle of the Middle Class,* 83–104 and appendix C, 257; Harry S. Stout and Catherine A. Brekus, "Declension, Gender, and the 'New Religious History,'" in Philip R. VanderMeer and Robert P. Swierenga, eds., *Belief and Behavior: Essays in New Religious History* (New Brunswick: Rutgers University Press, 1991), 15–37. At the same time, historians of religion have characterized the early nineteenth century as one of church democratization; see Sydney E. Ahlstrom, *A Religious History of the American People* (New Haven: Yale University Press, 1972), 387–509; Nathan O. Hatch, *The Democratization of American Christianity* (New Haven: Yale University Press, 1989).

Recently, historians of women have pointed to the limited nature of feminization and the gendered character of democratization. A study of missionaries suggests that, in the case of orthodox Calvinists, the Second Great Awakening was "less empowering for women [than] has generally been represented." See Genevieve McCoy, "The Women of the ABCFM Oregon Mission and the Conflicted Language of Calvinism," *Church History* 64 (March 1995): 62–82; quotation from p. 64. Other work asserts that it was primarily within marginal or dissenting religions, such as Shakerism, that women exercised institutional power. However, a study of Baptist churches found that becoming mainstream meant embracing patriarchalism and hierarchical relations. Spiritual equality, this historian notes, was a weak foundation for social equality; Susan Juster, *Disorderly Women: Sexual Politics and Evangelicalism in Revolutionary New England* (Ithaca: Cornell University Press, 1994), 12. Catherine A. Brekus also finds that the establishment of formerly dissenting churches sparked pressure to limit women's leadership and autonomy, in "'Let Your Women Keep Silence in the Churches': Female Preaching and Evangelical Religion in America, 1740–1845" (Ph.D. diss., Yale University, 1993). See also the collection of essays in Catherine Wessinger, ed., *Women's Leadership in Marginal Religions: Explorations Outside the Mainstream* (Urbana: University of Illinois Press, 1993).

The case for feminization has largely relied upon women's numerical dominance in the churches and upon the assumption that the emotionalism of the Second Great Awakening was evidence of feminization. The first contention was true as early as the seventeenth century, when no such conclusion of feminization is asserted, although Lonna Malmsheimer points to its long-term con-

sequences in "Daughters of Zion," 484–87; see also Cott, *Bonds of Womanhood,*
126. The second contention is also dubious, since the emotionalism of the revivals appealed to men as well as to women; indeed, the "new measures" of
Charles Grandison Finney were expressly intended to remind men (and women)
of the necessity of setting aside earthly cares for spiritual concerns; see Charles
Grandison Finney, "Measure to Promote Revivals," in William G. McLoughlin,
ed., *Lectures on Revivals of Religion by Charles Grandison Finney* (Cambridge,
Mass.: Harvard University Press, 1960), 250–76.

Taken together, these studies argue that the feminization of religion in the
early nineteenth century was more numerical than substantial, and that the
benefits of the democratization of churches were largely reserved for the men.
However, the events in Worcester illustrate the ways the forces of feminization
and democratization could come together. In contrast to dissenting denominations, the First Church confronted disestablishment from the other side of the
fence; it *was* the established church, now forced to make the case for a peculiar
claim upon its members. Orthodox Congregational women were thus faced
with novel opportunities to assert themselves.

5. In the early nineteenth century, conflicts between ministers and their
congregations were so common that they earned the sobriquet "difficulties;" see
also John J. Navin, "The Spirit of Reform in Hopkinton, 1829–1849," *Historical Journal of Massachusetts* 16 (summer 1988): 172–85. For the evolution of
religion generally, see Ahlstrom, *Religious History of the American People*; Edwin
Scott Gaustad, *A Religious History of America* (New York: Harper and Row, 1966);
William G. McLoughlin, *Revivals, Awakenings, and Reform: An Essay on Reli-
gion and Social Change in America, 1607–1977* (Chicago: University of Chicago
Press, 1978); William G. McLoughlin, *New England Dissent, 1630–1833: The
Baptists and the Separation of Church and State,* 2 vols. (Cambridge, Mass.: Harvard
University Press, 1971). For Worcester, see, for example, Brooke, *Heart of the
Commonwealth.*

6. In 1827, the estate of each Waldo sister was assessed at $35,500; when
they died two decades later, each was worth approximately $50,000. In 1846, a
widowed Elizabeth Salisbury controlled an estate valued at $125,200. When
Salisbury's husband died in 1829, the bulk of the estate went to their son, Stephen
Salisbury II, whose property in 1846 was assessed in excess of $320,000. Cen-
tral Church Records, folio vols. "W," vol. 4, Manuscript Collection, AAS (hereafter cited CCR); Papers of Daniel Waldo, Waldo Family Papers, box 2, folders
3, 4, 5; *List of Persons Assessed in the Town of Worcester, for the Town and County
Tax* (Boston: Samuel N. Dickinson and Co., 1846), 30, 31, 34.

Edward Pessen has estimated that, in the antebellum era, owning property
worth in excess of $50,000 placed an individual in the top one percent of the
population. Edward Pessen, *Riches, Class, and Power before the Civil War* (Lexington, Mass.: D.C. Heath, 1973), 36. For Rebecca Waldo's role as investor, see
Jeanne Whitney, "'An Art that Requires Capital': Agriculture and Mortgages in
Worcester County, Massachusetts, 1790–1850," (Ph.D. diss., University of
Delaware, 1991), 183. Daniel Waldo represented his sisters and Salisbury in the
early stages of the dispute; however, because he was not a church member, but

only a member of the parish, Waldo was not a party to the subsequent proceedings. A third Waldo sister, Elizabeth, later joined the Calvinist Church but was not involved in the schism.

7. For the theology of the New Divinity ministers, see Ahlstrom, *Religious History of the American People*, 403–14. For Samuel Austin, see Lincoln, *History of Worcester*, 157–61; William B. Sprague, *Annals of the American Pulpit*, (New York: R. Carter and Brothers, 1857; reprint, New York: Arno Press, 1969), 1:221–26; Leonard Bacon, *A Historical Discourse Delivered at Worcester, in the Old South Meeting House, September 22, 1863; The Hundredth Anniversary of Its Erection* (Worcester, Mass.: Edward R. Fiske, 1863), 12. In the 1790s, Worcester's First Church, which had long endorsed the Halfway Covenant, agreed to renounce it if Austin would be their pastor; Sprague, *Annals of the American Pulpit*, 1:223.

8. The town decided in favor of the Unitarians but the courts ruled for the First Church; see Charles Evans Butler, *Walking in the Way: A History of the First Congregational Church in Worcester 1716–1982* (Worcester, Mass.: The Society, 1987), 69–70, 72–74. For the disestablishment of Congregationalism see McLoughlin, *New England Dissent*, 2:1065–274.

9. Letter from the "qualified voters" to the Assessors of the First Parish, July 1, 1816, Old South Church Records, box 1, folder 10, Manuscript Collection, AAS; *Origin*, 4, 33. The First Church was later known as the Old South Church.

10. McLoughlin, *New England Dissent*, 1:661; 2:1072; see also William G. McLoughlin, *Soul Liberty: The Baptists' Struggle in New England, 1630–1833* (Hanover, New Hampshire: University Press of New England, 1991), 293–301. David Schuyler also suggests that who paid the minister's salary was pertinent to the question of feminization. The findings from Worcester support his insight that, with or without state sanction, church taxpayers (as opposed to church members) had a disproportionate influence over the minister; David Schuyler, "Inventing A Feminine Past," *New England Quarterly* 51 (September 1978): 291–308, 298.

11. See editor's note, *Remarks on the Late Publication of the First Church in Worcester, of which the Rev. Charles A. Goodrich Was Pastor, Relative to the "Origin and Difficulties" in That Church* (Worcester, Mass.: Manning and Trumbull, 1821), 121, (hereafter cited as *Remarks*). The pamphlet was the dissidents' response to *Origin*. Quotation from *Origin*, 9.

12. The first candidate was vetoed by opposition allegedly orchestrated by the Waldos; see *Origin*, 4–5; Butler, *Walking in the Way*, 73. Daniel Waldo never became a full church member, that is, he never underwent conversion. However, as a taxpayer, he participated actively in church affairs and was entitled to vote. See *Remarks*, 9.

13. *Remarks*, 9 (emphasis in original). The origin of this accusation is suggested in Goodrich's introduction to a book by a sixteenth-century English dissenter, in which Goodrich criticized Calvin's rule of Geneva. Calvin's "rude and fierce soldiery" against "popery," Goodrich asserted, led him to abolish "many most useful laws and practices . . . merely on account of their adoption by the church of Rome." Opinions such as these perhaps prompted the "cart-ropes"

remark that so scandalized the Waldos. Charles A. Goodrich, ed., *Actes and Monuments of the Church: Book of Martyrs, or, A History of the Lives, Sufferings and Triumphant Deaths of the Primitive as Well as Protestant Martyrs: From the Commencement of Christianity, to the Latest Periods of Pagan and Popish Persecution* (New York: William W. Reed, 1831), 47–48.

14. *Remarks*, 7–12; Daniel Waldo to the First Church, December 20, 1820, in *Remarks*, 9.

15. *Remarks*, 12; quotation from p. 7; see also 26–27; Elizabeth Salisbury concurred in her letter to the First Church, undated but January, 1819 in *Origin*, 32–33.

16. For the role of ministers, see David D. Hall, *The Faithful Shepherd: A History of the New England Ministry in the Seventeenth Century* (New York: Norton, 1974), 55–60. The Arminianism of the Second Great Awakening strengthened the role of the minister, who facilitated salvation through effective preaching; Hatch, *Democratization of American Christianity*, 17–46.

17. Minority report to the ecclesiastical council, December 1818, cited in *Origin*, 19–20. In 1816, Daniel Waldo, at fifty-three, was the eldest of the dissidents; Sarah Waldo was forty-nine, Elizabeth Salisbury was forty-eight, and Rebecca Waldo was forty-five; Waldo Lincoln, *Four Generations of the Waldo Family in America* (Boston: David Clapp and Son, 1898); Daniel Waldo to Charles A. Goodrich, April 29, 1817, Old South Church Records, box 1, folder 10. Samuel Austin, fifty-seven years old in 1816, had been a minister since 1784 and came to Worcester in 1790. The ties between the departed pastor and his supporters were strengthened when Austin's nephew and adopted son, John Hubbard, married Eliza Weir, the niece and adopted daughter of Elizabeth Salisbury. For the relations between the two families, see the letter from Jerusha Hopkins Austin to Elizabeth Salisbury, April 18, 1818, Salisbury Family Papers, box 18, folder 2; Sprague, *Annals of the American Pulpit*, 1:223–24; Meyer, *Salisbury Mansion*, 30; William Lincoln, *History of Worcester*, 160.

18. Austin's preaching was described by his contemporary Leonard Bacon in *Historical Discourse*, 45; Goodrich's characterization is from *Remarks*, 9, 27 (emphasis in original).

19. Louisa Jane Trumbull Diary, entry for May 11, 1835, Trumbull Family Papers, box 1, folder 6, Manuscript Collection, AAS. Rebekah Dean Salisbury (Worcester) to Catherine Dean Flint (Boston), May 7, 1839, Waldo Flint Papers, Manuscript boxes "F," box 6, folder 8, Manuscript Collection, AAS. See also the sermon by the Reverend Seth Sweetser, "No. 735, Preached on Sunday after the death of Miss Sarah Waldo," March 23, 1851, Seth Sweetser Papers, octavo vol. 2, Manuscript vols. "S," Manuscript Collection, AAS.

20. *Origin*, 6–7; the Reverend Auretius B. Hull (Worcester) to the Reverend Joseph Goffe (Milbury, Mass.), February 1824, Old South Church Records, box 2, folder 2. Hull succeeded Goodrich in the First Church.

21. For the intent of the brethren, see the discipline petition from church members to Charles A. Goodrich, March 1818, Old South Church Records, box 1, folder 11; letter from Charles A. Goodrich to Daniel Waldo, April 1817, cited in *Origin*, 7. The First Church noted that "After the above controversy

arose, discipline was inexpedient, and, considering the embarrassed state of the Church, might have been impossible. It was therefore conceded, that, until that question were at rest, nothing could properly be attempted." *Origin*, 25–26.

22. Samuel Austin (Worcester) to Betsey Flagg (Boylston, Mass.), August 3, 1814, Samuel Austin Papers, Manuscript Boxes "A," box 1, folder 6, Manuscript Collection, AAS. The ecclesiastical council granted Flagg a dismission and recommendation upon the condition that she apologize to the brethren, which she did. Thus, while Flagg was in a sense vindicated, it came at the cost of her acknowledging that she was also in the wrong. Susan Juster analyzes the gender implications of "crimes of the tongue" among Baptists in *Disorderly Women*, 88–107.

23. In 1816, women comprised 72 percent of the First Church membership, men 28 percent. The "voting majority" was thus itself a minority, since it was limited to the male members of the parish. "Old South Parish," *Proceedings of the Worcester Society of Antiquity*, n.s., 22 (1907), 174–75.

24. Butler, *Walking in the Way*, 74; *Remarks*, 12; *Origin*, 10.

25. Elizabeth Salisbury to Stephen Salisbury I, April 13, 1818 and April 2, 1818, respectively; Salisbury Family Papers, box 18, folder 2.

26. *Origin*, 12–13, quotation from 13 (emphasis in original). Letter from the Reverend Samuel Austin (Burlington, Vermont) to the First Church (Worcester), September 26, 1818, cited in *Origin*, 18–19.

27. William Lincoln, *History of Worcester*, 161–62; *Origin*, 20–21.

28. *Origin*, 24–25. According to the Mutual Council, the pro-Goodrich majority represented four-fifths of the congregation.

29. Because Daniel Waldo was not a member of the church (that is, was not converted) but only a member of the parish (that is, a taxpaying congregant), he was not subject to the proceedings. Charles A. Goodrich (Worcester) to Elizabeth Salisbury (Worcester), January 17, 1819, Salisbury Family Papers, box 19, folder 1.

30. *Origin*, 41.

31. Sarah Waldo and Rebecca Waldo to the First Church, undated but January, 1819; in *Remarks*, 31–32.

32. Elizabeth Salisbury to the First Church, undated but January, 1819; in *Origin*, 32–33.

33. Elizabeth Salisbury, Sarah Waldo, and Rebecca Waldo to the First Church, undated but January, 1819; in *Origin*, 39–40.

34. Elizabeth Salisbury, Sarah Waldo, and Rebecca Waldo to the First Church, undated but January, 1819; in *Origin*, 40. The records indicate that although men participated personally in church meetings and ecclesiastical councils, women participated via written petitions. This has had the ironic result of better documenting the women's views than the men's, which, given orally, were not recorded.

35. Elizabeth Salisbury, Sarah Waldo, and Rebecca Waldo to the First Church, undated but January, 1819; *Remarks*, 40–41.

36. CCR octavo vols. "W," vol. 5; Butler, *Walking in the Way*, 10.

37. "Records of the Ecclesiastical Council," August 2, 1820; CCR octavo

vols. "W," vol. 5. The First Church bitterly denounced this council on the grounds that it was an *ex parte*, that is private, council. Indeed, it was not a mutual council but one gathered at the dissenters' request. See the letter from the Reverend Auretius B. Hull (Worcester) to the Reverend Joseph Goffe (Milbury, Mass.), February, 1824, Old South Church Records, box 2, folder 2.

38. CCR octavo vols. "W," vol. 5, May 12, 1821; entry for March 25, 1820, in vol. 2, *Diary of Isaiah Thomas*, 65.

39. Although well out of the dispute by this point, Samuel Austin followed it with great interest; Samuel Austin to John Nelson, March 2, 1824, cited in U. Waldo Cutler, *The First Hundred Years of the Calvinist Church in Worcester, 1820–1920* (Worcester, Mass.: The Church, 1920), 18–19. It is unclear why the Calvinist Church did not select Austin as its pastor.

40. Anna McFarland and Lydia Taylor to Charles A. Goodrich, October 4, 1820, CCR octavo vols. "W," vol. 5; *Origin*, 80, 53; *Remarks*, 57.

41. See the tax lists for 1827, 1832, 1837, 1842, 1845; CCR folio vols. "W," vol. 4; *List of Persons Assessed in Worcester*.

42. Charles A. Goodrich to Anna McFarland and Lydia Taylor, October, 1820, CCR octavo vols. "W," vol. 5.

43. Anna McFarland and Lydia Taylor to the Calvinist Church, October 14, 1820, CCR octavo vols. "W," vol. 5.

44. Salisbury insisted that her son, a member of the Unitarian Church, be tutored by the orthodox Samuel Austin. Samuel S. Green, "Gleanings from the Sources of the History of the Second Parish, Worcester, Massachusetts," *Proceedings of the American Antiquarian Society*, n.s., 11 (1883): 301–317, 313.

45. Computed from the membership list, *Manual of the Calvinist Church* (Worcester, Mass.: Goddard, 1877). These data confirm the findings of Paul E. Johnson, Mary P. Ryan, and Harry S. Stout and Catherine A. Brekus in their studies of Rochester, Utica, and New Haven churches, respectively. Paul Johnson, *A Shopkeeper's Millennium: Society and Revivals in Rochester, New York 1815–1837* (New York: Hill and Wang, 1978), 95–115; Ryan, *Cradle of the Middle Class*, 257; Stout and Brekus, "Declension, Gender, and 'New Religious History,'" 30.

46. *Historical Sketch of the Central Church in Worcester with Its Charter, By-Laws and Members* (Worcester, Mass.: Central Church, 1880).

47. Article 3, "Articles of Association of the Calvinist Church in Worcester," April 11, 1822, CCR folio vols. "W," vol. 1; Cutler, *First Hundred Years*, 13. In 1825, 83 percent of church revenues came from the Waldos; Cutler, *First Hundred Years*, 23. The tax-free incentive was likely patterned upon the Second (Unitarian) Parish, which offered free services when it organized in the late eighteenth century; Green, "Gleanings," 301–17. The Calvinist Church added thirty-six new members during the tax-free period, a healthy increase but one that paled in comparison to its phenomenal growth in the late 1820s and early 1830s, after the offer had expired; *Manual of the Calvinist Church*, 9–11.

Not only did Waldo money subsidize the Calvinist Church for its first five years but the family's control was still more pervasive. Determined never again to be outvoted by a congregation, the Waldos literally *owned* the Calvinist Church—lock, stock, and pulpit. The Waldos' subsequent actions reveal that they did not intend to keep the property within the family but, betraying their suspicion of democratically inclined congregations, neither did they give it to the church. In 1826, Daniel Waldo drew up an indenture agreement with five male church members that established the Trustees of the Parochial Funds of the Calvinist Society. In exchange for one dollar, Waldo conveyed the property to this body in a perpetual trust on behalf of the Calvinist Society. The trustees were a part of the church, drawn from its membership, but free from its control. The trustees were not, however, free of the Waldos, and could perform none of their duties, such as selling pews, making improvements upon the property, or hiring and providing for the minister, without the family's consent. Barnard, "Central Church, Worcester, 1820–1903," 107–8; *Historical Sketch*, 6–7. See also the *Spy*, May 9, 1827; McLoughlin, *New England Dissent*, 2:1072.

48. CCR folio vol. 1, April 8, 1833; folio vol. 2, March 23, 1841; octavo vol. 10; folio vols. "W," vols. 1, 4, 5. By 1848, the tax rebate was raised to eight percent; folio vol. 2, March 27, 1848. The reduced value of property was its assessed value minus debts or other liabilities. Only those who had given their consent to join a religious society could be taxed. Churches therefore circulated "the Book," a log by which members agreed to pay their taxes. Women did not routinely sign the Calvinist Church's Book when they joined the church, whether as full members or as unconverted communicants.

49. Tax lists for 1827 and 1837, CCR folio vols. "W," vols. 4, 1.

50. Tax lists for 1827, 1832, 1837, 1842, 1845, CCR folio vols. "W," vols. 1, 4, 5.

51. CCR folio vols. "W," vol. 5.

52. For example, see the letter from Lucretia Bancroft recounting the woes of her husband, Aaron Bancroft, minister of Worcester's Unitarian church, in Horace Davis, "Mrs. Lucretia (Chandler) Bancroft. A Letter to Her Daughter Mrs. Gherardi, with Introduction," *Proceedings of the American Antiquarian Society*, n.s., 14 (1900): 130–34; Charles C. Smith, "Financial Embarrassments of the New England Ministers in the Last Century," *Proceedings of the American Antiquarian Society*, n.s., 7 (1891), 129–35.

53. CCR folio vols. "W," vol. 1, March 24, 1832, April 8, 1833; vol. 2, March 29, 1841 and April 4, 1842.

54. Letter from Daniel Waldo to the Reverend Seth Sweetser, October 16, 1838, CCR folio vol. "W," vol. 10; Membership lists, CCR folio vols. "W," vol. 2; Manuscript Boxes "W," box 4, folders 1–5.

55. Robert Doherty has suggested that "as many as 100,000 persons may have entered and left Worcester in the 1850s" in Robert Doherty, *Society and Power: Five New England Towns, 1800–1860* (Amherst: University of Massachusetts Press, 1977), 31.

56. CCR octavo vols. "W," vol. 8, February 25, 1830; vol. 10, April 1, 1836, November 20, 1833.

57. Membership lists rarely stated a reason for leaving a church but dismission certificates sometimes did. Taxpayers filed a certificate with the parish clerk to sever their official connections with the church and thus any further obligation to pay its tax. CCR Manuscript Boxes "W," box 4, folders 1, 3, 2, 4.

58. Daniel Waldo's notes for 1830, CCR folio vols. "W," vol. 2; Daniel Waldo's undated notes, CCR Manuscript Boxes "W," box 2, folder 8.

59. CCR octavo vols. "W," vol. 8, February 1, 1850.

60. Of 261 nominal members in 1841, 184 (70.5 percent) were women and 77 (29.5 percent) were men; of 173 resident members, 122 (70 percent) were women, 51 (30 percent) were men. CCR octavo vols. "W," vol. 8, April 19, 1841.

61. CCR octavo vols. "W," vol. 8, March 24, 1847; May 14, 1847; September 28, 1849.

62. CCR octavo vols. "W," vol. 8, September 28, 1849; vol. 6, June 4, 1858.

63. CCR octavo vols. "W," vol. 8, May 18, 1836; folio vols. "W," vol. 2, April 7, 1856.

64. CCR Manuscript Boxes "W," box 4, folder 4, April 9, 1847.

65. Johnson, *Shopkeeper's Millennium*, 121.

66. CCR Manuscript Boxes "W," box 6, folder 5; box 1, folder 7; box 2, folder 8; folio vols. "W," vol. 1, "Conditions of Sale of Pews," July, 1826; vol. 2, April 25, 1859.

67. CCR folio vols. "W," vol. 2; Manuscript Boxes "W," box 1, folder 7; Daniel Waldo's memo from 1832, CCR Manuscript Boxes "W," box 2, folder 8.

68. CCR folio vols. "W," vol. 2, April 7, 1856; will of Alfred D. Foster, August 7, 1847, Foster Family Papers, Manuscript Boxes "F," box 7, folder 3, Manuscript Collection, AAS. In the late 1850s, the Calvinist Church held ninety-two pews, only ten of which still belonged to the church; see the floor plan in CCR Manuscript Boxes "W," box 1, folder 7.

69. In 1854, the women of the church sewing circle made new carpets for the vestry; in 1860 the Church noted the "valuable assistance rendered by our ladies" who had contributed $450 toward new church furnishings. See the records of the Central Missionary Sewing Circle, CCR octavo vol. 6, October 10, 1854; January 17, 1854; February 3, 1860.

70. "Articles of Faith and Covenant adopted by the Calvinistic Church in Worcester," CCR octavo vols. "W," vol. 5.

71. The Calvinist Church argued that it must "protect itself against the intrusion of those . . . who might be willing to assume the relation of membership for the purpose of creating obstacles in the way of an united and harmonious action on the part of the existing members." CCR Manuscript Boxes "W," box 6, folder 1, "Report as to the By Laws of Calvinist Society," March and April, 1836, box 1, folder 7, April 7, 1856; octavo vols. "W," vol. 8, August 23, 1837; July 13, 1840; January 11, 1841; March 24, 1847; May 14, 1847.

72. "Articles of Faith and Covenant adopted by the Calvinist Church in Worcester," CCR octavo vols. "W," vol. 5.

73. CCR octavo vols. "W," vol. 8, May 25, 1836; April 19, 1841; May 2, 1839, March 5, 1847; see also the ad in the *Spy*, June 9, 1830.

74. For common fame, see also Glenn C. Altschuler and Jan M. Saltzgaber, *Revivalism, Social Conscience, and Community in the Burned-Over District: The Trial of Rhoda Bement* (Ithaca: Cornell University Press, 1983); T. Scott Miyakawa, *Protestants and Pioneers: Individualism and Conformity on the Ameri-*

can Frontier (Chicago: University of Chicago Press, 1964). For the significance of gossip in establishing reputations, see Hansen, *A Very Social Time:*, 114–36.

75. CCR octavo vols. "W," vol. 9, January 11, 1841; April 19, 1841.

76. For Goddard, see CCR octavo vols. "W," vol. 5, December 30, 1825; January 16, 1826; August 7, 1826; January 7, 1827; for Cutter, see octavo vols. "W," vol. 8, October 24, 1833; March 19, 1834; November 17, 1834; for Dakin and Conant, see octavo vols. "W," vol. 8, November 14, 1834 and December 14, 1834.

77. CCR octavo vols. "W," vol. 8, September 24, 1829; January 4, 1830; April 30, 1830; April 25, 1838; May 4, 1838.

78. For Child, see CCR octavo vols. "W," vol. 5, May 12, 1821; May 13, 1821; *Spy*, May 2, 1821; for Chapin, see octavo vols. "W," vol. 8, November 17, 1834; April 20, 1835; for Fenno, see folio vols. "W," vol. 2, June 23, 1841; *Spy*, July 2, 1823, July 18, 1827. Fenno's pew was assessed at $170 while the liens against it amounted to $13,000.

79. For Oaks, see CCR folio vols. "W," vol. 2, May 2, 1839; May 8, 1839; July 31, 1839; for Townsends, see folio vols. "W," vol. 2, April 20, 1840, and octavo vols. "W," vol. 8, January 11, 1841; for Howard, Brown, Taylor, and Howe, see folio vols. "W," vol. 2, April, 1835; February 12, 1834; February 19, 1834; octavo vols. "W," vol. 8, March 30, 1838; April 25, 1838; April 28, 1838; folio vols. "W," vol. 2, September, 1833; *Manual of the Calvinist Church*, 13, 22.

80. CCR folio vols. "W," vol. 2, April, 1833; September, 1833.

81. CCR folio vols. "W," vol. 2, June, 1832; octavo vols. "W," vol. 8, June 19, 1832; *Manual of the Calvinist Church*, 11.

82. For Moore, see CCR octavo vols. "W," vol. 8, March 8, 1844; March 23, 1844; March 9, 1846, and *Manual of the Calvinist Church*, 22; for Hutchinson, see octavo vols. "W," vol. 8, March 9, 1846, and *Manual of the Calvinist Church*, 14; for Peckham, see octavo vols. "W," vol. 8, March 18, 1842; April 27, 1842; March 7, 1844; March 23, 1844.

83. For Holder, see CCR folio vols. "W," vol. 2, December, 1832; April, 1840; for Clark, see folio vols. "W," vol. 2, March, 1841; April, 1841; July, 1841.

84. From 1820 through 1846, slightly more than six hundred persons joined the Calvinist Church; of these, eighteen, or less than three percent, were excommunicated. Growth slowed from 1847 through 1860 but so too did the excommunications: out of nearly three hundred new members, only five, or less than two percent, were excommunicated. From 1820 to 1860, 293 men joined the Calvinist Church, compared to 481 women; *Manual of the Calvinist Church*, 9–37.

85. The disciplinary practices of the Calvinist Church began to fade in the late 1830s and largely disappeared in the 1840s, a decade of enormous growth in Worcester. The church found itself spending increasing amounts of time and energy identifying, locating, and persuading its communicants to pay their church taxes and to attend services; moral discipline seems to have been a lower priority. Moreover, after disestablishment, churches became self-selecting voluntary societies. Those whose behavior was most likely to offend a congregation likely remained aloof from the churches and thus there was less need for discipline.

86. "Copy of the Hon. Daniel Waldo's Deed," July 29, 1826, CCR folio vols. "W," vols. 1 and 2.

87. CCR octavo vols. "W," vol. 5, March 28, 1823. For the election of John S.C. Abbott, pastor from 1830 to 1835, see octavo vol. 8, undated entry for late 1829; for David Peabody, pastor from 1835 to 1838, see octavo vol. 8, April 22, 1835; for Seth Sweetser, pastor from 1838 to 1878, see folio vols. "W," vol. 10, undated entry for 1838.

88. Congregational churches in England were also divided on the question of women's suffrage, with many deciding in the affirmative; see Timothy Larsen, "'How Many Sisters Make a Brotherhood?': A Case Study in Gender and Ecclesiology in Early Nineteenth-Century English Dissent," *Journal of Ecclesiastical History* 49 (April 1998): 282–311.

2. MISSIONARIES AND MORE

1. Diary of Caroline Barrett White, entry for March 5, 1850, Caroline Barrett White Papers, octavo vols. "W," vol. 1, Manuscript Collection, American Antiquarian Society (hereafter cited AAS).

2. Deborah van Broekhoven also argues that sewing circles were centers of political activism in "'Better than a Clay Club': The Organization of Anti-Slavery Fairs, 1835–60," *Slavery and Abolition* 19 (spring 1998): 24–45; and "Needles, Pens, and Petitions: Reading Women into Antislavery History," in David Roediger and Martin H. Blatt, eds., *The Meaning of Slavery in the North* (New York: Garland Publications, 1998): 125–55. See also Beverly Gordon, "Playing at Being Powerless: New England Ladies Fairs, 1830–1930," *Massachusetts Review* 26 (September 1986): 144-60; Nancy Hewitt, "The Social Origins of Women's Antislavery Politics in Western New York," in Alan M. Kraut, ed., *Crusaders and Compromisers: Essays on the Relationship of the Antislavery Struggle to the Antebellum Party System* (Westport, Conn.: Greenwood Press, 1979): 205–33; Amy Swerdlow, "Abolition's Conservative Sisters: The Ladies' New York City Anti-Slavery Societies, 1834–1840," in Jean Fagan Yellin and John C. Van Horne, eds., *The Abolitionist Sisterhood: Women's Political Culture in Antebellum America* (Ithaca: Cornell University Press, 1994): 31–44; Debra Gold Hansen, "The Boston Female Anti-Slavery Society and the Limits of Gender Politics," in *Abolitionist Sisterhood*, 45–65; Jean R. Soderlund, "Priorities and Power: The Philadelphia Female Anti-Slavery Society," in *Abolitionist Sisterhood*, 67–88; Lee Chambers-Schiller, "'A Good Work among the People:' The Political Culture of the Boston Antislavery Fair," in *Abolitionist Sisterhood*, 249–74.

3. Jane H. Pease and William H. Pease, *Ladies, Women, and Wenches: Choice and Constraint in Antebellum Charleston & Boston* (Chapel Hill: University of North Carolina Press, 1990), 119; Ryan, *Cradle of the Middle Class*, 217, 216; Hewitt, *Women's Activism*, 129, 253, see also pp. 22, 38–40, 223, 232; Hewitt, "Origins of Women's Antislavery Politics;" Anne Firor Scott, *Natural Allies: Women's Associations in American History* (Urbana: University of Illinois Press, 1993), 38. See also Keith Melder, "Ladies Bountiful: Organized Women's Be-

nevolence in Early 19th-Century America," *New York History* 48 (July 1967): 231–55; Kathleen D. McCarthy, "Parallel Power Structures: Women and the Voluntary Sphere," in Kathleen D. McCarthy, ed., *Lady Bountiful Revisited: Women, Philanthropy, and Power* (New Brunswick: Rutgers University Press, 1990), 6, 13.

In an important work on women and benevolence, Lori D. Ginzberg challenged the paradigm of separate spheres and noted that "The steps from female prayer and sewing meetings to auxiliaries to independent female organizations and institutions went virtually unnoticed and unremarked." Ginzberg did not, however, address how this process unfolded; *Women and the Work of Benevolence*, 38.

4. Deborah van Broekhoven compares sewing circles to political clubs in "'Better than a Clay Club,'" 40, and argues that "sewing may in fact have been as radical as petitioning," in "Needles, Pens, and Petitions," 145.

5. Louisa Jane Trumbull Diary, entry for December 12, 1829, Trumbull Family Papers, Manuscript Boxes "T," box 1, folder 6, Manuscript Collection, AAS; Abijah Bigelow (Washington, D.C.) to Hannah Gardner Bigelow (Worcester), January 31, 1811, and February 10, 1811, Bigelow Family Papers, folio vols. "B," vol. 1, Manuscript Collection, AAS; *Spy*, May 24, 1826.

For sewing, see Betty Ring, *Girlhood Embroidery: American Samplers and Pictorial Needlework, 1650–1850*, 2 vols. (New York: Alfred A. Knopf, 1993), especially vol. 1; Mary Jaene Edmonds, *Samplers and Samplermakers: An American Schoolgirl Art, 1700–1850* (New York: Rizzoli International, 1991), 10, 12, 16; Anne L. Macdonald, *No Idle Hands: The Social History of American Knitting* (New York: Ballantine Books, 1988), 17–23, 63; Cuesta Benberry, *Always There: The African-American Presence in American Quilts* (Louisville: Kentucky Quilt Project, 1992); Boydston, *Home and Work*, 12, 13, 41, 82, 83, 87, 125, 132, 133.

6. Anne M. Boylan, *Sunday School: The Formation of An American Institution, 1790–1880* (New Haven: Yale University Press, 1988), 39, 46; Louisa Jane Trumbull Diary, entry for May 6, 1836, Trumbull Family Papers, box 1, folder 6; Worcester *National Aegis*, May 21, 1851; Abby Kelley Foster (Cumberland, Rhode Island) to Stephen Foster (Worcester), April 17, 1847, Abby Kelley Foster Papers, Manuscript Boxes "F," box 2, folder 1, Manuscript Collection, AAS.

7. Nancy Avery White Diary, entry for April, 1808, White-Forbes Family Diaries, octavo vols. "W," vol. 1; entries for November 7, 1818, and November 6, 1818, octavo vols. "W," vol. 2; Eliza Earle Chase (Salem) to Lucy Chase (Worcester), undated but 1860s, Chase Family Papers, Manuscript Boxes "C," box 1, folder 5, Manuscript Collection, AAS.

8. Laurel Thatcher Ulrich, *Good Wives: Image and Reality in the Lives of Women of Northern New England, 1650–1750* (New York: Alfred A. Knopf, 1980); see also the essays in Joan M. Jensen and Sue Davidson, eds., *A Needle, A Bobbin, A Strike: Women Needleworkers in America* (Philadelphia: Temple University Press, 1984). For the Salisbury family correspondence, see Benjamin Thomas Hill, "Life at Harvard a Century Ago," *Proceedings of the American Antiquarian Society*, n.s., 20 (1910), 199, 214–15, 221–22, 205.

9. Rebekah Dean Salisbury (Worcester) to Catherine Dean Flint (Bos-

ton), November 19, 1838 and January 7, 1841, Waldo Flint Papers, box 6, folders 8 and 10; Lydia Stiles Foster (Worcester) to Mary Stiles Newcomb (Baton Rouge), March 21, 1838, Foster Family Papers, Manuscript Boxes "F," box 7, folder 1, Manuscript Collection, AAS.

10. *The Writings of Nancy Maria Hyde, of Norwich, Conn., Connected with A Sketch of Her Life* (Norwich: Russell Hubbard, 1816), entry for June 22, 1811, pp. 142–43; Maria Allen (Uxbridge, Mass.) to Lucy Chase (Worcester), April 28, undated but early 1840s, Chase Family Papers, box 2, folder 15; Ann E. Jennison Diary, entry for June 15, 1849, Jennison Family Papers, octavo vols. "J," vol. 1, Manuscript Collection, AAS; *Godey's Lady's Book*, January 1850; Macdonald, *No Idle Hands*, 52–62.

The literature on women and reading is extensive; see, for example, Douglas, *Feminization of American Culture*; Mary Kelley, *Private Woman, Public Stage: Literary Domesticity in Nineteenth-Century America* (New York: Oxford University Press, 1984); Mary Kelley, "Reading Women/Women Reading: The Making of Learned Women in Antebellum America," *Journal of American History* 83 (September 1996): 401–24; Ronald J. Zboray and Mary Saracino Zboray, "Books, Reading, and the World of Goods in Antebellum New England," *American Quarterly* 48 (December 1996): 587–622; Ronald J. Zboray and Mary Saracino Zboray, "Political News and Female Readership in Antebellum Boston and Its Region," *Journalism History* 22 (spring 1996): 2–14.

11. Receipt from Eliza Bancroft to Eliza Weir, June 23, 1812, John Davis Papers, Manuscript Boxes "D," box 1, folder 1, Manuscript Collection, AAS; *Spy*, May 17, 1826; May 14, 1828; quotation from January 10, 1827; October 31, 1827; Henry H. Chamberlin, "The Trade of Worcester, During the Present Century," *Proceedings of the Worcester Society of Antiquity*, n.s., 13 (1880): 27–39, 32. For the sewing trade, see Wendy Gamber, *The Female Economy: The Millinery and Dressmaking Trades, 1860–1930* (Urbana: University of Illinois Press, 1997); Christine Stansell, *City of Women, Sex and Class in New York City, 1789–1860* (Urbana: University of Illinois Press, 1982), 15, 107–109; Joan M. Jensen, "Needlework as Art, Craft, and Livelihood before 1900," in Jensen and Davidson, eds., *A Needle, A Bobbin, A Strike*, 3–19; Ava Baron and Susan E. Klepp, "'If I Didn't Have My Sewing Machine . . .': Women and Sewing Machine Technology," in Jensen and Davidson, eds., *A Needle, A Bobbin, A Strike*, 20–59.

12. Julie Roy Jeffrey, *Frontier Women: The Trans-Mississippi West, 1840–1880* (New York: Hill and Wang, 1979), 60; Rosalie Roos, *Travels in America, 1851–1855*, trans. and ed., Carl. L. Anderson (Carbondale: Southern Illinois University Press, 1982), 34; Adelaide Crossman Diary, entries for January 21, 1857, January 22, 1857, and November 30, 1857, Crossman Family Diaries, octavo vols. "C," vol. 3, Manuscript Collection, AAS; see also Boydston, *Home and Work*, 87; Laurel Thatcher Ulrich, "Wheels, Looms, and the Gender Division of Labor in Eighteenth-Century New England," *William & Mary Quarterly*, 3rd ser., 55 (January 1998): 3–38.

13. Louisa Jane Trumbull Diary, entry for December 19, 1834, Trumbull Family Papers, box 1, folder 6.

14. [William N. Blane], *An Excursion through the United States and Canada during the Years 1822–23 by An English Gentleman* (reprint, New York: Negro Universities Press, 1969), 258; Marianne Finch, *An Englishwoman's Experience in America* (originally published, 1853; reprint, New York: Negro Universities Press, 1969), 83; *Spy*, April 14, 1830.

15. Trollope, *Domestic Manners of the Americans*, ed. Donald Smalley (New York: Alfred A. Knopf, 1949), 284, 159, 223, 281–82; Edmonds, *Samplers and Samplermakers*, 149; Boylan, *Sunday School*, 69–70; Finch, *An Englishwoman's Experience*, 209. Finch also remarked upon Indian women sewing "as daintily as boarding-school misses," 116.

16. Cited in Charles E. Rosenberg, *The Care of Strangers: The Rise of America's Hospital System* (New York: Basic Books, 1987), 29; Worcester Lunatic Asylum Records, entries for October 21, 1841, and March 30, 1846, folio vols. "W," vol. 1, Manuscript Collection, AAS.

Michael Grossberg describes how, in the 1850 case of *True v. Raney*, parents seeking to annul their daughter's marriage offered as proof of her mental incompetence her inability to "wash or dress herself, spell or read, use money, tell time, knit or sew." Grossberg, *Governing the Hearth*, 115; Patricia Cline Cohen, "Unregulated Youth: Masculinity and Murder in the 1830s City," *Radical History Review* 52 (1992): 33–52, 41; Benberry, *Always There*, 21–29; Deborah Gray White, *Ar'n't I a Woman: Female Slaves in the Plantation South* (New York: Norton, 1984), 128; Rita Bode, "Dickinson's 'Don't Put Up My Thread & Needle,'" *The Explicator* 52 (spring 1994): 161–66.

17. Ulrich, *Good Wives*, 59; Laurel Thatcher Ulrich, "Housewife and Gadder: Themes of Self-Sufficiency and Community in Eighteenth-Century New England," in Carol Groneman and Mary Beth Norton, eds., *"To Toil the Livelong Day": America's Women at Work, 1780–1980* (Ithaca: Cornell University Press, 1987), 21–34; Macdonald, *No Idle Hands*, 26–43; Alfred F. Young, "The Women of Boston: 'Persons of Consequence' in the Making of the American Revolution, 1765–76," in Harriet B. Applewhite and Darline G. Levy, eds., *Women and Politics in the Age of the Democratic Revolution* (Ann Arbor: University of Michigan Press, 1990), 196–98, 208–13; Laurel Thatcher Ulrich, "'Daughters of Liberty': Religious Women in Revolutionary New England," in Ronald Hoffman and Peter J. Albert, eds., *Women in the Age of the American Revolution* (Charlottesville: University of Virginia Press, 1989), 211–43; Linda Kerber, *Women of the Republic: Intellect and Ideology in Revolutionary America* (Chapel Hill: University of North Carolina Press, 1980); Elaine Forman Crane, "Religion and Rebellion: Women of Faith in the American War for Independence," in Ronald Hoffman and Peter J. Albert, eds., *Religion in A Revolutionary Age* (Charlottesville: University Press of Virginia, 1994): 52–86; Jeffrey, *Frontier Women*, 86. In 1790, Martha Ballard of Maine described an evening tea that followed an afternoon's sewing; Ulrich, "Housewife and Gadder," 30.

Anne Boylan argues that sewing societies attracted more young women compared to other kinds of organizations, in "Timid Girls, Venerable Widows and Dignified Matrons: Life Cycle Patterns among Organized Women in New York and Boston, 1797–1840," *American Quarterly* 38 (winter 1986): 779–98, quotation from p. 784. Deborah Gray White finds that quiltings were popular among enslaved women; *Ar'n't I A Woman?*, 123. African American women also organized to raise money for political resistance; see Gayle T. Tate, "Political Consciousness and Resistance among Black Antebellum Women," *Women and Politics* 13 (1993): 67–89.

18. Nancy Avery White Diaries, entries for April 9, 1822; May 19, 1836; April 21, 1837; June 16, 1837; June 20, 1839; September 22, 1838; January 31, 1839, White-Forbes Family Diaries, vols. 6 and 4; Andrea Moore Kerr, *Lucy Stone: Speaking Out for Equality* (New Brunswick: Rutgers University Press, 1992), 21–22. White was not a member of Worcester's sewing circles but her diary reveals the process by which women integrated sewing circles into their busy lives. Moreover, White counted among her friends several who belonged to Worcester's circles; Nancy Avery White Diaries, entry for November 3, 1842, White-Forbes Family Diaries, vol. 6. For the social implications of clothing see Karen Halttunen, *Confidence Men and Painted Women: A Study of Middle Class Culture in America, 1830–1870* (New Haven: Yale University Press, 1982). According to Anne L. Macdonald the "oldest continuing sewing circle" was the Boston Fragment Society, organized in 1812; *No Idle Hands*, 104.

19. Nancy Avery White Diaries, entries for March 4, 1861; April 26, 1861, White-Forbes Family Diaries, vol. 8. For women's work in the Civil War, see, for example, Ginzberg, *Women and the Work of Benevolence*, 3–73; Macdonald, *No Idle Hands*, 98–113.

20. Charles A. Goodrich, *An Address, Delivered June 26, 1817, before the Female Reading and Charitable Society of the First Parish in Worcester, Mass.* (Worcester, Mass.: William Manning, 1817); appendices B and C, 19–20.

21. Goodrich, *Address*; appendices B, C, D, and E, 19–20; see also chapter 1.

22. "Records of the Worcester Female Association," Old South Church Records, octavo vols. 62, 63, and 64, Worcester Collection, AAS. The First Church was also known as the Old South Church.

23. "Records of the Worcester Female Association," Old South Church Records, octavo vols. 62, 63, and 64. The records do not include a membership list.

24. *Spy*, October 24, 1827.

25. *Constitution of the Worcester Female Samaritan Society* (Worcester, Mass.: Griffin and Morrill, 1827). The extant records are limited to the constitution and do not include a membership list.

26. Ibid.

27. Ibid.; "Mrs. Salisbury" is inscribed on the copy of the WFSS constitution at the AAS.

28. Analysis of the Center Missionary Sewing Circle is based upon the secretary's unpublished minutes; Central Church Records, octavo vols. "W," vols. 23 and 24 (hereafter cited as CMSC), Worcester Collection, AAS. The secretary kept notes of each meeting and also wrote an annual report. CMSC, December 10, 1841 (emphasis in original); December 20, 1844.

29. In January 1841, the *Missionary Herald* reported that the ABCFM was in debt by almost $5,000. CMSC, February 21, 1840; December 22, 1843;

January 9, 1852; October 22, 1841; December 20, 1844; January 9, 1852; December 10, 1841; October 22, 1841; April 4, 1843.

The women of nearby Hopkinton also formed a missionary sewing circle in 1839; see Navin, "The Spirit of Reform," 172–85.

30. CMSC, October 7, 1851.

31. Ibid., December 23, 1842; July 12, 1842; March 16, 1844; October 7, 1842; February 26, 1841; February 24, 1842; January 25, 1841; October 7, 1842; February 26, 1841; February 24, 1842; January 20, 1843; March 16, 1844; March 7, 1845; February 27, 1846; December 19, 1839, May 8, 1840; December 7, 1849.

The *Missionary Herald* printed obituaries of missionaries such as Angeline Castle and Louisa Munn, which appeared in June 1842. For women and missions, see, for example, Patricia Grimshaw, *Paths of Duty: American Missionary Wives in Nineteenth-Century Hawaii* (Honolulu: University of Hawaii Press, 1989); Patricia R. Hill, *The World Their Household: The American Woman's Foreign Mission Movement and Cultural Transformation, 1870–1920* (Ann Arbor: University of Michigan Press, 1985); Dana L. Robert, *American Women in Mission: A Social History of Their Thought and Practice* (Macon, Georgia: Mercer University Press, 1996). For women and biography, see Joanna Bowen Gillespie, "'The Clear Leadings of Providence': Pious Memoirs and the Problems of Self-Realization for Women in the Early Nineteenth Century," *Journal of the Early Republic* 5 (summer 1985): 197–221; Scott E. Casper, *Constructing American Lives: Biography and Culture in Nineteenth-Century America* (Chapel Hill: University of North Carolina Press, 1999).

32. Doherty, *Society and Power*, 24–25, 33; Lincoln, *History of Worcester*, 261.

33. Seth Sweetser, "Review of my ministry for 14 years," Seth Sweetser Papers, octavo vols. "S," vol. 2, December 19, 1852, Manuscript Collection, AAS; CMSC, January 31, 1854; December 24, 1847; December 30, 1845; December 30, 1845.

34. Only a few CMSC membership lists survive, with the first dating from 1849, a full ten years after the group's founding. Thus the total membership was likely much greater than indicated here. The data were compiled from the membership and tax lists of the CMSC, the Central Church Records, and city directories.

Of ninety-one known married members, the husband's occupation can be determined for sixty-four, or 70 percent. Eight, or 12.5 percent, were professionals; eighteen, or 28 percent, were merchants; seven, or 11 percent, were non-manual workers such as clerks; three, or 4.6 percent, were manufacturers; twenty-four, or 37.5 percent were artisans or skilled workers. Thirty-three of the sixty unmarried women can be identified as daughters of members. Twenty-three percent of the members belonged for more than five years; of these, the largest groups were married to skilled workers, 38 percent, or to merchants, 28.5 percent. An apparent influx of new members in the late 1840s skews the average length of membership, as do incomplete membership lists.

Defining the antebellum middle class is a challenge. Associating non-manual labor with the middle class, and manual labor with the working class, as Stuart Blumin has suggested, is helpful but occasionally misleading. Many of the husbands of CMSC members did not fit either category, such as Martin Lathe, an appropriately named machinist turned tool manufacturer, or Benjamin P. Rice, a baker who ran an extensive wholesale business. These men are perhaps better described as artisan-entrepreneurs. See Stuart Blumin, *The Emergence of the Middle Class: Social Experience in the American City, 1760–1900* (New York: Cambridge University Press, 1989), 66–107. Moreover, women were instrumental in creating a "middle class" sensibility; see, for example, C. Dallett Hemphill, "Middle Class Rising in Revolutionary America: The Evidence from Manners," *Journal of Social History* 30 (winter 1996): 317–44; Jacquelyn C. Miller, "An 'Uncommon Tranquility of Mind': Emotional Self-Control and the Construction of a Middle-Class Identity in Eighteenth-Century Philadelphia," *Journal of Social History* 30 (fall 1996): 129–48.

35. Diary of Brigham Nims of Roxbury, New Hampshire, quoted in Karen V. Hansen, "'Helped Put in a Quilt': Men's Work and Male Intimacy in Nineteenth-Century New England," in Judith Lorber and Susan A. Farrell, eds., *The Social Construction of Gender* (Newbury Park: Sage Publications, 1991); Robert Kendall Shaw, *Samuel Swett Green* (Chicago: American Library Association, 1926), 16; Levi Lincoln Newton (Cambridge, Mass.) to Hester Newton (Worcester), April 26, 1839, Newton Family Papers, Manuscript Boxes "N," box 2, folder 3, Manuscript Collection, AAS.

36. CMSC, January 6, 1843, January 6, 1843; December 10, 1855; membership lists for 1849, 1851, and 1856. Karen V. Hansen discusses mixed group socializing in *A Very Social Time*. For Martha Ballard, see Ulrich, "Housewife and Gadder," 30. Elizabeth Cady Stanton noted that the Daughters of Liberty sewed in the afternoons and the Sons of Liberty joined them after supper, in Elizabeth Cady Stanton, Susan B. Anthony, and Matilda Joslyn Gage, eds., *History of Woman Suffrage* (New York: Fowler and Wells; reprint, Arno Press, 1969), 1:203.

37. Central Church Records (hereafter cited CCR), octavo vols. "W," vol. 8, Worcester Collection, AAS, entry for September 25, 1839; "Records of the Tatnuck Ladies' Sewing Circle," octavo vols. "T," vol. 1, Worcester Collection, AAS; see also Laura Wasowicz, "The Tatnuck Ladies' Sewing Circle, 1847–1867," *Historical Journal of Massachusetts* 24 (winter 1996): 19–46; "East Haddam, Ct. Ladies & Gentleman Literary Association Records, 1847–1862," Manuscript Collection, AAS. For further examples of men attending sewing circles, see Lois A. Boyd and R. Douglas Brackenridge, *Presbyterian Women in America: Two Centuries of a Quest for Status* (Westport, Conn.: Greenwood Press, 1996), 1:5; Suzanne Yabsley, *Texas Quilts, Texas Women* (College Station: Texas A&M University Press, 1984), 13, 14.

38. CMSC, November 21, 1839; December 12, 1842; February 8, 1850; January 28, 1851; November 18, 1851; December 2, 1851; December 23, 1851; February 22, 1853.

39. Ibid., December 5, 1839; December 12, 1839; January 3, 1840; January 15, 1841; February 21, 1840; September 18, 1840; December 4, 1840 (emphasis

in original). On average, twenty-five women attended each of the eight meetings held in 1840 and worked at least four hours per meeting, for a total of 800 labor hours.

40. Ibid., December 10, 1841 (emphasis in original); February 21, 1840; January 15, 1841; March 12, 1841; July 16, 1841; December 10, 1841.

41. Lydia Stiles Foster (Worcester) to Mary Stiles Newcomb (Baton Rouge), February 9, 1843, Foster Family Papers, box 7, folder 1; CMSC, June 25, 1841; July 9, 1841; September 3, 1841; September 17, 1841; September 24, 1841; November 5, 1841; April 23, 1841; May 6, 1841; July 16, 1841; October 8, 1841; November 19, 1841; November 26, 1841; February 14, 1845; March 15, 1842; December 10, 1841; March 11, 1842; September 26, 1843.

42. CMSC, January 21, 1842 (emphasis in original).

43. Ibid., December 20, 1842; July 12, 1842; *Missionary Herald* August 1842; November 1842; July 1843. Cyrus Hamlin had a personal tie to the CMSC through Lydia Stiles Foster; Cyrus Hamlin (Constantinople) to Alfred D. Foster (Worcester), January 31, 1852, Foster Family Papers, box 7, folder 3.

44. CMSC, July 12, 1842; March 16, 1843; December 22, 1843; February 15, 1844; April 4, 1843; *Missionary Herald*, August 1842 and November 1842. "Such appropriations excite great interest . . . among the students of the Seminary," Hamlin wrote enthusiastically to the CMSC. "Christianity is presented to them in the light of disinterested benevolence, & they are thus made to feel its reality." Worcester later became a magnet for Armenian immigration; *The Armenians in Massachusetts* (Boston: Armenian Historical Society, 1937).

45. CMSC, July 29, 1843; December 22, 1843; March 11, 1842; October 6, 1843; August 16, 1844; January 11, 1853; December 14, 1853 (emphasis in original).

46. Ibid., February 11, 1851; December 20, 1844 (emphasis in original); CCR octavo vols. "W," vol. 8, April 19, 1841; *Spy* May 16, 1849. For the "business of benevolence," see Ginzberg, *Women and the Work of Benevolence*, 36–66.

47. CMSC, March 22, 1853; April 12, 1853; April 12, 1853; December 31, 1850; December 20, 1844; January 28, 1851; December 20, 1844; January 9, 1852.

48. CMSC, January 11, 1853; December 31, 1850; January 21, 1842; February 11, 1842; December 4, 1840; November 2, 1849.

49. Ibid., December 30, 1845 (emphasis in original); January 9, 1846; October 27, 1846; November 13, 1846; December 24, 1847; February 25, 1848; January 19, 1849. Between 1846 and 1848, average attendance at meetings declined from fifty members to fifteen; CMSC, January 7, 1848; January 19, 1849; April 5, 1849; November 2, 1849.

50. Ibid., January 11, 1850; February 11, 1851; Seth Sweetser, *Living to Do Good: A Sermon Occasioned by the Death of the Hon. Daniel Waldo* (Worcester, Mass.: Privately printed, 1845), 6, 12, 8, 9 (emphasis in original). For Sweetser's election, see CCR undated entry for 1838, folio vols. "W," vol. 10; CMSC, June 24, 1851 and January 9, 1852. Dorothea Dix taught school in Worcester from 1816 to 1818.

51. The secretary noted, "It was proposed to the consideration of the ladies,

whether a different kind of work might interest them more, and therefore be more profitable." CMSC, December 23, 1851; October 21, 1851; January 17, 1854; October 7, 1851; November 4, 1851; January 17, 1854; October 7, 1851.

52. Ibid., October 21, 1851; January 9, 1852; January 11, 1853; February 22, 1853; October 21, 1851; February 22, 1853; October 10, 1854; January 17, 1854; CCR octavo vols. "W," vol. 6, February 3, 1860; CMSC, January 11, 1853; September 30, 1856 (emphasis in original).

53. CMSC, December 10, 1841 (emphasis in original); December 23, 1842 (emphasis in original); December 23, 1842 (emphasis in original); December 20, 1844; December 10, 1841 (emphasis in original).

54. Ibid., February 3, 1852; April 12, 1853; May 24, 1853 (emphasis in original); January 11, 1853; December 11, 1855; December 23, 1842; January 25, 1853 (emphasis in original); March 7, 1854; June 1, 1852; October 19, 1852 (emphasis in original). In 1853, the CMSC furnished a room at the Sailor's Home in Boston and appropriated "a large part of our proceeds" that year for it; CMSC, January 11, 1853; February 22, 1853.

55. For assistance to the parish poor, see CCR octavo vols. "W," vol. 9, October 7, 1833; December 20, 1834; March 3, 1838; January 20, 1839; November 9, 1852.

In "'Where is the Real America?': Politics and Popular Consciousness in the Antebellum Era," *American Quarterly* 49 (June 1997): 225–67, Glenn C. Altschuler and Stuart M. Blumin argue that historians have overstated the political consciousness of antebellum Americans. If so, then the political (dis)interests of the CMSC were more representative of their era than of their gender. Moreover, recent studies find that women were more active in politics than previously thought; see, for example, Varon, *We Mean to Be Counted* and Ryan, *Women in Public.*

For women and the Civil War, see, for example, Jeanie Attie, "Warwork and the Crisis of Domesticity in the North," in Catherine Clinton and Nina Silber, eds., *Divided Houses: Gender and the Civil War* (New York: Oxford University Press, 1992): 247–59.

56. CMSC, January 11, 1850; January 11, 1853; March 23, 1854. For moralism and politics, see, for example, Paul Goodman, "Moral Purpose and Republican Politics in Antebellum America," *The Maryland Historian* 20 (fall/winter 1989): 5–39; Brooke, *Heart of the Commonwealth*; Edwards, *Angels in the Machinery*; Elizabeth B. Clark, "'The Sacred Rights of the Weak': Pain, Sympathy, and the Culture of Individual Rights in Antebellum America," *Journal of American History* 82 (September 1995): 463–93; Ronald P. Formisano, *The Transformation of Political Culture: Massachusetts Parties, 1790–1840* (New York: Oxford University Press, 1983); Eric Foner, *Free Soil, Free Labor, Free Men: The Ideology of the Republican Party before the Civil War* (New York: Oxford University Press, 1995), 114. For Nativism in Worcester, see Tyler Anbinder, *Nativism and Slavery: The Northern Know Nothings and the Politics of the 1850s* (New York: Oxford University Press, 1992), especially 20–51; Brooke, *Heart of the Commonwealth*, 383–88.

57. CMSC, October 10, 1854; October 24, 1854; see also Jeffrey, *Frontier Women*, 34–35.

58. CMSC, December 10, 1841; CCR octavo vols. "W," vol. 8, April 27, 1842, and May 9, 1842. In 1853, the *Palladium* noted, "Our citizens are lecture-crazy," November 23, 1853; Linda Blackman and Kim Etheridge, "The Worcester County Mechanics Association and Worcester's Cultural Enlightenment: 1853–1861," 94–112, unpublished manuscript, Interactive Qualifying Project, Worcester Polytechnic Institute, 1985, Worcester Collection, AAS; Edward P. Kimball, *Brinley Hall Album and Post 10 Sketch Book* (Worcester, Mass.: F.S. Blanchard, 1896). Elizabeth B. Clark argues that sympathy encouraged abolitionism and that this was especially true for evangelicals; "'The Sacred Rights of the Weak,'" 478–82.

59. CMSC, January 11, 1850; January 15, 1855; September 9, 1856 (emphasis in original); David M. Potter, *The Impending Crisis, 1848–1861* (New York: Harper Torchbooks, 1976), 199–200.

60. "Treasurer's Accounts, 1839–1840" and "Constitution of the Worcester Anti-Slavery Sewing Circle," Worcester Anti-Slavery Sewing Circle Record Book, 1839–1857, Manuscript Collection, Worcester Historical Museum, Worcester, Massachusetts. The WASSC's extant records consist of the constitution, the treasurer's accounts, and membership lists for 1839–1841, 1847–1849, 1853, and 1855–1857.

61. Membership lists for 1839–1841, 1847–1849, 1853, 1855–1857, Worcester Anti-Slavery Sewing Circle Record Book, Worcester Historical Museum. Even the extant membership lists are incomplete; the 1849 list, for example, includes only four names. It is therefore possible that the Hemenways remained members of the WASSC.

62. *Spy*, April 5, 1848; see also April 17, 1848; April 26, 1848; May 3, 1848. The ad also was signed by women outside of the city, as well as by several from Worcester who do not appear to have been members of the WASSC.

63. *Palladium*, April 26, 1848. Editor John S.C. Knowlton was fond of the phrase "Negrophilism" and hurled it at Martin Van Buren later that year; *Palladium*, September 6, 1848.

64. Stanton, *History of Woman Suffrage*, 1:256–57.

65. Sixteen WASSC members formally joined the Women's Rights Convention in 1850 and it is likely that still more attended. Not only are WASSC membership rosters missing for several years but the convention membership list included only those who formally joined, which represented about one in three in attendance. WASSC and Children's Friend Society members included Ann B. Earle, Mary Hadwen, Rebecca Goddard, Sarah A. Brown, and Mary Drew. Julia T. Harris and Ann B. Earle moved from membership in the WASSC to membership in the Female Employment Society.

On May 18, 1840 the WASSC noted "By cash received of Abby Kelley for Antislavery bags, books, cards, etc . . . 4.05." Worcester Anti-Slavery Sewing Circle Record Book, Worcester Historical Museum. "A.K. Foster" appears for the first time on the 1853 membership list; however, there is a four-year gap between the 1849 membership list and the 1853 membership list.

66. CCR octavo vols. "W," vol. 8, April 27, 1842; May 9, 1842.
67. Ann E. Jennison Diary, entries for June 15 and July 4, 1849, Jennison Family Papers, vol. 1; "Records of the Worcester Female Association, 1824–1864," Old South Church Records, octavo vols. 62 and 63.
68. Due to the incomplete record keeping typical of antebellum societies, the actual membership was likely much higher for both groups.
69. Anonymous Civil War Diary, 1861, Civil War Record Books, 1861–1865, box 5, folder 3, Worcester Collection, AAS; Soldiers' Relief Society Records, Manuscript Boxes "W" and octavo vols. "W," Manuscript Collection, AAS. For the sewing circles, see especially octavo vols. "W," vol. 1; for local fairs, see Sarah Theophilus Brown, ed., *Letters of Martha LeBaron Goddard, With Recollections by Nathan Haskell Dole* (Worcester, Mass.: Davis and Banister, 1901), 50–52.
70. "Fifth Annual Report of the Worcester Soldiers' Relief Committee," October 9, 1865, vol. 3, Soldier's Relief Society Records.
71. Seth Sweetser (Worcester) to Lucy Chase (Norfolk, Virginia), February 20, 1865, Chase Family Papers, box 2, folder 11.

3. MATERNAL POLITICS

1. Worcester Children's Friend Society, *First Annual Report of the Worcester Children's Friend Society* (Worcester, Mass.: n.p., 1850), 2–3. For the city's rapid growth in the 1840s and 1850s, see Doherty, *Society and Power.*
2. Unpublished records of the Worcester Children's Friend Society, octavo vols. "W," vol. 1, Manuscript Collection, American Antiquarian Society, Worcester, Massachusetts (hereafter cited as CFS, *Minutes*); *First Annual Report*, 3.
3. For an early overview of public support for poor and orphaned children, see Homer Folks, *The Care of Destitute, Neglected, and Delinquent Children* (Albany: Macmillan Company, 1900); for more recent work, see Leroy Ashby, *Endangered Children: Dependency, Neglect, and Abuse in American History* (New York: Twayne Publishers, 1997); Patricia Ferguson Clement, *Welfare and the Poor in the Nineteenth Century City: Philadelphia, 1800–1854* (Rutherford: Fairleigh-Dickinson University Press, 1988); Kenneth Cmiel, *A House of Another Kind: One Chicago Orphanage and the Tangle of Child Welfare* (Chicago: University of Chicago Press, 1995); Robert E. Cray, Jr., *Paupers and Poor Relief in New York City and Its Rural Environments, 1700–1830* (Philadelphia: Temple University Press, 1988); Joan Gittens, *Poor Relations: The Children of the State in Illinois, 1818–1990* (Urbana: University of Illinois Press, 1994); Peter C. Holloran, *Boston's Wayward Children: Social Services for Homeless Children, 1830–1930* (Rutherford: Fairleigh-Dickinson University Press, 1989); Michael Katz, *The Undeserving Poor: From the War on Poverty to the War on Welfare* (New York: Pantheon Books, 1989); Carol S. Lasser, "A 'Pleasingly Oppressive' Burden: The Transformation of Domestic Service and Female Charity in Salem, 1800–1840," *Essex Institute Historical Collections* 116 (July 1980): 156–75; Kathleen D. McCarthy, *Noblesse Oblige: Charity and Cultural Philanthropy in Chicago, 1849–*

1929 (Chicago: University of Chicago Press, 1982); Susan Lynne Porter, "The Benevolent Asylum—Image and Reality: The Care and Training of Female Orphans in Boston" (Ph.D. diss., Boston University, 1984); Susan L. Porter, "Victorian Values in the Marketplace: Single Women and Work in Boston, 1800–1850," in Susan L. Porter, ed., *Women of the Commonwealth: Work, Family, and Social Change in Nineteenth-Century Massachusetts* (Amherst: University of Massachusetts Press, 1994): 17–41; David J. Rothman, *The Discovery of the Asylum: Social Order and Disorder in the New Republic*, rev. ed. (Boston: Little, Brown and Company, 1990); Eric C. Schneider, *In the Web of Class: Delinquents and Reformers in Boston, 1810s-1930s* (New York: New York University Press, 1992); Peter L. Tyor and Jamil Zainaldin, "Asylum and Society: An Approach to Industrial Change," *Journal of Social History* 13 (fall 1979): 23–48. For a contemporary account of the problems of poor, orphaned, and abandoned children in New York City, see Charles Loring Brace, *The Dangerous Classes of New York, & Twenty Years' Work Among Them* (New York: Wynkoop and Hallenbeck, 1872).

For analysis of the social control thesis, see Clarke A. Chambers, "Toward a Redefinition of Welfare History," *Journal of American History* 73 (September 1986): 407–33; E. Wayne Carp, "Two Cheers for Orphanages," *Reviews in American History* 24 (spring 1996): 277–84. For the emphasis on class, see Schneider, *In the Web of Class*, 1 n. 1. Lori D. Ginzberg argues that gender was formative for antebellum reformers while class became dominant in the postbellum era in *Women and the Work of Benevolence*.

4. Scholars have noted women's role in the anti-institutional approach to childsaving but have not analyzed this development in terms of gender. Eric C. Schneider, for example, describes how the "ladies" of the postbellum Boston Children's Aid Society moved "boldly" to arrange placement for children in the face of male opposition but does not explain why; *In the Web of Class*, 68. Similarly, Timothy Hacsi argues that "most Protestant orphan asylums were founded by the type of women [Nancy] Hewitt calls benevolent" for whom "religion was important, often central," but does not otherwise analyze gender; Timothy A. Hacsi, "'A Plain and Solemn Duty': A History of Orphan Asylums in America," (Ph.D. diss., University of Pennsylvania, 1993), 56. See also Hewitt, *Women's Activism*; Lasser, "A 'Pleasingly Oppressive' Burden;" Lebsock, *Free Women of Petersburg*; Ryan, *Cradle of the Middle Class*; Porter, "The Benevolent Asylum;" Schneider, *In the Web of Class*; Holloran, *Boston's Wayward Children*.

5. For Charles Loring Brace, see Marilyn Irvin Holt, *The Orphan Trains: Placing Out in America* (Omaha: University of Nebraska Press, 1992); Stansell, *City of Women*, 198–216; Ashby, *Endangered Children*, 35–53; Thomas Bender, *Toward An Urban Vision: Ideas and Institutions in Nineteenth-Century America* (Lexington: University Press of Kentucky, 1975), 131–35. For the Boston Children's Mission see Holloran, *Boston's Wayward Children*, 42–49.

Not until 1882 did Massachusetts authorize boarding children in foster families, 152; Boston did not board children until 1889; Folks, *Care of Destitute, Neglected, and Delinquent Children*, 154–55. For a more recent history, see Ashby, *Endangered Children*.

6. For the significance of a maternalist ideology in connecting women to

the larger polity, see Katherine A. Lynch, "The Family and the History of Public Life," *Journal of Interdisciplinary History* 24 (spring 1994): 665–84, especially 676–79.

7. In 1852, there were approximately 10,000 vagrant children in New York City; Henry W. Thurston, *The Dependent Child: A Story of Changing Aims and Methods in the Care of Dependent Children* (New York: Columbia University Press, 1930), 97.

8. Charles Loring Brace, *The Best Method of Disposing of Our Pauper and Vagrant Children* (New York: Wynkoop, Hallenbeck and Tomas, 1859), 4, 11, 4–6 (emphasis in original).

9. The reports of the New York Children's Aid Society are available as *Annual Reports of the Children's Aid Society, Nos. 1–10, February 1854–February 1863* (reprint, New York: Arno Press, 1971). Brace was the society's founder, secretary, and author of the reports; CAS, *Sixth Annual Report*, 9 (emphasis in original); *First Annual Report*, 3; *Fourth Annual Report*, 11. The NYCAS attracted support from across the nation, including from Worcester; *Second Annual Report*, 54, 58.

10. CAS, *First Annual Report*, 8; Brace, *Best Method*, 13. Brace had numerous sources for children, including agents paid to find parents willing to send their children to what the CAS assured them would be better homes in the West. CAS, *First Annual Report*, 8; Stansell, *City of Women*, 210–12; CAS, *Third Annual Report*, 21; *Fifth Annual Report*, 13; Thurston, *Dependent Child*, 121; CAS, *Third Annual Report*, 8; *Fifth Annual Report*, 7; *Seventh Annual Report*, 28; *First Annual Report*, 4; *Second Annual Report*, 11–12. Christine Stansell questions Brace's statistics, suggesting that "where orphans were lacking, [the CAS] manufactured them;" *City of Women*, 210.

11. Brace, *Best Method*, 13; CAS, *Third Annual Report*, 9; *Fifth Annual Report*, 16; *Second Annual Report*, 15; *Fourth Annual Report*, 10; *Seventh Annual Report*, 8; *Fifth Annual Report*, 15, 63. Brace was not as interested in the problems of vagrant and homeless girls. While the CAS built a home for newsboys, it left the care and training of girls to unfunded women volunteers; CAS, *Fifth Annual Report*, 17. Brace offered no data to support his claim that girls were especially troublesome.

12. Brace, *Best Method*, 14; CAS, *Third Annual Report*, 10, 21; *Fifth Annual Report*, 13. For attitudes toward indentures, see Ashby, *Endangered Children*, 6–16, and for the CAS's lack of oversight, 50–51. Stephen B. Presser characterizes Brace's approach as "a rather radical departure" that contributed to the evolution of adoption law, and credits Brace with inspiring an 1873 New York adoption law. Presser offers insight into the development of adoption law but does not question Brace's views, in "The Historical Background of the American Law of Adoption," *Journal of Family Law* 11 (1971): 443–516.

13. CAS, *Sixth Annual Report*, 10; Brace, *Best Method*. In 1852, Brace noted that 25 percent of New York City's criminals were under the age of twenty-one; *First Annual Report*, 5; see also Holt, *Orphan Trains*.

14. Brace, *Best Method*, 14–15.

15. Ibid., 22; appendix, letter from "J.L.," Newton, New Jersey, December

14, 1859; letter from "G.D.," Hudson, Ohio, June 29, 1859; letter from "M.P.H.," Warren, Ohio, December 1, 1859; see also Holt, *Orphan Trains*, 94–96.

16. Brace, *Best Method*, appendix, letter from the "Rev. Edward T.," Kalamazoo, Michigan, December 9, 1859 (emphasis in original); appendix, letter from "W.W.," Hiram, Ohio, 1859.

17. Brace, *Best Method*, appendix, letter from "J.R.B.," Hudson, Ohio, November 25, 1859; CAS, *Fourth Annual Report*, 9; Ashby, *Endangered Children*, 50–51.

18. For Brace in Worcester, see Central Church Records, octavo vols. "W," vol. 24, September 9, 1856, Manuscript Collection, AAS; Blackman and Etheridge, "The Worcester County Mechanics Association," 100; CFS, Article 2, Constitution of the Children's Friend Society, *Appeal to the Public* (Worcester, Mass.: n.p., 1849), 5.

On May 3, 1848, the *Spy* reported that an infant had been literally left on a doorstep. There is no evidence, however, that this was anything but highly unusual. The editor's comment that "We are falling into *city habits* very readily" (emphasis in original) testified to a perception that particular kinds of troubles, such as child abandonment, accompanied urbanization.

Several studies of women and social reform discuss orphan asylums but none in depth; see Mary P. Ryan's analysis of the Utica Orphan Asylum in *Cradle of the Middle Class*, 186–229; Nancy A. Hewitt discusses the Rochester Orphan Asylum in *Women's Activism and Social Change*, 88–90, 94–95, 99, 114–115, 145–145, 175, 183, 194–195, 200–204, 220–21; Suzanne Lebsock describes the Petersburg orphan asylum in *Free Women of Petersburg*, 195–236. Susan Lynne Porter, in her analysis of the Boston Female Asylum, raises similar issues to those addressed here and argues that women's experience of dependency made it more difficult for them to view poor children and their families as deviant. Porter describes the ideology of the founders of the BFA as "benevolent maternalism;" Porter, "The Benevolent Asylum;" see also Porter, "Victorian Values in the Marketplace." Carol S. Lasser analyzes the Salem Female Charitable Society in "A 'Pleasingly Oppressive' Burden." Christine Stansell points out that the men and women of New York City's Children's Aid Society had different notions of how to resolve the problems of their city. CAS founder Charles Loring Brace and his salaried male assistants supported draining the dangerous elements out of the city; the unpaid women sought to strengthen working-class domestic life "to abolish class conflicts," Stansell, *City of Women*, 210, 214; see also Rothman, *Discovery of the Asylum*, 206–36; Holloran, *Boston's Wayward Children*, 248, 251; Schneider, *In the Web of Class*, 11–14, 23–31.

19. CFS, *Appeal to the Public*, 3–4.

20. Ibid.

21. See, for example, the Philadelphia House of Refuge, *An Appeal to the Public on Behalf of A House of Refuge for Coloured Juvenile Delinquents* (Philadelphia: T.K. and P.G. Collins, 1846); Hartford Orphan Asylum for Boys, *To the Citizens of Hartford: A Sketch of the Orphan Asylum for Boys* (Hartford: Elihu Gear, 1844).

22. See appendix A, tables 1 and 2. Data on CFS managers were compiled

from the society's annual reports, city directories, city tax lists, collections of vital statistics, local histories, church records, and family papers. Data on birthplace are available for sixty-one, or 84 percent, of the women; of these, thirty, or 49 percent, were from the city or county of Worcester. Of the remaining thirty-one women, eleven were from Massachusetts and three were from other northern states.

23. See appendix A, table 3. Biographical data were developed from the Collection of Worcester Vital Statistics, Worcester Room, Worcester Public Library; Emory Washburn, *Memoir of Hon. Levi Lincoln* (Cambridge, Mass.: John Wilson and Son, 1869); William Lincoln and Charles Hersey, *History of Worcester, Massachusetts, from its Earliest Settlement to September, 1836* (Worcester, Mass.: Charles Hersey, 1862), 202; Thomas R. Navin, *The Whitin Machine Works since 1831: A Textile Machinery Company in an Industrial Village* (Cambridge, Mass.: Harvard University Press, 1950), 5–20; H.G. Kittredge and A.C. Gould, *History of the American Card-Clothing Industry* (Worcester, Mass.: T.K. Earle Manufacturing, 1886), 16–20.

For the antebellum economy see, for example, Winifred B. Rothenberg, "The Emergence of a Capital Market in Rural Massachusetts, 1730–1838," *Journal of Economic History* 45 (December 1985): 781–808, and "The Emergence of Farm Labor Markets and the Transformation of the Rural Economy: Massachusetts, 1750–1855," *Journal of Economic History* 48 (September 1988): 537–66; Christopher Clark, *The Roots of Rural Capitalism: Western Massachusetts, 1780–1860* (Ithaca: Cornell University Press, 1990); Jonathan Prude, *The Coming of Industrial Order: Town and Factory Life in Rural Massachusetts, 1810–1860* (New York: Cambridge University Press, 1983).

24. The "pepperbox" was reputedly popular with Mississippi riverboat gamblers and was referred to in Mark Twain's *Roughing It*; cited in H.H. Thomas, *The Story of Allen and Wheelock Firearms* (Cincinnati: C.J. Krehbiel, 1965), 1–2; George Sumner Barton, *A Line of Men One Hundred Years Long: The Story of Rice, Barton & Fales, Inc.* (Worcester, Mass.: Rice, Barton and Fales, 1937), 20–23; *Worcester Almanac, Directory, and Business Advertiser, for 1845* (Worcester, Mass.: Henry J. Howland, 1845), 75; *List of Persons Assessed*, 25–26.

25. Rebecca Lincoln Newton, Marcia Knowlton, Fanny Bradley, and Maria Morse were the mothers of Hester Newton Wetherell, Sarah Knowlton Brown, Maria Bradley Wyman, and Maria Bigelow Morse, respectively. Sarah Griggs was the stepmother of Almira Griggs. Fanny Bradley joined the CFS after daughter Maria Bradley Wyman.

26. *National Aegis*, May 23, 1840. Contemporaries often exaggerated the equality of the city's economy. Several businesses were quite large and employed hundreds of workers; see Charles C. Buell, "The Workers of Worcester: Social Mobility and Ethnicity in a New England City, 1850–1880," (Ph.D. diss., New York University, 1974), 37–45; Robert J. Kolesar, "Politics and Policy in a Developing Industrial City: Worcester, Massachusetts, in the Late Nineteenth Century," (Ph.D. diss., Clark University, 1987), 36–78.

27. See appendix A, table 4; data compiled from *List of Persons Assessed in the Town of Worcester*. By the late 1840s, the fortunes of those at the top of the tax list had grown. An 1849 list of those worth more than $10,000 included

twenty-five CFS member families; in 1846, there had been twenty-two in this category. Moreover, the fortunes of the wealthiest were quite substantial: in 1850, Ann King Colton's husband was assessed at more than $50,000, Ann Buffum Earle's husband was assessed at more than $30,000, and Mary Brown, widowed in 1848, was assessed at $25,000; *Spy*, September 4, 1850.

28. *Spy*, April 25, 1832; City Ordinance No. 14, May 22, 1848, cited in *The Worcester Almanac, Directory, and Business Advertiser for 1849* (Worcester, Mass.: Henry J. Howland, 1849). For analysis of tax assessments, see Edward Pessen, "The Egalitarian Myth and the American Social Reality: Wealth, Mobility, and Equality in the 'Era of the Common Man,'" *American Historical Review* 76 (October 1971): 989–1034.

29. Peter J. Coleman, *Debtors and Creditors in America: Insolvency, Imprisonment for Debt, and Bankruptcy, 1607–1900* (Madison: State Historical Society of Wisconsin, 1974), 287, 285; Edward J. Balleisen, "Vulture Capitalism in Antebellum America: The 1841 Federal Bankruptcy Act and the Exploitation of Financial Distress," *Business History Review* 70 (winter 1996): 473–516; the statistics of business failure are from p. 476. Balleisen argues that politicians were slow to legislate bankruptcy relief and that the legislation was soon repealed. Paul Goodman argued that concern for the social effects of bankruptcy spurred the homestead exemption laws in "The Emergence of Homestead Exemption in the United States: Accommodation and Resistance to the Market Revolution, 1840–1880," *Journal of American History* 80 (September 1993): 470–98.

30. Christopher Columbus Baldwin, *Diary of Christopher Columbus Baldwin, 1829–1835* (Worcester, Mass.: American Antiquarian Society, 1901), 7, 33, 39; Eliza Bancroft Davis (Worcester) to John Davis (Washington, D.C.), undated but likely 1832, John Davis Papers, Manuscript Boxes "D," box 1, folder 4, Manuscript Collection, AAS; "Valuation List and Assessments for the Year 1834," Worcester Collection, box 1, folder 3, Manuscript Collection, AAS.

31. David A. Gerber, "Cutting Out Shylock: Elite Anti-Semitism and the Quest for Moral Order in the Mid-Nineteenth-Century Market Place," *Journal of American History* 69 (December 1982): 615–37; Wendy Gamber, "A Precarious Independence: Milliners and Dressmakers in Boston, 1860–1890," *Journal of Women's History* 4 (spring 1992): 60–88; Jeanne Whitney, "An Art That Requires Capital,'" 52–95.

32. Franklin P. Rice, *The Worcester Book: A Diary of Noteworthy Events in Worcester, Massachusetts, from 1657 to 1883* (Worcester, Mass.: Putnam, Davis and Company, 1884), 33, 38; *National Aegis*, September 18, 1850; *Spy*, November 10, 1847; *National Aegis*, August 15, 1849; [Clarendon Wheelock], *Carl's Tour in Main Street* (Worcester, Mass.: Sanford and Davis, 1888), 17–19; see also Toby L. Ditz, "Shipwrecked; or, Masculinity Imperiled: Mercantile Representations of Failure and the Gendered Self in Eighteenth-Century Philadelphia," *Journal of American History* 81 (June 1994): 51–80. Daniel A. Cohen finds that economic failure contributed to a rise in family violence in "Homicidal Compulsion and the Conditions of Freedom: The Social and Psychological Origins of Familicide in America's Early Republic," *Journal of Social History* 28 (summer 1995): 725–64.

33. Quoted in Waldo Lincoln, *The Worcester County Institution for Savings, 1828–1928* (Worcester, Mass.: WCIS, 1928), 73 n. 1.

34. For women in business, see Gamber, *The Female Economy*; Lucy Eversveld Murphy, "Business Ladies: Midwestern Women and Enterprise, 1850–1880," *Journal of Women's History* 3 (spring 1991): 65–89; for the invention of the gendered corporation, see Berthoff, "Conventional Mentality," 753–84. For women's legal rights, see Norma Basch, *In the Eyes of the Law: Women, Marriage, and Property in Nineteenth-Century New York* (Ithaca: Cornell University Press, 1982), especially 15–41, 70–112.

35. Stories in the popular press occasionally argued otherwise. In Lydia Sigourney's "The Father—An Instructive Sketch," a bankrupt family moves to the country and the wife and daughters take charge of the family economy. By embroidering, raising flowers, plaiting straw, painting maps, and sewing, the women pay off the family's debts and live happily ever after. Although it presents a highly unlikely solution to economic crisis, the story suggests that women were reluctant to accept the limits of their economic power. *Spy*, July 5, 1848.

36. Mary C. Todd (Fitchburg, Mass.) to Lucy Chase (Worcester), December 3, 1837, Chase Family Papers, Manuscript Boxes "C," box 1, folder 14, Manuscript Collection, AAS; Louisa Jane Trumbull Diary, entry for April 16, 1837, Trumbull Family Papers, Manuscript Boxes "T," box 1, folder 6, Manuscript Collection, AAS. The recurring panics also produced a body of literature that sought to make sense of it all; see Ann Fabian, "Speculation on Distress: The Popular Discourse of the Panics of 1837 and 1857," *Yale Journal of Criticism* 3 (1989): 127–42.

37. At least fifteen, or 27 percent, of the husbands of CFS members had declared bankruptcy, several more than once; George H. Harvey, *Court of Insolvency, County of Worcester. Index of Cases and Records, 1838–1897* (Worcester, Mass.: n.p., 1897). Because this source covered only Worcester, and because many CFS managers moved there as adults, the actual percentage of bankruptcies is likely greater. Nathaniel Paine, "Random Recollections of Worcester, 1839–1843," *Proceedings of the Worcester Society of Antiquity*, n.s., 6 (1880), 112; "The Lumber Business of Worcester," *Proceedings of the Worcester Society of Antiquity*, n.s., 5 (1879): 13–33; Chamberlin, "Trade of Worcester," 27–39, 32–33. Carol S. Lasser's study of the Salem Female Charitable Society also reveals the economic vulnerability of its founders, although Lasser draws different conclusions from her data; Lasser, "A 'Pleasingly Oppressive' Burden," 164.

38. CFS, *Thirty-Seventh Annual Report*, 4, 96.

39. Frances Trollope, *Domestic Manners*, 349–50; see also Charles Olliffe, *American Scenes: Eighteen Months in the New World*, trans. Ernest Falbo and Lawrence A. Wilson, (Painesville, Ohio: Lake Erie College Studies, 1964), 3:115.

40. *Palladium*, April 11, 1849. Residential data were developed from the city directories. See appendix A, table 5.

41. Anthony R. Taylor, *Worcester's Architectural Neighborhoods* (Worcester, Mass.: Worcester Historical Museum, 1984), 5–6, 9–13, 16–19.

42. See Frances Trollope's use of the term in *Domestic Manners of the Americans*, 283.

43. Data were collected from Franklin P. Rice, comp., *Worcester Births, Marriages, and Deaths* (Worcester, Mass.: Worcester Society of Antiquity, 1894); the vital statistics in the Worcester Room, Worcester Public Library; as well as the series of vital statistics of Massachusetts towns compiled by Franklin P. Rice. The figure of 2.8 children per woman is low, given prevailing fertility rates, and is likely the result of undercounting. The data were derived mostly from published sources; data uncovered by chance or from family histories makes it clear that these records were not comprehensive. In addition, many joined the CFS after their childbearing years and after they had moved to Worcester from other locations; their children were not included in Worcester town records and thus not included in the figures given here.

44. Eliza Bancroft Davis (Worcester) to John Davis (Washington, D.C.), December 14, 1831, John Davis Papers, box 1, folder 3; Rebekah Dean Salisbury (Worcester) to Catherine Dean Flint (Boston), December 1, 1841, Waldo Flint Papers, Manuscript Boxes "F," box 6, folder 10, Manuscript Collection, AAS; Matilda Butterworth Chase (Leicester, Mass.) to Anthony Chase (Worcester), undated but possibly 1840, Chase Family Papers, Manuscript Boxes "C," box 1, folder 7, Manuscript Collection, AAS.

45. Clayne L. Pope, "Adult Mortality in America before 1900: A View from Family Histories," in Claudia Goldin and Hugh Rockoff, eds., *Strategic Factors in Nineteenth Century American Economic History: A vol. to Honor Robert W. Fogel* (Chicago: University of Chicago Press, 1992), 268, 281, 283; see also John Komlos, "The Height and Weight of West Point Cadets: Dietary Change in Antebellum America," *Journal of Economic History* XLVII (December 1987): 897–927. For deaths in Worcester, see the *Spy*, January 7, 1829; January 19, 1831; January 3, 1849.

The "puzzle" of declining life expectancies in an era when the gross national product was growing at approximately 4.8 percent annually was pointed out by Robert Fogel; Pope, "Adult Mortality in America before 1900," 294. Barbara Logue suggests a link between economic development and the death rate in "In Pursuit of Prosperity: Disease and Death in a Massachusetts Commercial Port, 1660–1850," *Journal of Social History* 25 (winter 1991): 309–43.

46. Mary C. Beaudry, "Public Aesthetics Versus Personal Experience: Worker Health and Well-Being in 19th-Century Lowell, Massachusetts," *Historical Archaeology* 27 (1993): 94–95, 97; Joseph M. Carlin, "Pleasures of the Table: Eating and Drinking in the Early Republic," *Nutrition Today* 33 (March-April 1998): 71–76; Adelaide Isham Crossman Diary, undated entry for 1857, Crossman Family Diaries, octavo vols. "C," vol. 3, Manuscript Collection, AAS; Rebekah Dean Salisbury (Worcester) to Catherine Dean Flint (Boston), January 8, 1841, Waldo Flint Papers, box 6, folder 10; Rebekah Dean Salisbury (Worcester) to Catherine Dean Flint (Boston), October 26, 1840; March 9, 1840; Waldo Flint Papers box 6, folder 9; *Spy*, July 5, 1848; Stephen Salisbury (Cambridge, Mass.) to Elizabeth Tuckerman Salisbury (Worcester), June 26, 1817, cited in Hill, "Life at Harvard," 232. Ironically, the temperance movement, which dramatically decreased alcohol consumption between 1830 and 1860, may have contributed to poor health by reducing the daily caloric intake

of the newly temperate; see Mark Thornton, "Alcohol Consumption and the Standard of Living in Antebellum America," *Atlantic Economic Journal* 23 (June 1995), 156.

47. The *National Aegis* commented, "A much greater number of females have died from consumption than males, for five years and eight months, the excess being 18.98 per cent," October 8, 1851.

48. Sheila M. Rothman, *Living in the Shadow of Death: Tuberculosis and the Social Experience of Illness in American History* (New York: Basic Books, 1994), 2, 131, 13, 8, 120, 17; "Tuberculosis," *Clinical Reference Systems* (December 1997), 2250. From May to December, 1842, of 60 adult deaths, 23 (38 percent) died of consumption, "Record of Deaths in Worcester, Mass., May 10, 1842—December 30, 1849," folio vols. "W," vol. 7, Worcester Collection, Manuscript Collection, AAS.

49. Maria Allen (Worcester) to Lucy Chase (Philadelphia), September 24, 1843, Chase Family Papers, box 1, folder 2.

50. Levi Lincoln Newton (Worcester) to Hester Newton (Boston), February 12, 1844, Newton Family Papers, box 2, folder 3, Manuscript Collection, AAS; Thomas Chase (Worcester) to Lucy Chase (Philadelphia), December 9, 1843, Chase Family Papers, box 1, folder 10.

51. The cause of death is available for only twenty-seven, or 34 percent, of the managers; of these, tuberculosis was the cause of six deaths, or 22 percent. Rebecca Lincoln Newton (Richmond, Virginia) to Rejoice Newton (Worcester), May 9, 1847, Newton Family Papers, box 2, folder 3.

52. Receipt for Dr. John Green, Newton Family Papers, box 2, folder 1; receipt for pharmacist James Green, Newton Family Papers, box 2, folder 2; CFS, *Sixth Annual Report*, 14. For bleeding, see, for example, Shigehisa Kuriyama, "Interpreting the History of Bloodletting," *Journal of the History of Medicine and Allied Sciences* 50 (January 1995): 11–46.

53. Louisa Jane Trumbull Diary, entry for May 6, 1836, Trumbull Family Papers, box 1, folder 6; Rothman, *Living In the Shadow of Death*, 17.

54. Rothman, *Living In the Shadow of Death*, 65. Rothman applied this observation to both men and women but presented evidence only for men.

55. CFS, *Sixth Annual Report*, 12; Robert L. Bratton and Robert E. Nesse, "St. Anthony's Fire: Diagnosis and Management of Erysipelas," *American Family Physician* 51 (February 1, 1995): 401–4.

56. *Palladium*, January 6, 1841, cited in Thomas, *Story of Allen and Wheelock Firearms*, 6.

57. Rice, *Worcester Book*, 50–51; Duane H. Hurd, *History of Worcester County, Massachusetts* (Philadelphia: J.W. Lewis and Co., 1889), 2:1539; Buell, "Workers of Worcester," 60.

58. Leonard Moody Parker (Boston) to F.H. Kinnicutt (Worcester), March 19, 1837, Leonard Moody Parker Papers, Manuscript Boxes "P," Manuscript Collection, AAS.

59. Paine, "Random Recollections," 119; Eliza Bancroft Davis (Worcester) to John Davis (Washington, D.C.), February 6, 1832, John Davis Papers, box 1, folder 4; Eliza Bancroft Davis (Worcester) to John Davis (Washington, D.C.),

undated but likely June, 1831 (emphasis in original), John Davis Papers, box 1, folder 3. For William Lincoln, see also Hurd, *History of Worcester County*, 2:1526; Charles H. Chase, "William Lincoln," *Proceedings of the American Antiquarian Society*, n.s., 7 (1891):424–36; Lydia Stiles Foster (Worcester) to Mary Stiles Newcomb (Baton Rouge), February 9, 1843, Foster Family Papers, box 7, folder 1; see also the Newton Family Papers, especially box 2, folder 3.

60. Thirty-one, or 42 percent, of the managers opened their homes to boarders between 1848 and 1860. Some, like Charlotte Foxcroft, did so to earn money; others, such as Mary Brown, did so for companionship; still others, such as Ann Earle, did so out of compassion. The incidence of boarding appears to have been representative of the era. Tamara K. Hareven estimates that from one-half to one-third of all antebellum urban households included boarders at some point and argues that "The family selected those aspects of traditional culture that were most useful in coping with new conditions and adopted them to new needs." Tamara K. Hareven, "The History of the Family and the Complexity of Social Change," *American Historical Review* 96 (February 1991): 95–124, especially 105, 115; see also John Modell and Tamara K. Hareven, "Urbanization and the Malleable Household: An Examination of Boarding and Lodging in American Families," *Journal of Marriage and the Family* 35 (August 1973): 467–79; Steven Ruggles, "The Transformation of American Family Structure," *American Historical Review* 99 (February 1994): 103–28; Howard P. Chudacoff, "New Branches on the Tree: Household Structure in Early Stages of the Family Cycle in Worcester, Massachusetts, 1860–1880," *Proceedings of the American Antiquarian Society*, n.s., 86 (1977): 303–20. For the importance of disaggregating family history to reveal the internal dynamics of family life, see Lynch, "The Family and the History of Public Life," 665–84. For a discussion of the difficulties conceptualizing "the family," see Stephanie Coontz, *The Social Origins of Private Life: A History of American Families, 1600–1900* (New York: Verso, 1988), especially 12–18.

4. "RACHEL WEEPING FOR HER CHILDREN"

1. Unpublished records of the Worcester Children's Friend Society, octavo vols. "W," vol. 1, Manuscript Collection, American Antiquarian Society, Worcester, Massachusetts (hereafter cited as CFS, *Minutes*); quote from the Worcester Children's Friend Society, *Appeal to the Public*, 5.

2. *First Annual Report of the Worcester Children's Friend Society*, 4.

3. CFS, *Minutes*, August, 1858; November, 1858; December, 1863; July, 1864; April, 1849; October, 1858; *Eleventh Annual Report of the Managers of the Worcester Children's Friend Society* (Worcester, Mass.: Edward R. Fiske, 1860), 9; *Ninth Annual Report of the Worcester Children's Friend Society* (Worcester, Mass.: Earle & Drew, 1858), 5. Not until 1930, when a male social worker was hired to supervise the older boys, did a man become part of the society's daily affairs; *Fiftieth Annual Report of the Children's Friend Society* (Worcester, Mass.: O.B. Wood, 1899), 8.

4. The churches involved were Protestant and included the Society of Friends and the Universalists. Neither the Catholic Church nor the African Methodist Episcopal Zion Church were included. CFS, *Minutes*, March, 1851; July 1853. For Ichabod Washburn, see Henry T. Cheever, ed., *Autobiography and Memorials of Ichabod Washburn* (Boston: D. Lothrop and Company, 1879).

5. CFS, *First Annual Report*, 11; *Fourth Annual Report of the Worcester Children's Friend Society* (Worcester, Mass.: n.p., 1853), 14; *Seventh Annual Report of the Worcester Children's Friend Society* (Worcester, Mass.: Henry J. Howland, 1856), 15.

6. CFS, *Tenth Annual Report of the Worcester Children's Friend Society* (Worcester, Mass.: Edward R. Fiske, 1859), 12; *Fourth Annual Report*, 15; *Seventeenth Annual Report of the Managers of the Worcester Children's Friend Society* (Worcester, Mass.: Edward R. Fiske, 1866), 7; *Seventh Annual Report*, 16; *Fourth Annual Report*, 13; *Third Annual Report of the Worcester Children's Friend Society* (Worcester, Mass.: n.p., 1852), 7; *Sixteenth Annual Report of the Managers of the Worcester Children's Friend Society* (Worcester, Mass.: Edward R. Fiske, 1865), 7; *Second Annual Report of the Worcester Children's Friend Society* (Worcester, Mass.: n.p., 1851), 11, 12; *Fifth Annual Report of the Worcester Children's Friend Society* (Worcester, Mass.: Henry J. Howland, 1854), 10, 16; *Seventh Annual Report*, 15; *Third Annual Report*, 9–12, 7; *Eighth Annual Report of the Worcester Children's Friend Society* (Worcester, Mass.: Edward R. Fiske, 1857), 13; *Tenth Annual Report*, 11.

7. CFS, *Seventeenth Annual Report*, 7; *Spy*, March 16, 1867; *Third Annual Report*, 7; *Eighth Annual Report*, 14; *Fifth Annual Report*, 14; *Eleventh Annual Report*, 12; *Sixth Annual Report*, 13.

8. CFS, *Sixth Annual Report*, 5 (emphasis in original); *Second Annual Report*, 10; *Eighth Annual Report*, 6; Worcester *Palladium*, November 19, 1851; *Second Annual Report*, 12; *Third Annual Report*, 7, 14; *Eighth Annual Report*, 14; *Minutes*, April, 1870; *Eighth Annual Report*, 13; *Fourteenth Annual Report*, 6–7. Other legacies included $523 from the estate of F.W. Gale in 1856, *Eighth Annual Report*, 13; $1,880 from the estate of Mary B. Merrick, *Minutes*, October 1866; $1,000 from Advisor Ichabod Washburn, $10,000 from the estate of Pliny Merrick in 1870, *Minutes*, April, 1870. The largest donation in the nineteenth century came from the estate of its longtime Treasurer Hester Newton Wetherell, who left the society $20,000 upon her death in 1898.

9. CFS, *Twelfth Annual Report*, 6–7; *Minutes*, February, 1859; *Second Annual Report*, 9; *Twelfth Annual Report*, 6–7; *Sixteenth Annual Report*, 8; *Tenth Annual Report*, 12; *Eleventh Annual Report*, 6, 10, 12. For a contemporary assessment of Worcester's fairs, see Brown, *Letters of Martha LeBaron Goddard*, 4–7, 50–51, 74.

10. CFS, *Tenth Annual Report*, 12; *Fifth Annual Report*, 8–9; *Second Annual Report*, 7; *Sixth Annual Report*, 5; *Ninth Annual Report*, 5, 11; *Fifth Annual Report*, 8–9 (emphasis in original).

11. CFS, *Sixteenth Annual Report*, 7; *Fourth Annual Report*, 12–13; *Eighth Annual Report*, 7, 15; *Sixteenth Annual Report*, 7; Treasurer's Reports: *Third An-*

nual Report, Fourth Annual Report, Fifth Annual Report, Sixth Annual Report; Tenth Annual Report, 11–12.

12. CFS, *First Annual Report,* 9; *Minutes,* October, 1858; *Eleventh Annual Report,* 6; *Fifth Annual Report,* 24; *Eighth Annual Report,* 9. It is also possible that the managers did not think the city would adequately subsidize the CFS, for in the 1850s city officials were intent on reducing spending; see Kolesar, "Politics and Policy," 94 and appendix E, 329–32.

13. CFS, *Tenth Annual Report,* 4–5; for the city's offer, see *Minutes,* November, 1858.

14. CFS, *Eleventh Annual Report,* 10; *Minutes,* June 1859. The annual report did not explicitly criticize city officials, whose cooperation the CFS still needed, but the women's opinion of the city's actions is suggested by the atypical curtness of the language as well as by what was *not* expressed, namely, gratitude. Timothy A. Hacsi argues that antebellum state or municipal governments "often" provided some support to private orphan asylums, "'A Plain and Solemn Duty': A History of Orphan Asylums in America," (Ph.D. diss., University of Pennsylvania, 1993), 64–65.

15. CFS, *Seventh Annual Report,* 8–9.

16. CFS, *Second Annual Report,* 7; *Seventh Annual Report,* 30; *Eighth Annual Report,* 23; *Seventh Annual Report,* 28; see also Porter, "The Benevolent Asylum." Porter's study indicates that the Worcester women's assessment of the Boston Female Asylum was fairly accurate; 257–59. For the asylum movement, see Rothman, *Discovery of the Asylum;* for the development of non-institutional approaches, see Peter L. Tyor and Jamil S. Zainaldin, "Asylum and Society," 23–48, especially 26–32.

17. CFS, *Second Annual Report,* 5; *Seventh Annual Report,* 33; *Eighth Annual Report,* 23.

18. Joseph Ben-Or, "The Law of Adoption in the United States: Its Massachusetts Origins and the Statute of 1851," *New England Historical and Genealogical Register* 130 (October 1976): 259–69, data from p. 266; see also Presser, "The Historical Background of the American Law of Adoption," 443–516; Lloyd Bonfield, "Marriage, Property & the 'Affective Family,'" *Law and History Review* 1 (fall 1983): 297–312; C.M.A. McCauliffe, "The First English Adoption Law and Its American Precursors," *Seton Hall Law Review* 16 (1986): 656–77; Grossberg, *Governing the Hearth,* especially 268–77.

19. "Indenture Agreement between Rejoice Newton, Charles White, Daniel Waldo Lincoln, and Joseph Mason, June 18, 1851," Newton Family Papers, Manuscript Boxes "N," box 2, folder 1, Manuscript Collection, AAS. For Articles of Indenture, see Grossberg, *Governing the Hearth,* 259–65. David J. Rothman argues that indentures attempted "to erect legal barriers against parental intervention" and that reformers sought unquestioned control; *Discovery of the Asylum,* 221. For an overview of childsaving, see Ashby, *Endangered Children.*

20. CFS, *Minutes,* May, 1849; March, 1849.

21. CFS, *First Annual Report,* 5; see also Ginzberg, *Women and the Work of Benevolence,* 36–66.

22. "An act to incorporate the Worcester Children's Friend Society," *Massachusetts State Laws*, chapter 88, 1849; for women's legal rights, see Basch, *In the Eyes of the Law* and Grossberg, *Governing the Hearth*.

23. CFS, *Tenth Annual Report*, 15; *Minutes*, April, 1849.

24. CFS, *Minutes*, June, 1849.

25. In 1849, Earle and Buffum were the Visiting Committee for January, June, and December; Brown served in February and July. CFS, *Minutes*, February, 1850; August 1853.

26. "An Act in Addition to an Act to Incorporate the Worcester Children's Friend Society," *Massachusetts Special Laws*, chapter 61, 1851.

27. CFS, *Minutes*, 1851.

28. See appendix A, table 6; CFS, *Eighth Annual Report*, 11. From 1849 to 1860, the *Minutes* named slightly more than 200 children, but many by family group, e.g., "the O'Grady children." Because it is unclear how many O'Gradys there were, if we deem any family group to equal at least two children, a total of 204 can be considered a conservative estimate. Corroborative evidence is scarce and estimates vary. The *Twenty-First Annual Report* counted 525 children from 1849 to 1870 (p. 6) while the *Twenty-Fifth Annual Report* indicates 825 from 1849 to 1874 (p. 5).

Suzanne Lebsock describes the Petersburg Female Orphan Asylum as "small," with "only fifteen or at the outside twenty girls in residence;" *The Free Women of Petersburg: Status and Culture in a Southern Town, 1784–1860* (New York: Norton, 1984), 211. The Salem Female Charitable Society cared for only eighty-two girls in thirty-six years; Lasser, "A 'Pleasingly Oppressive' Burden," 156–175, figure from p. 167. Susan Porter's analysis of the Boston Female Asylum includes more children but covers a much longer time span: 386 children in forty years; "The Benevolent Asylum," 202.

29. See appendix A, table 7. It was much more common for asylums to assist only one sex, such as the Boston Female Asylum, the Salem Female Charitable Society, the Petersburg Female Orphan Asylum, the Boston Asylum for Indigent Boys, or the Hartford Orphan Asylum for Boys. Others, such as the New York Children's Aid Society or the Boston Children's Mission, did not exclude girls but gave preference to boys.

In 1879, the CFS noted that twenty-seven of the thirty-three children at the home were boys for "there is a premium on girls. A bright, active girl, if indentured here, is soon snatched away." Unattributed newspaper clipping of the CFS meeting of January 25, 1879, Worcester Children's Friend Society envelope, Newspaper Clipping File, Worcester Historical Museum.

30. Timothy J. Meagher, "'Irish All the Time': Ethnic Consciousness Among the Irish in Worcester, Massachusetts, 1880–1905," *Journal of Social History* 19 (winter 1985): 273–303; Vincent E. Powers, "Invisible Immigrants: The Pre-Famine Irish Community in Worcester, Massachusetts, from 1826 to 1860," (Ph.D. diss., Clark University, 1976); Timothy Meagher, "Irish, American, Catholic: Irish-American Identity in Worcester, Massachusetts, 1880 to 1920," in Timothy Meagher, ed., *From Paddy to Studs: Irish-American Communities in the Turn of the Century Era, 1880–1920* (Westport, Conn.: Greenwood Press,

1986): 75–92; Thomas H. O'Connor, "The Irish in New England," *New England Historical and Genealogical Register* 139 (July 1985): 187–95; Buell, "The Workers of Worcester," 48–79; Hasia R. Diner, *Erin's Daughters in America: Irish Immigrant Women in the Nineteenth Century* (Baltimore: Johns Hopkins University Press, 1983), 41.

31. *Spy*, February 17, 1847; February 24, 1847.

32. CFS, *First Annual Report*, 7–8; *Third Annual Report*, 8.

33. Hewitt, *Women's Activism*, 88–90. See appendix A, table 8; CFS, *Eighth Annual Report*, 25.

34. CFS, *Eleventh Annual Report*, 20; *First Annual Report*, 7; Edward Everett Hale, *Letter on Irish Emigration* (Boston: Phillips, Sampson and Co., 1852), 36; see also Edward Everett Hale, Jr., ed., *The Life and Letters of Edward Everett Hale*, (Boston: Little, Brown and Co., 1917), 1:2, 186, 212, 218, 230, 237–38.

35. CFS, *First Annual Report*, 7; *Third Annual Report*, 12; *Ninth Annual Report*, 13.

36. Duane H. Hurd, *History of Worcester County, Massachusetts*, 2:1478; Margaret A. Erskine, *Heart of the Commonwealth, Worcester: An Illustrated History* (Woodland Hills, Calif.: Windsor Publications, 1981), 62; Hurd, *History of Worcester County*, 2:1517; Timothy Meagher, "'Why Should We Care for A Little Trouble or A Walk through the Mud': St. Patrick's and Columbus Day Parades in Worcester, Massachusetts, 1845–1915," *New England Quarterly* 57 (March 1984): 5–26; Buell, "Workers of Worcester," 86–179; Hurd, *History of Worcester County*, 2:1528; Timothy J. Meagher, "The Delayed Development of Parochial Education among Irish Catholics in Worcester," *Historical Journal of Massachusetts* 12 (January 1984): 44–59; Roy Rosenzweig, *Eight Hours for What We Will: Workers and Leisure in An Industrial City, 1870–1920* (New York: Cambridge University Press, 1983). Hasia R. Diner argues that Irish immigrant families were afflicted by high rates of male desertion and that social services for women were lacking; *Erin's Daughters*, 59, 120–22. For Nativism in Worcester, see Anbinder, *Nativism and Slavery*, especially 20–51; Buell, "Workers of Worcester," 67–71.

37. Statistics were compiled from the series published by the Commonwealth of Massachusetts, *Abstract of the Returns of the Overseers of the Poor in Massachusetts, for 1837* (Boston: Secretary of the Commonwealth of Massachusetts, 1838) [and for 1840, 1841, 1842, 1843, 1844, 1845, 1846, 1847, 1848, 1849, 1850, 1851]; "Report of the Overseers of the Poor," *City Document, No. 12 . . . the Annual Reports of the Several City Officers, for the Municipal Year Ending Jan. 4, 1858* (Worcester, Mass.: Edward R. Fiske, 1858); *Report of . . . the Overseers of the Poor* (Worcester, Mass.: *National Aegis*, 1847), 17.

Claudia Goldin and Robert A. Margo found that antebellum wages increased but that shocks to wages "had persistent effects on real wages in the short run, lasting as long as five years" and led to urban unemployment, in "Wages, Prices, and Labor Markets before the Civil War," in Goldin and Rockoff, eds., *Strategic Factors*, 67–93, quote from p. 69. Similarly, Kenneth L. Sokoloff and Georgia C. Villaflor found a rise in real wages from 1820 to 1860 in the New England manufacturing sector but conclude that the economy "remained quite vulnerable to extreme fluctuations in agricultural conditions and other such disturbances," in "The Market for Manufacturing Workers during Early Industrialization: The American Northeast, 1820 to 1860," in Goldin and Rockoff, eds., *Strategic Factors*, 29–65, quote from p. 62. For the emergence of the market, see Sellers, *The Market Revolution*.

38. *Palladium*, October 21, 1857; November 25, 1857; December 2, 1857; January 7, 1857.

39. See appendix A, table 9. Stansell, *City of Women*, 12.

40. CFS, *Seventh Annual Report*, 14.

41. CFS, *Minutes*, June, 1854; October, 1854; May 1857; January, 1854; November, 1856; August, 1854; August, 1859; May, 1858; May, 1853; April, 1854 (emphasis in original); March, 1853. For boarding services, see the brief discussion of Boston's Temporary Home for the Destitute, in Tyor and Zainaldin, "Asylum and Society;" Ashby, *Endangered Children*, 28; Hacsi, "'A Plain and Solemn Duty,'" 49.

The official number of boarding cases was 38, or 18.6 percent. Because boarding often was an informal arrangement, the total was likely much greater than indicated here. Twenty cases (12 percent) specified poverty as the reason for the child's arrival at the home. However, because the CFS's purpose was to help the poor, and because most parents gave up their children only reluctantly, it is likely that poverty accounted for most of the children at the home. Moreover, with the exception of a handful of cases of abandonment and orphanage, the records never cited any other explanation.

42. CFS, *Minutes*, February, 1849; July, 1850; November, 1850; August, 1859; July, 1853; September, 1853; February, 1854. As a point of comparison, in the 1840s Worcester's domestic servants earned seven to nine shillings a week; Mrs. E.O.P. Sturgis, "Chestnut Street, about 1840," *Proceedings of the Worcester Society of Antiquity*, n.s., 18 (1902), 89.

43. CFS, *Minutes*, January, 1853; April, 1853; June, 1854; July, 1854; September, 1854; September, 1859; June, 1860; August, 1853.

44. CFS, *Minutes*, March 1849; April, 1860; May, 1860; January, 1854; February, 1854; September 1854; August, 1853; June, 1851; August, 1851; April, 1850; November, 1851; January, 1853. For women's contributions to the family economy, see Boydston, *Home and Work*.

45. CFS, *Minutes*, February, 1855; April, 1856; April, 1859.

46. The children who were apprenticed were males in their mid-teens for whom adoptive homes could not be found.

David J. Rothman in particular has argued that indentures reflected the desire of reformers to control the poor. Rothman does not analyze how indentures worked in practice and only briefly characterizes them as "rigid;" *Discovery of the Asylum*, 221–25. For a comparison, see Ashby, *Endangered Children*, 51. When historians do examine indentures, it is usually in the context of arranging increasingly obsolete apprenticeships; see, for example, Lebsock, *Free Women of Petersburg*, 202–12. For apprenticeship, see W.J. Rorabaugh, *The Craft Apprentice: From Franklin to the Machine Age in America* (New York: Oxford University Press, 1986); Christopher Clark, ed., *The Diary of an Apprentice Cabi-*

netmaker: Edward Jenner Carpenter's "Journal," 1844–45 (Worcester, Mass.: American Antiquarian Society, 1988).

47. CFS, *Minutes*, April, 1854; September, 1854; December, 1859; May, 1853; January, 1855; March, 1855.

48. CFS, *Fourth Annual Report*, 6 (emphasis in original).

49. CFS, *Minutes*, March, 1851; *Fourth Annual Report*, 8. The details of the Kelly case were drawn from the *Fourth Annual Report*, 7–10, unless otherwise noted.

50. *Spy*, July 16, 1851.

51. CFS, *Fourth Annual Report*, 7–10.

52. CFS, *Minutes*, April, 1852; May, 1852; June, 1852; March, 1853; April, 1853.

53. CFS, *Minutes*, June, 1850; August, 1850; June, 1849; August, 1849.

54. Eric C. Schneider also points out the practical limits on antebellum welfare organizations, noting "it is easy to exaggerate their power and impact upon families," *In the Web of Class*, 9.

55. CFS, *Minutes*, February, 1859; April, 1859; May, 1854; August, 1854; July, 1857; November, 1857; May, 1858.

56. CFS, *Minutes*, April, 1857; August, 1857; September, 1857; February, 1855; September, 1855; October, 1856. The records do not indicate the nature of the suspicions the board harbored about Mrs. Ashton.

57. CFS, *Minutes*, June, 1849; April, 1854; April, 1850; December, 1853; September, 1857; January, 1858; May, 1858; January, 1853; *Fourth Annual Report*, 11; *Minutes*, March, 1853; February, 1854; August, 1854; May, 1855; August, 1854; June, 1855; March, 1856; February, 1849; March, 1849; April, 1849.

58. Barbara Brenzel found a similar dynamic at work at the nearby Lancaster School for Girls in *Daughters of the State: A Social Portrait of the First Reform School for Girls in North America, 1856–1905* (Cambridge, Mass.: MIT University Press, 1983), 7–8.

59. CFS, *Minutes*, March, 1849; July, 1853.

60. CFS, *Fourth Annual Report*, 6; *Third Annual Report*, 11; *Ninth Annual Report*, 10.

61. CFS, *Ninth Annual Report*, 9–10.

62. CFS, *Second Annual Report*, 6; *Twenty-seventh Annual Report*, 3; *Minutes*, October, 1849, to September, 1854; *Tenth Annual Report*, 8.

63. For the newly affectionate family, see Ruth M. Bloch, "American Feminine Ideals in Transition: The Rise of the Moral Mother, 1785–1815," *Feminist Studies* 4 (June 1978): 101–26; Ruth M. Bloch, "The Gendered Meanings of Virtue in Revolutionary America," *Signs* 13 (autumn 1987): 37–58; Cott, *Bonds of Womanhood*, 160–68; Douglas, *Feminization of American Culture*, 44–79; Dye and Smith, "Mother Love," 329–53; Grossberg, *Governing the Hearth*, xi-xii, 6, 8–9, 17, 24–27; Sylvia D. Hoffert, "'A Very Peculiar Sorrow': Attitudes toward Infant Death in the Urban Northeast, 1800–1860," *American Quarterly* 39 (winter 1987): 601–16; Jan Lewis, "Mother's Love: The Construction of an Emotion in Nineteenth-Century America," in Andrew E. Barnes and Peter N. Stearns, eds., *Social History and Issues in Human Consciousness* (New York: New York

University Press, 1989): 209–29; Jan Lewis, *The Pursuit of Happiness: Family and Values in Jefferson's Virginia* (New York: Cambridge University Press, 1983); Mary P. Ryan, *The Empire of the Mother: American Writings about Domesticity, 1830–1860* (New York: Institute for Research in History and Haworth Press, 1982), 45–60; Rosemarie Zagarri, "Morals, Manners, and the Republican Mother," *American Quarterly* 44 (June 1992): 192–215.

64. Grossberg, *Governing the Hearth*, 270–77; CFS, *Twenty-Fifth Annual Report*, 5. The Boston Female Asylum, the Charleston Orphan House, and the Orphan Asylum of Petersburg all bound out the children under their care as workers.

65. CFS, *Fifth Annual Report*, 8; *Seventh Annual Report*, 34.

66. CFS, *Minutes*, March, 1853 (emphasis in original); *Ninth Annual Report*, 13.

67. CFS, *Fourth Annual Report*, 12; *Minutes*, May, 1858; March, 1853; September, 1853; September, 1853.

68. CFS, *Fifth Annual Report*, 13; *Minutes*, May, 1859; July, 1858. The figure of sixty-two adoptions from 1849 to 1854 is probably optimistic; the *Minutes* record numerous instances where the managers assumed adoption would occur only to have to find another home for the child. Toward the end of the period under study, the managers ceased keeping a log of placements and turned the task over to the matron, Tamerson White. If White kept records, they are not extant, but it seems more likely that she did not. Asked if she had kept track of what happened to the children, White reportedly replied, "I have not. I have looked after each child as long as it seemed necessary for me to do so, but have been too busy with my work to note results." Quoted in C.A.K. Poole, "The Cottager," Worcester Children's Friend Society envelope, Pamphlet Collection, Worcester Historical Museum. For adoption, see Ben-Or, "The Law of Adoption"; Presser, "The Historical Background of the American Law of Adoption"; McCauliffe, "The First English Adoption Law and Its American Precursors"; Grossberg, *Governing the Hearth*, 268–77.

69. CFS, *Fifth Annual* Report, 4; unattributed newspaper clippings, Worcester Children's Friend Society envelope, Newspaper Clipping File, Worcester Historical Museum; "Report of the Secretary, Mrs. Rebecca B. Wheeler, Annual Meeting, 1886," Worcester Children's Friend Society envelope, Pamphlet Collection, Worcester Historical Museum. For the difficulties caused by an incompetent or ill-tempered matron, see Porter, "The Benevolent Asylum."

In the fall of 1849, the sheriff of Worcester County, John Waldo Lincoln, brother of Manager Rebecca Lincoln Newton, donated a large house on Pine Street in a working-class neighborhood. The children stayed here only until they were placed with relatives, or a foster or adoptive family. Sometimes the stay was brief, sometimes it was longer, but the home was not intended to be a permanent home for any child.

70. CFS, *Third Annual Report*, 10; Article 8, Constitution of the CFS, *Appeal to the Public* (Worcester, Mass.: n.p., 1849), 6. For women and teaching, see Kathryn Kish Sklar, *Catharine Beecher: A Study in American Domesticity* (New Haven: Yale University Press, 1973), 180–82; Richard M. Bernard and Maris

A. Vinovskis, "The Female School Teacher in Ante-Bellum Massachusetts," *Journal of Social History* 10 (spring 1977): 332–45; Joel Perlmann, Silvana R. Siddali, and Keith Whitescarver, "Literacy, Schooling, and Teaching among New England Women, 1730–1820," *History of Education Quarterly* 37 (summer 1997): 118–39; Julie A. Mattaei, *An Economic History of Women in America: Women's Work, the Sexual Division of Labor, and the Development of Capitalism* (New York: Schocken Books, 1982), 179–81; Lebsock, *Free Women of Petersburg*, 172–76. Catherine M. Scholten commented that "every woman who gave birth automatically acquired a teaching certificate," in *Childbearing in American Society, 1650–1850* (New York: New York University Press, 1985), 75.

71. CFS, *Eighth Annual Report*, 5; *First Annual Report*, 6–7.

72. CFS, *Tenth Annual Report*, 8; *Sixth Annual Report*, 8–9.

73. CFS, *Eighth Annual Report*, 5; *Seventh Annual Report*, 6.

74. CFS, *Minutes*, February, 1850; *Second Annual Report*, 9.

75. CFS, *Minutes*, May 1859; *Eighteenth Annual Report*, 7, 8; White quotation from *Fiftieth Annual Report*, 47. Adopting a child made White a respectable but unmarried mother. CFS, *Minutes*, October, 1874; *Ninth Annual Report*, 13; *Thirty-second Annual Report*, 5.

The classic discussion of dress as a marker of social and economic status is Alexis de Tocqueville, *Democracy in America*; for more recent work, see Halttunen, *Confidence Men*.

76. CFS, *Minutes*, May, 1859; *Second Annual Report*, 6; February, 1859; May, 1863; *Sixteenth Annual Report*, 4–5.

77. CFS, *Fiftieth Annual Report*, 46; *Minutes*, June, 1859; *Seventh Annual Report*, 7; *Minutes*, February, 1860; March, 1860. According to the published report, revoking a foster family's custodial care "rarely occur[s]." In fact, the Board meetings discussed many such cases.

78. For stories of imperiled orphans, see, for example, *National Aegis*, March 14, 1849, and January 1, 1851. The murder of Prudence Arnold was covered in the *Spy*, February 7, 1849, and February 14, 1849; *National Aegis*, February 7, 1849, and February 2, 1850. For domestic violence see, for example, Ashby, *Endangered Children*; Linda Gordon, *Heroes of Their Own Lives: The Politics and History of Family Violence, Boston, 1880–1900* (New York: Viking, 1988); Elizabeth Pleck, *Domestic Tyranny: The Making of American Social Policy against Family Violence from Colonial Times to The Present* (New York: Oxford University Press, 1987).

79. CFS, *Tenth Annual Report*, 7.

80. CFS, *Minutes*, March, 1849; August, 1849; February, 1850; March, 1850. The *Minutes* habitually couched such discussions in oblique phrases; thus, the nature of Tommy Wright's complaint is unclear.

81. Susan Porter states that the Boston Female Asylum indentured children "without warranty" and refused to take them back; "Benevolent Asylum," 179. Peter C. Holloran adds that the BFA accepted only "Yankee girls; Catholic, Black, and illegitimate girls were usually refused . . . as were girls with a criminal in the family;" *Boston's Wayward Children*, 35.

82. CFS, *Minutes*, February, 1854; *Sixth Annual Report*, 13; *Minutes*, June, 1850.

83. CFS, *Twenty-seventh Annual Report*, 5. The *Minutes* do not detail debates over policy issues such as accepting or rejecting infants, but it is apparent that such applications provoked considerable discussion; *Minutes*, August, 1849; December, 1853; *Second Annual Report*, 6.

84. CFS, *Minutes*, March, 1849; June 1857; March, 1853; March, 1854; June, 1860; *Twelfth Annual Report*, 3; *Minutes*, March, 1854; August, 1860.

85. CFS, *Tenth Annual Report*, 9; *Twelfth Annual Report*, 4.

86. CFS, *Minutes*, March, 1853; September, 1853; *Third Annual Report*, 12; *Thirteenth Annual Report*, 8; September, 1853.

87. Caleb Wall, *Reminiscences of Worcester from the Earliest Period, Historical and Genealogical* (Worcester, Mass.: Tyler and Seagrave, 1877), 155; Worcester *Aegis and Gazette*, October 5, 1884. The decision to build separate schools for blacks and whites was discussed in the meetings of the Board of Selectmen, November 14 and November 21, 1831; Franklin P. Rice, ed., *Worcester Town Records, 1817–1832* (Worcester, Mass.: Worcester Society of Antiquity, 1883), 342, 350; *Inscriptions from the Burial Ground on Mechanic Street* (Worcester, Mass.: Worcester Society of Antiquity, 1879), 68, 96; Business card for William Brown, Brown Family Papers, folder 1, Manuscript Collection, AAS.

88. For antislavery, see James Mooney, "Antislavery in Worcester County, Massachusetts: A Case Study," (Ph.D. diss., Clark University, 1971). Mooney addresses women's activism briefly, 183–213; for Levi Lincoln, 4. See also Erskine, *Heart of the Commonwealth*, 45; Nelson, *History of Worcester County*, 169–70; Hurd, *History of Worcester County*, 2:1444–45; *The Liberator*, September 20, 1839, cited in Mooney, "Antislavery in Worcester County," 87; *Spy*, August 20, 1858, and September 3, 1858. For an amusing account of the riot by one who was in the thick of it, see Thomas Wentworth Higginson, *Cheerful Yesterdays* (Boston: Houghton, Mifflin and Company, 1898), 162–65.

89. Membership lists, "Worcester Anti-Slavery Sewing Circle Record Book, 1839–1857," Manuscript Collection, Worcester Historical Museum; *Spy*, April 30, 1851; Blackman and Etheridge, "The Worcester County Mechanics Association"; Elihu Burritt (Hamburg, Germany) to Mrs. Edward (Ann Buffum) Earle (Worcester), November 18, 1850, Edward Earle Papers, Manuscript Boxes "E," box 1, folder 3, Manuscript Collection, AAS; CFS, *Seventeenth Annual Report*, 4.

90. Alonzo Hill, *In Memoriam: A Discourse Preached in Worcester, Oct. 5, 1862, on Lieut. Thomas Jefferson Spurr, Fifteenth Massachusetts Volunteers; Who, Mortally Wounded at the Battle of Antietam, Died in Hagerstown, Sept. 27th Following* (Boston: J. Wilson, 1862), quotes from 25, 3; Abijah P. Marvin, *History of Worcester in the War of the Rebellion* (Cleveland: Arthur H. Clark, 1870), 459–62.

91. Ann B. Earle (Worcester) to Lydia Chase (Norfolk, Virginia), March 24, 1864, Chase Family Papers, box 1, folder 2, Manuscript Collection, AAS; Hurd, *History of Worcester County*, 2:1692–94.

92. Leon Litwack, *North of Slavery: The Negro in the Free States, 1790–1860* (Chicago: University of Chicago Press, 1961). It was unusual for white orphan asylums to accept black children, prompting the formation of separate orphan-

ages in cities with large African American populations. See, for example, Philadelphia House of Refuge, *Appeal to the Public on Behalf of A House of Refuge for Coloured Juvenile Delinquents* (Philadelphia: T.K. and P.G. Collins, 1846) and *The Twenty-Sixth Annual Report of the Association for the Care of Colored Orphans* (Philadelphia: William K. Bellows, 1862).

93. CFS, *Minutes*, April, 1852; December, 1852; April, 1857; May, 1857. The outcome of the case was not recorded.

94. The census of 1850 counted 637 "colored" persons in Worcester county, most of whom lived in the city of Worcester. The city's total population in 1850 was 17,049; thus, blacks constituted at most 3.7 percent of the population. I found reference to only three black children out of approximately 204 children cared for at the CFS during this period. Black children thus represented only 1.5 percent of the children at the CFS even though blacks constituted 3.7 percent of the whole population. Since African Americans made up a disproportionate percentage of the city's poor families, the underrepresentation of black children at the CFS is likely greater than these numbers indicate. The three African American children I found references to were discussed only briefly and it is possible that there were others. However, given the lack of evidence of a greater presence of African American children at the home, a fact which most likely would have been noted, I doubt there could have been many more.

95. CFS, *Minutes*, June, 1849; *Spy*, June 27, 1849; CFS, *Minutes*, October, 1853; August, 1854; November, 1854; *Second Annual Report*, 7; *Seventh Annual Report*, 7; *Palladium*, March 12, 1851; Albert B. Southwick, *The Journals of Stephen C. Earle, 1853–1856* (Worcester, Mass.: Worcester Bicentennial Commission, 1976), 47. For the State Reform School for Boys, see Schneider, *In the Web of Class*, 45–50; Leroy Ashby notes that reformatories housed dependent as well as delinquent children, *Endangered Children*, 25. The Lancaster School for Girls was not built until 1856; see Brenzel, *Daughters of the State*; Schneider, *In the Web of Class*, 72–84.

96. CFS, *Minutes*, November, 1852; March, 1853. For a brief discussion of the evolution of the meaning of "friend," see Cott, *Bonds of Womanhood*, 186; CFS *Minutes*, April, 1854; May, 1854; June, 1859; May, 1850; January, 1856. The CFS preferred to accept children no older than twelve; *Second Annual Report*, 7; *Minutes*, March, 1856; April, 1856.

97. CFS, *Minutes*, December, 1849; February, 1853; March, 1853; May, 1853; February, 1854; September, 1854; July, 1855.

98. CFS, *Minutes*, October, 1853; December, 1853; March, 1854; September, 1854; January, 1855; February, 1855; March, 1855; June, 1855; July, 1855; September, 1857.

99. CFS, *Second Annual Report*, 7; *Minutes*, February, 1855.

100. Lebsock, *Free Women of Petersburg*, 228. The Worcester Children's Friend Society is still in existence. It ceased placing children decades ago, but continues to act as a resource for troubled and needy families and as an advocate for children's interests.

5. FROM FEMINISM TO FEMALE EMPLOYMENT

1. Some years two conventions were held; there was none in 1857, nor were any held during the Civil War. Although the term "feminist" is anachronistic when applied to the antebellum era, I use it intentionally to underscore the movement's commitment to the legal, economic, and social equality of women, a goal shared by later generations of feminists. For a similar perspective, see Marilley, *Woman Suffrage*, 6–7.

For antebellum feminism, see DuBois, *Feminism and Suffrage*; Eleanor Flexner, *Century of Struggle: The Woman's Rights Movement in the United States* (Cambridge, Mass.: Harvard University Press, 1975); Hoffert, *When Hens Crow*; Jean V. Matthews, *Women's Struggle for Equality: The First Phase, 1828–1876* (Chicago: Ivan R. Dee, 1997); Melder, *Beginnings of Sisterhood*; Stanton, Anthony, and Gage, *History of Woman Suffrage*, for the Worcester conventions, see volume 1, 215–46 and appendix, chapter VIII, 820–26; Wellman, "Seneca Falls Women's Rights Convention," 9–37.

2. Historians have tended to characterize the 1850s as a decade of decline in women's independent activism; see, for example, Boydston, *Home and Work*; Ginzberg, *Women and the Work of Benevolence*; Ryan, *Cradle of the Middle Class*.

3. Baldwin, *Diary of C. C. Baldwin* (Worcester, Mass.: American Antiquarian Society, 1901), 235; Hurd, *History of Worcester County*, 2:1448, 1450–51; Baldwin, *Diary of C.C. Baldwin*, 182; 312–13.

The site was decided upon at a Boston antislavery meeting in May, 1850, but the job of organizing it fell to Sarah H. Earle of Worcester; see Paulina W. Davis, comp., *A History of the National Woman's Rights Movement, for Twenty Years, with the Proceedings of the Decade Meeting Held at Apollo Hall, October 20, 1870, from 1850 to 1870* (New York: Journeymen Printers' Co-operative Association, 1871), 12; see also Stanton, Anthony, and Gage, *History of Woman Suffrage*, 1:216; Matthews, *Women's Struggle for Equality*, 66–83. For Worcester's role as a "junction city" connecting Boston to the hinterlands, see Doherty, *Society and Power*, 20–21.

4. *National Aegis*, October 23, 1850; *Worcester Sunday Telegram*, September 17, 1950.

5. *National Aegis*, June 19, 1850; September 18, 1850; *Spy*, October 9, 1850; Albert B. Southwick, *Once-Told Tales of Worcester County* (Worcester, Mass.: Worcester Telegram and Gazette, 1985), 44; *The Proceedings of the Woman's Rights Convention, Held at Worcester, October 15th and 16th, 1851* (New York: Fowlers and Wells, 1852), 27; *Palladium*, October 30, 1850 (emphasis in original); October 22, 1851; *New York Herald*, October 25, 1850; *Daily Mail*, October 25, 1850; see also the *New York Christian Inquirer*, cited in Stanton, Anthony, and Gage, *History of Woman Suffrage*, 1:243–45. Elizabeth Cady Stanton wrote that "hundreds" had to be turned away due to space limitations; *History of Woman Suffrage*, 1:242. The *New York Herald* facetiously suggested that the obese sideshow girl "ought, by all means, have been made president of the Convention." *Spy*, October 30, 1850; Boston *Daily Chronotype*, October 24, 1850; *Palladium*, October 8, 1851; October 22, 1851; *National Aegis*, August 27, 1851; October 8, 1851.

6. *Spy,* October 30, 1850, October 22, 1851; *National Aegis,* October 22, 1851; *New York Herald,* October 25, 1850; *Spy,* October 30, 1850; *National Aegis,* June 19, 1850 and October 22, 1851; see also the *Palladium,* October 22, 1851.

The *Herald* initially published a favorable account of the convention on October 24, 1850, in which it noted: "P.S.—Do not be deceived by the reports in some of the Boston papers. Some of them have sent reporters here to carica-ture the proceedings. Shame on a corrupt and venal press." Two days later, Oc-tober 26, 1850, the *Herald* joined in the shameful and venal caricaturing, insisting that "such monstrous sentiments, not an individual present, apart from the Convention, seemed to consider entitled to any other considerations than those of pity and disgust." By the close of the convention, the editor was beside him-self, denouncing with splenetic fury the "Pie-Bald Fanatics" and their "motley gathering of fanatical mongrels, of old grannies, male and female, of fugitive slaves and fugitive lunatics" who had spent two days discussing "the most hor-rible trash" involving "all the most monstrous and disgusting principles of so-cialism, abolition, amalgamation, and infidelity;" *New York Herald,* October 28, 1850. Horace Greeley's *New York Daily Tribune* was much more favorable; see the remarks following a letter to the editor, November 2, 1850. For the Boston *Daily Mail,* see October 24, 1850.

7. Of a total of 268 members, eighty-five, or 31.7 percent, were from Worcester. Due to the absence of titles and the frequent use of initials in lieu of first names, the sex of only sixty-six, or 78 percent, of the members from Worcester can be determined. Of these, at least forty-six, or 70 percent, were women; twenty, or 30 percent, were men. The family occupations of thirty-one female convention members can be determined; sixteen of the women were self-sup-porting. *The Proceedings of the Woman's Rights Convention, Held at Worcester, Oc-tober 23d & 24th, 1850* (Boston: Prentiss and Sawyer, 1851), 80–84; Worcester city directories, 1848–1853.

I am grateful to Mr. Robert J. Cormier of Shrewsbury, Mass., who gener-ously shared with me his data on the conventions.

8. *Proceedings* (1850), 30; occupational data compiled from the Worcester city directories.

9. For schoolteaching, see Bernard and Vinovskis, "The Female School Teacher," 332–45; Barbara Miller Solomon, *In the Company of Educated Women: A History of Women and Higher Education in America* (New Haven: Yale Univer-sity Press, 1985), 33; James M. Wallace, "The Feminization of Teaching in Mass-achusetts: A Reconsideration," in Susan L. Porter, ed., *Women of the Commonwealth: Work, Family, and Social Change in Nineteenth-Century Massachusetts* (Amherst: University of Massachusetts Press, 1994): 43–61.

The salaries of Worcester's public school teachers were compiled from mu-nicipal reports published as *City Documents, 1848–1856* (Worcester, Mass.: Henry J. Howland [1856]) and *City Document No. 13 . . . with the Annual Reports of the Several City Officers, for the Municipal Year Ending Jan. 3, 1859* (Worcester, Mass.: Henry J. Howland, 1859), 117–18; *City Document No. 14 . . . with the Annual Reports of the Several City Officers, for the Municipal Year Ending Jan. 2, 1860* (Worcester, Mass.: Henry J. Howland, 1860), 121–22.

10. *National* Aegis, August 6, 1851; *Proceedings* (1850), 24, 21 (emphasis in original), 28.

11. *Proceedings* (1850), 4; *Proceedings* (1851), 7–8; *Proceedings* (1850), 8; *Proceedings* (1851), 8, 12, 35, 48; *Proceedings* (1850), 4, 5, 7, 8, 10, 44, 45; *Daily Chronotype*, October 24, 1850. For analysis of the "upward tending spirit of the times," see Dolores Greenberg, "Energy, Power, and Perceptions of Social Change in the Early Nineteenth Century," *American Historical Review* 95 (June 1990): 693–714.

12. Melder, *Beginnings of Sisterhood*, 10; DuBois, *Feminism and Suffrage*, 37; *Proceedings* (1850), 46; *Proceedings* (1851), 27–28; *Proceedings* (1850), 11, 40, 45, 4; *Proceedings* (1851), 46; *Proceedings* (1850), 53–54, 55.

13. *Proceedings* (1851), 78, 27–29, 87.

14. *Proceedings* (1850), 44 (emphasis in original), 59, 55 (emphasis in original), 33–34, 43, 43, 57, 59.

15. *Proceedings* (1850), 37, 36 (emphasis in original); *Proceedings* (1851), 92.

16. *Proceedings* (1851), 20; *Proceedings* (1850), 45–46, 47, 49. Linking women's economic exploitation and prostitution was a common tactic, especially among moral reformers; see Carroll Smith-Rosenberg, *Religion and the Rise of the American City: The New York City Mission Movement, 1812–1870* (Ithaca: Cornell University Press, 1971), 97–124.

17. The 1851 convention did not keep a membership list, so the appeal of the convention to those in the city of Worcester cannot be measured.

18. *Proceedings* (1851), 7, 9, 10, 13; see also Stanton, Anthony, and Gage, *History of Woman Suffrage*, 1:234–37; *New York Herald*, October 28, 1850; *Proceedings* (1851), 33, 35. In 1837, Harriet Martineau published *Society in America*, which included a pungent critique of gender relations.

19. Ibid., 27–28, 30, 53, 47, 68 (emphasis in original). For women's property rights, see, for example, Dianne Avery and Alfred S. Konefsky, "The Daughters of Job: Property Rights and Women's Lives in Mid-Nineteenth-Century Massachusetts," *Law and History Review* 10 (fall 1992): 323–56.

20. *New York Herald*, October 25, 1850; *Daily Chronotype*, October 25, 1850; *Daily Mail*, October 25, 1850; *Daily Tribune*, October 25, 1850. For local opinion of Foster, see *National Aegis*, January 2, 1850. See also Nancy H. Burkett, *Abby Kelley Foster and Stephen S. Foster* (Worcester, Mass.: Worcester Bicentennial Commission, 1976); Joel Bernard, "Authority, Autonomy, and Radical Commitment: Stephen and Abby Kelley Foster," *Proceedings of the American Antiquarian Society*, n.s., 90 (1980): 347–86; Keith Melder, "Abby Kelley and the Process of Liberation," in Yellin and Van Horne, eds., *The Abolitionist Sisterhood*, 231–48; Dorothy Sterling, *Ahead of Her Time: Abby Kelley and the Politics of Antislavery* (New York: Norton, 1991).

21. *Proceedings* (1851), 111–12, 99, 100, 102, 105.

22. Melder, *Beginnings of Sisterhood*, 38–43; Wellman, "Seneca Falls Women's Rights Convention," 10–11; Boylan, "Women and Politics in the Era before Seneca Falls," 363.

23. The CFS published its annual reports, opened its books to the public,

and held annual public meetings, suggesting a general understanding that the society was a public trust. CFS, *Third Annual Report*, 9.

24. The Relief of the Poor was composed of male representatives from each of the Protestant churches in Worcester, including the African Methodist Episcopal Zion Church. "Report of the Treasurer," 1848; "Report of the Relief of the Poor," 1854; Handbill, December 7, 1854; "Plan of Organization," undated; Circular, "To the Citizens of Worcester," 1847, Relief of the Poor, Institutional Pamphlets Collection, AAS.

25. In 1848, the ROP assisted 153 families, including 400 children; in 1852, 169 families and more than 300 children. "To the Citizens of Worcester," 1848; "Report of The Treasurer," 1852; Relief of the Poor, Institutional Pamphlets Collection, AAS; *Spy*, January 3, 1857. For antebellum welfare policies, see Hale, *Letters on Irish Emigration*, 41–42; Glenn C. Altschuler and Jan M. Saltzgaber, "Clearinghouse for Paupers: The Poorfarm of Seneca County, New York, 1830–1860" *Journal of Social History* 17 (summer 1984): 573–600; and Glenn C. Altschuler and Jan M. Saltzgaber, "The Limits of Responsibility: Social Welfare and Local Government in Seneca County, New York, 1860–1875" *Journal of Social History* 21 (spring 1978): 515–37.

26. Of a total of 103 families assisted, 45 were headed by widows, while in an additional 20 the husband was either unable to work, or was absent. "Report of the Relief of the Poor," 1856, Relief of the Poor, Institutional Pamphlets Collection, AAS. For local reaction, see *Palladium*, January 1, 1857; October 21, 1857; November 25, 1857; December 2, 1857; December 9, 1857; *Spy*, January 3, 1857. The history of the Worcester FES strengthens Susan Porter Benson's interpretation of a similar organization in Providence, Rhode Island. Benson argues that the women of the Providence Employment Society transformed the approaches of male activists to suit their own purposes, extended to the public sphere their domestic skills, joined as part of a network of family and friends, and acted independently of their male relatives. Benson suggests that while gender separated the women from their male relatives, class distanced them from poor women. Neither fish nor fowl, the women of the Providence Employment Society lived in a culture that tolerated these contradictions, permitting them to "unify their domestic and public lives" in a way that was potentially feminist. Susan Porter Benson, "Business Heads and Sympathizing Hearts: The Women of the Providence Employment Society, 1837–1858," *Journal of Social History* 12 (winter 1978): 302–12.

27. Southwick, *Once-Told Tales of Worcester*, 54.

28. *Report of the Worcester Female Employment Society, Presented by the Executive Board at the First Annual Meeting, October 13, 1856* (Worcester, Mass.: Henry J. Howland, 1856), 5.

29. FES, *Report* (1856), 6–7; *Report of the Worcester Female Employment Society Presented by the Executive Board at the Third Annual Meeting, October 11, 1859* (Worcester, Mass.: William R. Hooper, 1859), 6; FES, *Report* (1856), 8, 10–11, 5. For sewing as an occupation, see Ava Baron and Susan E. Klepp, "'If I Didn't Have My Sewing Machine . . .': Women and Sewing Machine Technology," 20–59; Gamber, *The Female Economy*.

30. *Report of the Worcester Female Employment Society, Presented by the Executive Board at the Second Annual Meeting, October 12, 1857* (Worcester, Mass.: Henry J. Howland, 1857), 4, 5, 8, 11, 7; *Report of the Worcester Female Employment Society Presented by the Executive Board at the Third Annual Meeting, October 11, 1859* (Worcester, Mass.: William R. Hooper, 1859), 5.

31. FES, *Report* (1857), 4, 7, 6.

32. *Proceedings* (1851), 100; FES, *Report* (1857), 9, 10.

33. FES, *Report* (1857), 10.

CONCLUSION

1. Rosenzweig, *Eight Hours for What We Will*, 11.

2. George M. Frederickson, *The Inner Civil War: Northern Intellectuals and the Crisis of the Union* (New York: Harper and Row, 1965), 183–216.

Select Bibliography

MANUSCRIPT COLLECTIONS

Charles Allen Papers, Manuscript Collection, American Antiquarian Society (AAS).
Samuel Austin Papers, Manuscript Collection, AAS.
Bangs Family Papers, Manuscript Collection, AAS.
Bigelow Family Papers, Manuscript Collection, AAS.
Central Church Records, Worcester Collection, AAS.
Chase Family Papers, Manuscript Collection, AAS.
Clapp Family Letters, Manuscript Collection, AAS.
Crossman Family Diaries, Manuscript Collection, AAS.
John Davis Papers, Manuscript Collection, AAS.
Diaries Collection, Manuscript Collection, AAS.
Denny Family Papers, Manuscript Collection, AAS.
Edward Earle Papers, Manuscript Collection, AAS.
Flint Family Papers, Manuscript Collection, AAS.
Waldo Flint Family Papers, Manuscript Collection, AAS.
Abigail Kelley Foster Papers, Manuscript Collection, AAS.
Foster Family Papers, Manuscript Collection, AAS.
Jennison Family Papers, Manuscript Collection, AAS.
National Aegis Business Records, Worcester Collection, AAS.
Newton Family Papers, Manuscript Collection, AAS.
Old South Church Records, Worcester Collection, AAS.
Paine Family Papers, Manuscript Collection, AAS.
Leonard Moody Parker Papers, Manuscript Collection, AAS.
Records of the First Baptist Church, 1830–1840, Worcester Collection, AAS.
Records of Worcester Churches, 1821–1900, Worcester Collection, AAS.
Relief of the Poor, Institutional Pamphlets Collection, AAS.
Salisbury Family Papers, Manuscript Collection, AAS.
Soldiers' Relief Society Records, Worcester Collection, AAS.
Elizabeth Smith Diary, 1820–1854, Diaries Collection, AAS.
Seth Sweetser Papers, Manuscript Collection, AAS.
Trumbull Family Papers, Manuscript Collection, AAS.
Washburn Family Papers, Manuscript Collection, AAS.
John W. Wetherell Papers, Manuscript Collection, AAS.
Caroline Barrett White Papers, Manuscript Collection, AAS.
White-Forbes Family Papers, Manuscript Collection, AAS.

Worcester Antislavery Sewing Circle Record Book, Manuscript Collection, Worcester Historical Museum.
Worcester Children's Friend Society Records, Pamphlet Collection, Worcester Historical Museum
Worcester Children's Friend Society Records, Worcester Collection, AAS.
Worcester Lunatic Asylum Records, Manuscript Collection, AAS.
Worcester Vital Statistics, Microfilm Compilation, Worcester Room, Worcester Public Library.

NEWSPAPERS

Worcester *National Aegis*
Worcester *Spy*
Worcester *Palladium*

PRIMARY WORKS

Abbott, John S.C. *The Mother at Home: Or, the Principles of Maternal Duty.* Boston: Crocker and Brewster, 1833.
African Methodist Episcopal Zion Church. *The Fiftieth Anniversary of the A.M.E.Z. Church.* Worcester, Mass.: N.p., 1898.
Allen, Joseph. *The Worcester Association and Its Antecedents: A History of Four Ministerial Associations: The Marlborough, the Worcester (Old), the Lancaster, and the Worcester (New) Associations.* Boston: Nichols and Noyes, 1868.
Articles of Faith and Covenant, Adopted by Several Baptist Churches in the County of Worcester. Worcester, Mass.: Moses W. Grout, 1832.
Austin, Samuel. *Dissertations upon Several Fundamental Articles of Christian Theology.* Worcester, Mass.: William Manning, 1826.
Bacon, Leonard. *A Historical Discourse Delivered at Worcester, in the Old South Meeting House, September 22, 1863; The Hundredth Anniversary of its Erection.* Worcester, Mass.: Edward R. Fiske, 1863.
Baldwin, Christopher Columbus. *Diary of Christopher Columbus Baldwin.* Worcester, Mass.: American Antiquarian Society, 1901.
Bancroft, Aaron. *A Sermon Delivered in Worcester, January 31, 1836, by Aaron Bancroft, D.D., at the Termination of Fifty Years of His Ministry.* Worcester, Mass.: Clarendon Harris, 1836.
Beecher, Lyman. *The Faith Once Delivered to the Saints: A Sermon Delivered at Worcester, Mass., Oct. 15, 1823, at the Ordination of the Rev. Loammi Ives Hoadly to the Pastoral Office over the Calvinist Church and Society in that Place.* Boston: Crocker and Brewster, 1823.
[Blane, William J.] *An Excursion through the United States and Canada during the Years 1822–23 by An English Gentleman.* Reprint, New York: Negro Universities Press, 1969.
Brace, Charles Loring. *The Best Method of Disposing of Our Pauper and Vagrant Children.* New York: Wynkoop, Hallenbeck and Thomas, 1859.

————. *The Dangerous Classes of New York, & Twenty Years Work Among Them.* New York: Wynkoop and Hallenbeck, 1872.

Brown, Sarah Theo., ed. *Letters of Martha LeBaron Goddard, With Recollections by Nathan Haskell Dole.* Worcester, Mass.: Davis and Banister, 1901.

————. *Letters of Theophilus Brown.* Worcester, Mass.: Putnam, Davis and Co., 1898.

Catalogue of the Members of the First Church, (Old South) Worcester, Feb. 5, 1861. Worcester, Mass.: N.p., 1861.

Central [Calvinist] Society of Worcester. *Addresses at the Commemoration of the 75th Anniversary of the Organization of the Central Church.* Worcester, Mass.: N.p., 1896.

————. *Articles of Faith and Covenant Adopted by the Calvinist Church in Worcester.* Worcester, Mass.: N.p., 1834.

————. *Historical Sketch of the Central Society in Worcester with its Charter & By-Laws & Members et cetera.* Worcester, Mass.: Lucius P. Goddard, 1880.

————. *Manual of the Calvinist Church, Worcester, Massachusetts.* Worcester, Mass.: Lucius P. Goddard, 1877.

————. *Remarks on the Late Publication of the First Church in Worcester, of Which the Rev. Charles A. Goodrich Was Pastor, Relative to the "Origin and Difficulties" in That Church.* Worcester, Mass.: Manning and Trumbull, 1821.

Cheever, Henry T., ed. *The Autobiography and Memorials of Ichabod Washburn.* Boston: D. Lothrop and Company, 1878.

Children's Aid Society [of New York]. *Annual Reports of the Children's Aid Society, Nos. 1–10, February 1854–February 1863.* Reprint, New York: Arno Press, 1971.

Congdon, Albert. *The Worcester Business Directory and Advertiser.* Boston: Dutton and Wentworth, 1843.

Finch, Marianne. *An Englishwoman's Experience in America.* Reprint, New York: Negro Universities Press, 1969.

Goodrich, Charles A., ed. *Actes and Monuments: Book of Martyrs, or, A History of the Lives, Sufferings and Triumphant Deaths of the Primitive as Well as Protestant Martyrs: From the Commencement of Christianity, to the Latest Periods of Pagan and Popish Persecution.* New York: William W. Reed, 1831.

Goodrich, Charles A. *An Address, Delivered June 26, 1817, before the Female Reading and Charitable Society of the First Parish in Worcester, Mass.* Worcester, Mass.: Printed by William Manning, 1817.

Hale, Edward Everett. *Letters on Irish Emigration.* Boston: Phillips, Sampson and Co., 1852.

Hale, Edward Everett, Jr., ed. *The Life and Letters of Edward Everett Hale.* 2 vols. Boston: Little, Brown and Co., 1917.

Harvey, George H., comp. *Court of Insolvency, County of Worcester. Index of Cases and Records, 1838–1897.* Worcester, Mass.: N.p., 1897.

Higginson, Mary Thacher, ed. *Letters and Journals of Thomas Wentworth Higginson, 1846–1906.* Boston: Houghton Mifflin Co., 1921.

Higginson, Thomas Wentworth. *Cheerful Yesterdays.* Boston: Houghton, Mifflin and Company, 1898.

Hill, Alonzo. *In Memoriam: A Discourse Preached in Worcester, Oct. 5, 1862, on Lieut. Thomas Jefferson Spurr, Fifteenth Massachusetts Volunteers; Who, Mortally Wounded at the Battle of Antietam, Died in Hagerstown, Sept. 27th Following.* Boston: J. Wilson, 1862.

————. *Memorial Sermon of Charles Allen. Preached September 12, 1869.* Worcester, Mass.: N.p., n.d. [1869].

Hill, Benjamin Thomas. "Life at Harvard a Century Ago." *Proceedings of the American Antiquarian Society,* n.s., 20 (1910): 197–248.

History, Manual and Membership of the Worcester Mission Chapel Church, Organized, Dec. 23, 1864. Worcester, Mass.: E.R. Fiske, 1865.

Howland, Henry J. *The Worcester Almanac, Directory, and Business Advertiser for 1845.* Worcester, Mass.: Henry J. Howland, 1845 [and for 1849, 1850, 1851, 1852, 1853, 1855, 1856, 1867, 1868, 1869, 1860].

————. *The Worcester Almanac, Directory, and Business Advertiser for 1848.* Worcester, Mass.: S.A. Howland, 1848.

Lincoln, William. *History of Worcester, Massachusetts.* Worcester, Mass.: Moses D. Phillips and Co., 1837.

Lincoln, William and Hersey, Charles. *History of Worcester, Massachusetts, from its Earliest Settlement to September, 1836.* Worcester, Mass.: Charles Hersey, 1862.

List of Persons Assessed in the Town of Worcester, for the Town and County Tax. Boston: Samuel N. Dickinson, 1846.

Massachusetts, Commonwealth of. *Abstract of the Returns of the Overseers of the Poor in Massachusetts, for 1837.* Boston: Secretary of the Commonwealth of Massachusetts, 1838 [and for 1840, 1841, 1842, 1843, 1844, 1845, 1846, 1847, 1848, 1849, 1850, 1851].

————. *Returns Relating to the Poor in Massachusetts, for the Year Ending November 1, 1852.* Boston: Secretary of the Commonwealth, 1852 [and for 1853, 1854, 1855, 1856].

A Memorial of Levi Lincoln, the Governor of Massachusetts, from 1825 to 1834. Boston: J.E. Farwell and Co., 1868.

Ministry at Large [Worcester, Mass.]. *Second Annual Report of the Ministry at Large in the City of Worcester. For the Year Ending May 31st, 1851.* Worcester, Mass.: Henry J. Howland [1851].

————. *Third Annual Report of the Ministry at Large in the City of Worcester. For the Year Ending May 31st, 1852.* Worcester, Mass.: C.B. Webb, 1852.

Minutes of the Worcester Baptist Association. Held at the Baptist Meeting-House in Harvard, (Mass.) August 16 and 17, 1820. Worcester, Mass: Manning and Trumbull, 1820.

[Old South Church]. *The First Church Old South of Worcester Massachusetts. Bi-Centennial Celebration.* Worcester, Mass: N.p., 1916.

————. *Manual of the Old South Church in Worcester, 1854.* Worcester, Mass.: Henry J. Howland, 1854.

————. *Origin and Progress of the Late Difficulties in the First Church in Worcester, Mass.* Worcester, Mass.: Manning and Trumbull, 1820.

Olliffe, Charles. *American Scenes: Eighteen Months in the New World.* 3 vols. Trans-

lated by Ernest Falbo and Lawrence A. Wilson. Painesville, Ohio: Lake
Erie College Studies, 1964.

Rice, Franklin P., comp. *Vital Records of Charlton, Massachusetts.* Worcester, Mass.:
Franklin P. Rice, 1905.

———. *Vital Records of Millbury, Massachusetts.* Worcester, Mass.: Franklin P.
Rice, 1903.

———. *Vital Records of Spencer, Massachusetts.* Worcester, Mass.: Franklin P.
Rice, 1909.

———. *Vital Records of Sutton, Massachusetts.* Worcester, Mass.: Franklin P. Rice,
1907

———. *Worcester Births, Marriages, and Deaths.* Worcester, Mass.: Worcester
Society of Antiquity, 1894.

———. *Worcester Newspaper Index, 1793–1848.* Worcester, Mass.: N.p., 1898.

———. *Worcester Town Records, 1801–1816.* Worcester, Mass.: Worcester Society of Antiquity, 1891.

———. *Worcester Town Records, 1817–1832.* Worcester, Mass.: Worcester Society of Antiquity, 1883.

———. *Worcester Town Records, 1832–1848.* Worcester, Mass.: Worcester Society of Antiquity, 1895.

Rice, Franklin P., ed. *Reminiscences of the Reverend George Allen of Worcester.*
Worcester, Mass.: Putnam and Davis, 1883.

Roos, Rosalie. *Travels in America, 1851–1855.* Translated and edited by Carl L.
Anderson. Carbondale: Southern Illinois University Press, 1982.

Smalley, Elam. *The Worcester Pulpit, with Notices Historical and Biographical.*
Boston: Phillips, Sampson and Co., 1851.

Southwick, Albert B., ed. *The Journals of Stephen C. Earle, 1853–1858.* Worcester, Mass.: Worcester Bicentennial Commission, 1976.

———. *Once-Told Tales of Worcester County.* Worcester, Mass.: Worcester Telegram and Gazette, 1985.

Sprague, William B. *Annals of the American Pulpit.* 9 vols. New York: R. Carter
and Brothers, 1857–1869. Reprint, New York: Arno Press, 1969.

Stanton, Elizabeth Cady, Susan B. Anthony, and Matilda Joslyn Gage, eds.
History of Woman Suffrage. Volume I, 1848–1861. 2 vols. New York: Fowler
and Wells, 1881. Reprint, New York: Arno Press, 1969.

Sweetser, Seth. *Living To Do Good: A Sermon Occasioned by the Death of the Hon.
Daniel Waldo; Preached on Sunday, July 13, 1845.* Worcester, Mass.: Printed
for private distribution, 1845.

Thomas, Isaiah. *Catalogue of Books to be Sold by Thomas, Son & Thomas, at Their
Bookstore, in Worcester, Massachusetts.* Worcester, Mass.: Thomas, Son & Thomas, 1796.

———. *Diary of Isaiah Thomas, 1805–1820.* 2 vols. Worcester, Mass.: American Antiquarian Society, 1909.

Trollope, Frances. *Domestic Manners of the Americans.* Donald Smalley, ed. New
York: Alfred A. Knopf, 1949.

United States Bureau of the Census. *Census of the United States, 2nd–10th, 1800–*

1880, Worcester County. Washington, D.C.: Washington National Archives and Records Services, 1934.

Washburn, Emory. *Memoir of Hon. Levi Lincoln.* Cambridge, Mass.: Press of John Wilson and Son, 1869.

Wheelock, Clarendon, and John S.C. Knowlton. *Carl's Tour in Main Street.* Worcester, Mass.: Sanford and Davis, 1889.

Willard, Joseph A. *Memoir of William Lincoln.* Cambridge, Mass.: Metcalf and Company, 1848.

Women's Rights Convention. *The Proceedings of the Woman's Rights Convention, Held at Worcester, October 23d & 24th, 1850.* Boston: Prentiss and Sawyer, 1851.

————. *The Proceedings of the Woman's Rights Convention, Held at Worcester, October 15th and 16th, 1851.* New York: Fowlers and Wells, 1852.

Worcester Children's Friend Society. *Appeal to the Public.* Worcester, Mass.: N.p., 1849.

————. *First Annual Report of the Worcester Children's Friend Society, 1849.* Worcester, Mass.: N.p., 1850 [and for 1850, 1851, 1852, 1853, 1854, 1855, 1856, 1857, 1858, 1859, 1860, 1861, 1862, 1863, 1865, 1866, 1867, 1868, 1869, 1870, 1871, 1873, 1874, 1876, 1881, 1886, 1899, 1903].

Worcester County Statistical Record and Military Roll of Honor for the Year 1861. Worcester, Mass.: Edward R. Fiske, [1862].

Worcester County Institution for Savings. *Act of Incorporation; Laws Concerning Savings Banks; By-Laws; Catalogue of Members, &c., &c.* Worcester, Mass.: Edward R. Fiske, 1855.

————. *Constitution and By-Laws of the Worcester County Institution for Savings, in the Town of Worcester.* Worcester, Mass.: S.H. Colton & Co., 1828.

————. *Worcester County Institution for Savings, Officers for 1832.* Worcester, Mass.: N.p., 1832.

Worcester Female Employment Society. *Report of the Worcester Female Employment Society, presented by the Executive Board at the First Annual Meeting, October 13, 1856.* Worcester, Mass.: Henry J. Howland, 1856.

————. *Report of the Worcester Female Employment Society, presented by the Executive Board at the Second Annual Meeting, October 12, 1857.* Worcester, Mass.: Henry J. Howland, 1857.

————. *Report of the Worcester Female Employment Society, presented by the Executive Board at the Third Annual Meeting, October 11, 1858.* Worcester, Mass.: William R. Hooper, 1858.

[Worcester Female Samaritan Society]. *Constitution of the Worcester Female Samaritan Society.* Worcester, Mass.: Griffin and Morrill, 1827.

Worcester Medical Association. *Fee Table and Resolves Adopted by the Worcester Medical Association; with a Catalogue of the Members, January 1st, 1854.* Worcester, Mass.: Charles Hamilton, 1854.

Worcester Society of Antiquity. "Records of the Second Parish." *Bulletin of the Worcester Society of Antiquity, Worcester, Mass.* 16 (October 1898).

Worcester South Conference. *Worcester South Chronicles: A Brief History of the*

Congregational Churches of the Worcester South Conference of Massachusetts, 1670–1876. Worcester, Mass.: Lucius P. Goddard, 1879.

Worcester Village Directory, Containing the Names of the Inhabitants, Their Dwelling Houses and Places of Business. Worcester, Mass.: Clarendon Harris, 1829.

Worcester, Mass. *City Documents, 1848–1856.* Worcester, Mass.: Henry J. Howland, [1856].

———. *City Document, No. 11. Inaugural Address of Hon. George W. Richardson . . . with the Annual Reports of the Several City Officers, for the Municipal Year Ending Jan. 5, 1857.* Worcester, Mass.: Charles Hamilton, 1857.

———. *City Document, No. 12. Inaugural Address of Hon. Isaac Davis . . . with the Annual Reports of the Several City Officers, for the Municipal Year Ending Jan. 4, 1858.* Worcester, Mass.: Edward R. Fiske, 1858.

———. *Ordinances of the City of Worcester; with the City Charter, and Other City Laws. Published by Order of the City Council.* Worcester, Mass.: Charles Hamilton, 1854.

———. *Report of the Overseers of the Poor of the Town of Worcester, April 1, 1839.* Worcester, Mass.: Spooner and Howland, [1839].

———. *Report of the Selectmen of Worcester, March 1838.* Worcester, Mass.: Henry J. Howland, [1838].

———. *Report of the Selectmen of Worcester, February 1839.* Worcester, Mass.: Colton and Howland, [1839].

———. *Reports of the Municipal Officers: Submitted to the Town of Worcester, May 1840.* Worcester, Mass.: T.W. and J. Butterfield, [1840].

———. *Reports of the Municipal Officers: Submitted to the Town of Worcester, May, 1841.* Worcester, Mass.: T.W. and J. Butterfield, [1841].

———. *Reports Submitted to the Town of Worcester, at the Annual March Meeting, 1843.* Worcester, Mass.: Henry J. Howland, [1843].

———. *Reports Submitted to the Town of Worcester, at the Annual March Meeting, 1844.* Worcester, Mass.: Church and Fiske, [1844].

———. *Reports Submitted to the Town of Worcester, at the Annual March Meeting, 1845: And the By-Laws of the Town.* Worcester, Mass.: Henry J. Howland, [1845].

———. *Reports of the Selectmen and Overseers of the Poor, Submitted to the Town of Worcester, at the Annual April Meeting, 1846.* Worcester, Mass.: T.W. Butterfield, [1846].

———. *Report of the Town School Commission, Supplemental Report on the Paving of Main Street. Report of the Overseers of the Poor. Report and Return of the Fire Department.* Worcester, Mass.: National Aegis Office, 1847.

———. *Tables Showing the Population, Valuation, Taxes, Appropriations and Other Statistics of the City of Worcester, Mass. From 1850 to 1876. Prepared by the Auditor.* Worcester, Mass.: Charles Hamilton, 1876.

Zellers, Bruce, and Sue Hamel. "Worcester Central School District Valuation and Assessment Lists, 1803." Unpublished typescript, Worcester Collection, box 1, folder 3, Manuscript Collection, AAS.

SECONDARY WORKS

Worcester and Worcester County

Atlas of the City of Worcester. Rutland, VT: Charles E. Tuttle, Company, 1971.
Barnard, Frederick J. *Corporation and Legal History of the Central Church Worcester, Mass.* Worcester, Mass: Blanchard Press, 1905.
Barton, George Sumner. *A Line of Men One Hundred Years Long: The Story of Rice, Barton & Fales, Inc.* Worcester, Mass.: Rice, Barton and Fales, Inc., [1937].
Bergin, Paul F., M.D. "A History of the Worcester District Medical Society and the Worcester Medical Society, 1794–1954," unpublished manuscript, Worcester Medical Library, Inc., 1954; Worcester History Collection, AAS.
Bernard, Joel. "Authority, Autonomy, and Radical Commitment: Stephen and Abby Kelley Foster." *Proceedings of the American Antiquarian Society*, n.s., 90 (1988): 347–86.
Blackman, Linda, and Kim Etheridge. "The Worcester County Mechanics Association and Worcester's Cultural Enlightenment: 1853–1861," unpublished manuscript, Interactive Qualifying Project, Bachelor of Science Degree, Worcester Polytechnic Institute, 1985, Worcester History Collection, AAS.
Brenzel, Barbara, *Daughters of the State: A Social Portrait of the First Reform School for Girls in North America, 1856–1905.* Cambridge, Mass.: MIT University Press, 1983.
Brooke, John L. *The Heart of the Commonwealth: Society and Political Culture in Worcester County, Massachusetts, 1713–1861.* New York: Cambridge University Press, 1989.
Buell, Charles C. "The Workers of Worcester: Social Mobility and Ethnicity in a New England City, 1850–1880." Ph.D. diss., New York University, 1974.
Burkett, Nancy H. *Abby Kelley Foster and Stephen S. Foster.* Worcester, Mass.: Worcester Bicentennial Commission, 1976.
Butler, Charles Evans. *Walking In the Way: A History of the First Congregational Church in Worcester, 1716–1982.* Worcester, Mass.: The Society, 1987.
Chamberlin, Henry H. "The Trade of Worcester, During the Present Century." *Proceedings of the Worcester Society of Antiquity*, n.s., 13 (1880): 27–39.
———. *Worcester Main Street, Sixty-Three Years Ago.* Worcester, Mass.: Franklin P. Rice, 1886.
Chasan, Joshua. "Civilizing Worcester: The Creation of Institutional and Cultural Order, Worcester, Massachusetts, 1848–1876." Ph.D. diss., University of Pittsburgh, 1974.
Chase, Charles A. *Nobility Hill: Worcester, Mass.* Worcester, Mass.: Blanchard Press, 1900.
———. "William Lincoln." *Proceedings of the American Antiquarian Society*, n.s., 2 (1883): 424–36.
Chudacoff, Howard P. "New Branches on the Tree: Household Structure in

Early Stages of the Family Cycle in Worcester, Massachusetts, 1860–1880."
Proceedings of the American Antiquarian Society, n.s., 86 (1977): 303–20.
Clark, Christopher. *The Roots of Rural Capitalism: Western Massachusetts, 1780–
1860*. Ithaca: Cornell University Press, 1990.
Clark, Christopher, ed. *Diary of an Apprentice Cabinetmaker: Edward Jenner
Carpenter's "Journal," 1844–45*. Worcester, Mass.: American Antiquarian
Society, 1988.
Cutler, U. Waldo. *The First Hundred Years of the Central Church in Worcester,
1820–1920*. Worcester, Mass.: Published by the Church, 1920.
———. *Jottings from Worcester's History*. Worcester, Mass.: Worcester Historical
Society, 1932.
Davis, Horace. "Mrs. Lucretia (Chandler) Bancroft. A Letter to Her Daughter
Mrs. Gherardi, with Introduction." *Proceedings of the American Antiquarian
Society*, n.s., 14 (1900): 125–59.
Doherty, Robert. *Society and Power: Five New England Towns, 1800–1860*.
Amherst: University of Massachusetts Press, 1977.
Feingold, Norma. *Woman's Work: The Worcester Experience, 1830–1916*. Worces-
ter, Mass.: Worcester Historical Museum, 1986.
First Church Old South of Worcester Massachusetts. Bi-Centennial Celebration.
Worcester, Mass.: N.p., 1916.
Green, Samuel Swett. "Gleanings from the Sources of the History of the Sec-
ond Parish, Worcester, Massachusetts." *Proceedings of the American Anti-
quarian Society*, n.s., 2 (1883): 301–20.
Greenwood, Richard D. *The Five Heywood Brothers (1826–1951): A Brief His-
tory of the Heywood-Wakefield Company during 125 Years*. New York: The
Newcomen Society in North America, 1951.
Hathaway, Samuel. *A Sketch of Historical Reality with the Blendings of the Ro-
mance of Ideality*. Worcester, Mass.: F.S. Blanchard & Co., 1897.
History of the Town of Hingham, Massachusetts. Hingham, Mass.: Published by
the Town, 1893.
Hurd, Duane H. *History of Worcester County, Massachusetts*. 2 vols. Philadelphia:
J.W. Lewis and Co., 1889.
Kittredge, N.G. and A.C. Gould. *History of the American Card-Clothing Indus-
try*. Worcester, Mass.: T.K. Earle Manufacturing Company, 1886.
Kimball, Edward P. *Brinley Hall Album and Post 10 Sketch Book*. Worcester, Mass.:
F.S. Blanchard, 1896.
Knowlton, Elliot B., ed. *Worcester's Best: A Guide to the City's Architectural Heri-
tage*. Worcester, Mass.: Worcester Heritage Preservation Society, 1984.
Kolesar, Robert J. "Politics and Policy in a Developing Industrial City: Worces-
ter, Massachusetts, in the Late Nineteenth Century." Ph.D. diss., Clark
University, 1987.
Kring, Walter D. *The Fruits of Our Labors: The Bicentennial History of the First
Unitarian Church of Worcester, 1785–1985*. Worcester, Mass.: The First
Unitarian Church of Worcester, 1985.
Lincoln, Waldo. *Four Generations of the Waldo Family in America*. Boston: David
Clapp and Son, 1898.

————. *The Worcester County Institution for Savings, 1828–1928.* Worcester, Mass.: Privately printed for the WCIS, 1928.

Lyman, Richard B., Jr. "'What Is Done in My Absence?' Levi Lincoln's Oakham, Massachusetts, Farm Workers, 1807–20." *Proceedings of the American Antiquarian Society*, n.s., 99 (1989): 151–87.

Marvin, Abijah P. *History of Worcester in the War of the Rebellion.* Cleveland: Arthur H. Clark, 1870.

Meagher, Timothy. "Irish, American, Catholic: Irish-American Identity in Worcester, Massachusetts, 1880 to 1920." In *From Paddy to Studs: Irish-American Communities in the Turn of the Century Era, 1880–1920,* edited by Timothy Meagher. Westport, Conn.: Greenwood Press, 1986, 75–92.

————. "'Irish All the Time': Ethnic Consciousness among the Irish in Worcester, Massachusetts, 1880–1905." *Journal of Social History* 19 (winter 1985): 273–303.

————. "'Why Should We Care for A Little Trouble or A Walk through the Mud': St. Patrick's and Columbus Day Parades in Worcester, Massachusetts, 1845–1915." *New England Quarterly* 58 (March 1985): 5–26.

Meyer, Susan M. *The Salisbury Mansion: A Plan for Furnishings.* Worcester, Mass.: Worcester Historical Museum, 1986.

Mooney, James. "Antislavery in Worcester County, Massachusetts: A Case Study." Ph.D. diss., Clark University, 1971.

Moynihan, Kenneth J. "Meetinghouse vs. Courthouse: The Struggle for Legitimacy in Worcester, 1783–1788." In *Shays' Rebellion: Selected Essays,* edited by Martin Kaufman. Westfield, Mass.: Westfield State College, 1987.

Navin, John J. "The Spirit of Reform in Hopkinton, 1829–1849." *Historical Journal of Massachusetts* 16 (summer 1988): 172–85.

Navin, Thomas R. *The Whitin Machine Works since 1831: A Textile Machinery Company in An Industrial Village.* Cambridge, Mass.: Harvard University Press, 1950.

Nutt, Charles. *History of Worcester and Its People.* 4 vols. New York: Lewis Historical Publishing Company, 1919.

"The Old South Parish." *Proceedings of the Worcester Society of Antiquity* 22 (1907): 163–79.

Paine, Nathaniel. *Random Recollections of Worcester, Mass., 1839–1843.* Worcester, Mass.: F.P. Rice, 1885.

Powers, Vincent E. "'Invisible Immigrants': The Pre-Famine Irish Community in Worcester, Massachusetts, from 1826 to 1860." Ph.D. diss., Clark University, 1976.

Prude, Jonathan. *The Coming of Industrial Order: Town and Factory Life in Rural Massachusetts, 1810–1860.* New York: Cambridge University Press, 1983.

Rice, Franklin P. *Romance and Humor in Worcester's History.* Worcester, Mass.: F.P. Rice, 1896.

————. *Time Notes of Franklin P. Rice.* Worcester, Mass.: F.P. Rice, 1915.

————. *The Worcester District in Congress, from 1789 to 1857.* Worcester, Mass.: F.P. Rice, 1889.

————. *Worcester Newspaper Index, 1793–1848.* Worcester, Mass: F.P. Rice., 1848.

———. *The Worcester Book: A Diary of Noteworthy Events in Worcester, Massachusetts, from 1657 to 1883.* Worcester, Mass.: Putnam, Davis, and Co., 1884.
Roe, Alfred S. *Worcester Methodism: Its Beginnings.* Worcester, Mass.: Franklin P. Rice, 1889.
Rosenzweig, Roy. *Eight Hours for What We Will: Workers and Leisure in an Industrial City, 1870–1920.* New York: Cambridge University Press, 1983.
Sawyer, Herbert M. *History of the Department of Police Service of Worcester, Mass., from 1674 to 1900.* Worcester, Mass.: The Worcester Police Relief Association, 1900.
Shaw, Robert K. *All Saints Church, Worcester, Massachusetts: A Centennial History, 1835–1935.* Worcester, Mass.: The Society, 1935.
———. *Samuel Swett Green.* Chicago: American Library Association, 1926.
Stevens, Charles E. *Worcester Churches.* Worcester, Mass.: Lucius P. Goddard, 1890.
Stiles, Major F.G. "Exchange Street Sixty and More Years Ago." *Proceedings of the Worcester Society of Antiquity* 16 (1898), 491–96.
———. "Recollections of Central and Thomas Streets in the Thirties of 1800." *Proceedings of the Worcester Society of Antiquity* 16 (1898), 542–54.
———. "Recollections of Front Street, Worcester, in the Thirties." *Proceedings of the Worcester Society of Antiquity* 14 (1896), 300–13.
———. "Recollections of Mechanic Street, from 1830 to 1840." *Proceedings of the Worcester Society of Antiquity* 16 (1898), 60–73.
Sturgis, Mrs. O.P. "Old Worcester—Chestnut Street, About 1840." *Proceedings of the Worcester Society of Antiquity* 18 (1902), 69–90.
Taylor, Anthony R. *Worcester's Architectural Neighborhoods.* Worcester, Mass.: Worcester Historical Museum, 1984.
Thomas, H.H. *The Story of Allen and Wheelock Firearms.* Cincinnati: C.J. Krehbiel Company, 1965.
Tymeson, Mildred M. *Worcester Bankbook: From Country Barter to County Bank, 1804–1955.* Worcester, Mass.: Worcester County National Bank, 1966.
Wall, Caleb A. *Reminiscences of Worcester from the Earliest Period, Historical and Genealogical.* Worcester, Mass.: Tyler & Seagrave, 1877.
Washburn, Charles G. *Industrial Worcester.* Worcester, Mass.: Davis Press, 1917.
———. *Sketch of the Development of the Manufacturing Industries of Worcester.* N.p., n.d.
Wasowicz, Laura. "The Tatnuck Ladies' Sewing Circle, 1847–1867." *Historical Journal of Massachusetts* 24 (winter 1996): 19–46.
Weil, Francois. "Capitalism and Industrialization in New England, 1815–1845." *Journal of American History* 84 (March 1998): 1334–54.
———. "The Coming of the French Canadians to New England." Paper presented at a Colloquium of the American Antiquarian Society, Worcester, Mass., November, 1990.
Wheeler, Henry M. "Reminiscences of Thomas Street Schools and School-House 60 Years and More Ago." *Proceedings of the Worcester Society of Antiquity* 19, 82–116.
Whitney, Jeanne Ellen Whitney. "An Art That Requires Capital": Agriculture

and Mortgages in Worcester County, Massachusetts, 1790–1850." Ph.D diss., University of Delaware, 1991.

General

Ahlstrom, Sidney E. *A Religious History of America*. New Haven: Yale University Press, 1972.

Alexander, Ruth M. "'We Are Engaged as a Band of Sisters': Class and Domesticity in the Washingtonian Temperance Movement, 1840–1850." *Journal of American History* 75 (December 1988): 763–85.

Altschuler, Glenn C., and Stuart M. Blumin. "'Where is the Real America?': Politics and Popular Consciousness in the Antebellum Era." *American Quarterly* 49 (June 1997): 225–67.

Altschuler, Glenn C., and Jan M. Saltzgaber. "Clearinghouse for Paupers: The Poorfarm of Seneca County, New York, 1830–1860." *Journal of Social History* 17 (summer 1984): 573–600.

———. "The Limits of Responsibility: Social Welfare and Local Government in Seneca County, New York, 1860–1875." *Journal of Social History* 21 (spring 1988): 515–37.

———. *Revivalism, Social Conscience, and Community in the Burned-Over District: The Trial of Rhoda Bement*. Ithaca: Cornell University Press, 1983.

Ashby, Leroy. *Endangered Children: Dependency, Neglect, and Abuse in American History*. New York: Twayne Publishers, 1997.

Avery, Dianne, and Alfred S. Konefsky. "The Daughters of Job: Property Rights and Women's Lives in Mid-Nineteenth-Century Massachusetts." *Law and History Review* 10 (fall 1992): 323–56.

Baker, Paula. "The Domestication of Politics: Women and American Political Society, 1780–1920." *American Historical Review* 89 (June 1984): 627–32.

Balleisen, Edward J. "Vulture Capitalism in Antebellum America: The 1841 Federal Bankruptcy Act and the Exploitation of Financial Distress." *Business History Review* 70 (winter 1996): 473–516.

Banner, James M. *To the Hartford Convention: The Federalists and the Origins of Party Politics in the Early Republic, 1789–1815*. New York: Alfred A. Knopf, 1970.

Banner, Lois. "Religious Benevolence as Social Control: A Critique of an Interpretation." *Journal of American History* 60 (June 1973): 23–41.

Bartlett, Samuel C. *Historical Sketches of the Missions of the American Board*. Boston: ABCFM, 1876; Collected and reprinted, New York: Arno Press, 1972.

Basch, Norma. "Equity vs. Equality: Emerging Concepts of Women's Political Status in the Age of Jackson." *Journal of the Early Republic* 3 (fall 1983): 297–318.

———. *In the Eyes of the Law: Women, Marriage, and Property in Nineteenth-Century New York*. Ithaca: Cornell University Press, 1982.

Benberry, Cuesta. *Always There: The African-American Presence in American Quilts*. Louisville: The Kentucky Quilt Project, 1992.

Bender, Thomas. *Toward An Urban Vision: Ideas and Institutions in Nineteenth-Century America*. Lexington: University Press of Kentucky, 1975.

Ben-Or, Joseph. "The Law of Adoption in the United States: Its Massachusetts Origins and the Statute of 1851." *New England Historical and Genealogical Register* 130 (October 1976): 259–69.

Benson, Susan Porter. "Business Heads and Sympathizing Hearts: The Women of the Providence Employment Society, 1837–1858." *Journal of Social History* 12 (winter 1978): 302–12.

Berg, Barbara J. *The Remembered Gate: Origins of American Feminism: The Woman and the City, 1800–1860.* New York: Oxford University Press, 1978.

Bernard, Richard M., and Maris A. Vinovskis. "The Female School Teacher in Ante-Bellum Massachusetts." *Journal of Social History* 10 (spring 1977): 332–45.

Blumin, Stuart. *The Emergence of the Middle Class: Social Experience in the American City, 1760–1900.* New York: Cambridge University Press, 1989.

Bonfield, Lloyd. "Marriage, Property, and the 'Affective Family.'" *Law and History Review* 1 (fall 1983): 297–312.

Boydston, Jeanne. *Home and Work: Housework, Wages, and the Ideology of Labor in the Early Republic.* New York: Oxford University Press, 1990.

Boylan, Anne M. *Sunday School: The Formation of An American Institution, 1790–1880.* New Haven: Yale University Press, 1988.

———. "Timid Girls, Venerable Widows and Dignified Matrons: Life Cycle Patterns among Organized Women in New York and Boston, 1797–1840." *American Quarterly* 38 (winter 1986): 779–98.

———. "Women and Politics in the Era before Seneca Falls." *Journal of the Early Republic* 10 (fall 1990): 363–82.

———. "Women in Groups: An Analysis of Women's Benevolent Organizations in New York and Boston, 1797–1840." *Journal of American History* 71 (December 1984): 497–515.

Brekus, Catherine A. "'Let Your Women Keep Silence in the Churches': Female Preaching and Evangelical Religion in America, 1740–1845." Ph.D. diss., Yale University, 1993.

Casper, Scott E. *Constructing American Lives: Biography and Culture in Nineteenth-Century America.* Chapel Hill: University of North Carolina Press, 1999.

Chambers, Clarke A. "Toward a Redefinition of Welfare History." *Journal of American History* 73 (September 1986): 407–33.

Clark, Elizabeth B. "'The Sacred Rights of the Weak': Pain, Sympathy, and the Culture of Individual Rights in Antebellum America." *Journal of American History* 82 (September 1995): 463–93.

Clement, Patricia Ferguson. *Welfare and the Poor in the Nineteenth-Century City.* Rutherford, New Jersey: Farleigh-Dickinson University Press, 1988.

Clinton, Catherine, and Nina Silber, eds. *Divided Houses: Gender and the Civil War.* New York: Oxford University Press, 1992.

Cmiel, Kenneth. *A House of Another Kind: One Chicago Orphanage and the Tangle of Child Welfare.* Chicago: University of Chicago Press, 1995.

Coleman, Peter. *Debtors and Creditors in America: Insolvency, Imprisonment for Debt, and Bankruptcy, 1607–1900.* Madison: The State Historical Society of Wisconsin, 1974.

Coontz, Stephanie. *The Social Origins of Private Life: A History of American Families, 1600–1900*. New York: Verso, 1988.

Cott, Nancy F. *The Bonds of Womanhood: Woman's Sphere in New England, 1780–1835*. New Haven: Yale University Press, 1977.

———. "Passionlessness: An Interpretation of Victorian Sexual Ideology, 1790–1850." *Signs* 4 (winter 1978): 219–36.

———. "Young Women in the Second Great Awakening in New England." *Feminist Studies* 3 (fall 1975): 15–29.

Crane, Elaine Forman. "Religion and Rebellion: Women of Faith in the American War for Independence." In Ronald Hoffman and Peter J. Albert, eds., *Religion in a Revolutionary Age*. Charlottesville: University Press of Virginia, 1994, 52–86.

Cray, Robert E., Jr. *Paupers and Poor Relief in New York City and Its Rural Environments, 1700–1830*. Philadelphia: Temple University Press, 1988.

Cross, Whitney. *The Burned-Over District: The Social and Intellectual History of Enthusiastic Religion in Western New York*. Ithaca: Cornell University Press, 1950.

Diner, Hasia R. *Erin's Daughters in America: Irish Immigrant Women in the Nineteenth Century*. Baltimore: Johns Hopkins University Press, 1983.

Doherty, Robert. "Social Bases for the Presbyterian Schism of 1837–1838: The Philadelphia Case." *Journal of Social History* 2 (fall 1968): 69–79.

Douglas, Ann. *The Feminization of American Culture*. New York: Alfred A. Knopf, 1977.

Dublin, Thomas. *Transforming Women's Work: New England Lives in the Industrial Revolution*. Ithaca: Cornell University Press, 1994.

DuBois, Ellen. *Feminism and Suffrage: The Emergence of an Independent Women's Movement in America, 1848–1869*. Ithaca: Cornell University Press, 1978.

Dye, Nancy Schrom, and Daniel Blake Smith. "Mother Love and Infant Death, 1750–1920." *Journal of American History* 73 (September 1986): 329–53.

Edelstein, Tilden G. *Strange Enthusiasm: A Life of Thomas Wentworth Higginson*. New Haven: Yale University Press, 1968.

Edmonds, Mary Jaene. *Samplers and Samplermakers: An American Schoolgirl Art, 1700–1850*. New York: Rizzoli International, 1991.

Edwards, Rebecca. *Angels in the Machinery: Gender in American Party Politics from the Civil War to the Progressive Era*. New York: Oxford University Press, 1997.

Epstein, Barbara L. *The Politics of Domesticity: Women, Evangelism, and Temperance in Nineteenth-Century America*. Middletown, Conn.: Wesleyan University Press, 1981.

Estes, J. Worth, and David M. Goodman. *The Changing Humors of Portsmouth: The Medical Biography of an American Town, 1623–1983*. Boston: Francis A. Countway Library of Medicine, 1986.

Fabian, Ann. "Speculation on Distress: The Popular Discourse of the Panics of 1837 and 1857." *Yale Journal of Criticism* 3 (1989): 127–42.

Flexner, Eleanor. *Century of Struggle: The Woman's Rights Movement in the United States*. Cambridge, Mass.: Harvard University Press, 1975.

Folks, Homer. *The Care of Destitute, Neglected, and Delinquent Children.* Albany, New York: Macmillan Company, 1900.

Formisano, Ronald P. *The Transformation of Political Culture: Massachusetts Parties, 1790–1840.* New York: Oxford University Press, 1983.

Freedman, Estelle. "Separatism as Strategy: Female Institution Building and American Feminism, 1870–1930." *Feminist Studies* 5 (fall 1979): 512–29.

Gamber, Wendy. *The Female Economy: The Millinery and Dressmaking Trades, 1860–1930.* Urbana: University of Illinois Press, 1997.

———. "A Precarious Independence: Milliners and Dressmakers in Boston, 1860–1890." *Journal of Women's History* 4 (spring 1992): 60–88.

Gaustad, Edwin Scott. *A Religious History of America.* New York: Harper and Row, 1966.

Gerber, David A. "Cutting Out Shylock: Elite Anti-Semitism and the Quest for Moral Order in the Mid-Nineteenth-Century Market Place." *Journal of American History* 69 (December 1982): 615–37.

Gillespie, Joanna Bowen. "'The Clear Leadings of Providence': Pious Memoirs and the Problems of Self-Realization for Women in the Early Nineteenth Century." *Journal of the Early Republic* 5 (summer 1985): 197–221.

Ginzberg, Lori D. *Women and the Work of Benevolence: Morality, Politics, and Class in the Nineteenth-Century United States.* New Haven: Yale University Press, 1990.

Gittens, Joan. *Poor Relations: The Children of the State in Illinois, 1818–1990.* Urbana: University of Illinois Press, 1994.

Goldin, Claudia. "The Gender Gap in Historical Perspective." In Peter Kilby, ed., *Quantity & Quiddity: Essays in U.S. Economic History.* Middletown, Conn.: Wesleyan University Press, 1987, 135–70.

Goodman, Paul. "The Emergence of Homestead Exemption in the United States: Accommodation and Resistance to the Market Revolution, 1840–1880." *Journal of American History* 80 (September 1993): 470–98.

———. "Moral Purpose and Republican Politics in Antebellum America, 1830–1840." *The Maryland Historian* 20 (fall/winter 1989): 5–39.

———. *Towards a Christian Republic: Anti-Masonry and the Great Transition in New England, 1826–1836.* New York: Oxford University Press, 1988.

———. "The Social Basis of New England Politics in Jacksonian America." *Journal of the Early Republic* 6 (spring 1986): 23–58.

Gordon, Beverly. "Playing at Being Powerless: New England Ladies Fairs, 1830–1930." *Massachusetts Review* 26 (September 1986): 144–60.

Greenberg, Dolores. "Energy, Power, and Perceptions of Social Change in the Early Nineteenth Century." *American Historical Review* 95 (June 1990): 693–714.

Grimshaw, Patricia. "Christian Woman, Pious Wife, Faithful Mother, Devoted Missionary: Conflicts in Roles of American Missionary Women in Nineteenth-Century Hawaii." *Feminist Studies* 9 (fall 1983): 489–521.

Grossberg, Michael. *Governing the Hearth: Law and Family in Nineteenth Century America.* Chapel Hill: University of North Carolina Press, 1985.

Hacsi, Timothy A. "'A Plain and Solemn Duty': A History of Orphan Asylums in America." Ph.D. diss., University of Pennsylvania, 1993.

Halttunen, Karen. *Confidence Men and Painted Women: A Study of Middle Class Culture in America, 1830–1870.* New Haven: Yale University Press, 1982.

Hansen, Karen V. "'Helped Put in A Quilt': Men's Work and Male Intimacy in Nineteenth-Century New England." *Gender & Society* 3 (September 1989): 334–54.

———. *A Very Social Time: Crafting Community in Antebellum New England.* Berkeley: University of California Press, 1994.

Hareven, Tamara K. "The History of the Family and the Complexity of Social Change." *American Historical Review* 96 (February 1991): 95–124.

Hatch, Nathan O. *The Democratization of American Christianity.* New Haven: Yale University Press, 1989.

Hemphill C. Dallett. "Middle Class Rising in Revolutionary America: The Evidence from Manners." *Journal of Social History* 30 (winter 1996): 317–44.

Hewitt, Nancy A. *Women's Activism and Social Change: Rochester, New York, 1822–1872.* Ithaca: Cornell University Press, 1984.

———. "The Social Origins of Women's Antislavery Politics in Western New York." In Alan M. Kraut, ed. *Crusaders and Compromisers: Essays on the Relationship of the Antislavery Struggle to the Antebellum Party System.* Westport, Conn.: Greenwood Press, 1979, 205–33.

Hoffert, Sylvia D. *Private Matters: American Attitudes toward Childbearing and Infant Nurture in the Urban North, 1800–1860.* Urbana: University of Illinois Press, 1989.

———. "'A Very Peculiar Sorrow': Attitudes Toward Infant Death in the Urban Northeast, 1800–1860." *American Quarterly* 39 (winter 1987): 601–16.

———. *When Hens Crow: The Women's Rights Movement in Antebellum America.* Bloomington: Indiana University Press, 1995.

Holloran, Peter C. *Boston's Wayward Children: Social Services for Homeless Children, 1830–1930.* Rutherford, New Jersey: Fairleigh-Dickinson University Press, 1989.

Holt, Marilyn Irvin. *The Orphan Trains: Placing Out in America.* Omaha: University of Nebraska Press, 1992.

Jensen, Joan and Sue Davidson, eds. *A Needle, A Bobbin, A Strike: Women Needle Workers in America.* Philadelphia: Temple University Press, 1984.

Johnson, Paul E. *A Shopkeeper's Millennium: Society and Revivals in Rochester, New York, 1815–1837.* New York: Hill and Wang, 1978.

Juster, Susan. *Disorderly Women: Sexual Politics and Evangelicalism in Revolutionary New England.* Ithaca: Cornell University Press, 1994.

Kaestle, Carl F. *Pillars of the Republic: Common Schools and American Society, 1780–1860.* New York: Hill and Wang, 1983.

Katz, Michael B. *In the Shadow of the Poorhouse: A Social History of Welfare in America.* New York: Basic Books, 1986.

Kelley, Mary. *Private Women, Public Stage: Literary Domesticity in Nineteenth-Century America.* New York: Oxford University Press, 1984.

————. "Reading Women/Women Reading: The Making of Learned Women in Antebellum America." *Journal of American History* 83 (September 1996): 401–24.

Kerber, Linda K. "Separate Spheres, Female Worlds, Woman's Place: The Rhetoric of Women's History." *Journal of American History* 75 (June 1988): 9–39.

Kerr, Andrea Moore. *Lucy Stone: Speaking Out for Equality*. New Brunswick: Rutgers University Press, 1992.

Kessler-Harris, Alice. *Out to Work: A History of Wage-Earning Women in the United States*. New York: Oxford University Press, 1982.

Kornblith, Gary. "From Artisan to Businessmen: Master Mechanics in New England, 1789–1850." Ph.D. diss., Princeton University, 1983.

Larsen, Timothy. "'How Many Sisters Make a Brotherhood?': A Case Study in Gender and Ecclesiology in Early Nineteenth-Century English Dissent." *Journal of Ecclesiastical History* 49 (April 1998): 282–311.

Lasser, Carol. "Gender, Ideology, and Class in the Early Republic." *Journal of the Early Republic* 10 (fall 1990): 331–37.

————. "'Let Us Be Sisters Forever': The Sororal Model of Nineteenth-Century Female Friendship." *Signs* 14 (autumn 1988): 158–81.

————. "A 'Pleasingly Oppressive' Burden: The Transformation of Domestic Service and Female Charity in Salem, 1800–1840." *Essex Institute Historical Collections* 116 (July 1980): 156–75.

Leavitt, Judith Walzer. *Brought to Bed: Childbearing in America, 1750–1950*. New York: Oxford University Press, 1986.

Lebsock, Suzanne. *The Free Women of Petersburg: Status and Culture in a Southern Town, 1784–1860*. New York: Norton, 1984.

Lynch, Katherine A. "The Family and the History of Public Life." *Journal of Interdisciplinary History* 24 (spring 1994): 664–84.

Lystra, Karen. *Searching the Heart: Women, Men, and Romantic Love in Nineteenth-Century America*. New York: Oxford University Press, 1989.

Macdonald, Anne L. *No Idle Hands: The Social History of American Knitting*. New York: Ballantine Books, 1988.

McCarthy, Kathleen D. *Noblesse Oblige: Charity and Cultural Philanthropy in Chicago, 1849–1929*. Chicago: University of Chicago Press, 1982.

————. "Parallel Power Structures: Women and the Voluntary Sphere." In *Lady Bountiful Revisited: Women, Philanthropy, and Power*, edited by Kathleen D. McCarthy. New Brunswick: Rutgers University Press, 1990, 1–33.

McCauliffe, C.M.A. "The First English Adoption Law and Its American Precursors." *Seton Hall Law Review* 16 (1986): 656–77.

McCoy, Genevieve. "The Women of the ABCFM Oregon Mission and the Conflicted Language of Calvinism." *Church History* 64 (March 1995): 62–82.

McLoughlin, William G. *New England Dissent, 1630–1833: The Baptists and the Separation of Church and State*. 2 vols. Cambridge, Mass.: Harvard University Press, 1971.

————. *Revivals, Awakenings, and Reform: An Essay on Religion and Social Change in America, 1607–1977*. Chicago: University of Chicago Press, 1978.

————. *Soul Liberty: The Baptists' Struggle in New England, 1630–1833.* Hanover, New Hampshire: University Press of New England, 1991.

Malmsheimer, Lonna M. "Daughters of Zion: New England Roots of American Feminism." *New England Quarterly* 50 (September 1977): 484–504.

Marilley, Suzanne M. *Woman Suffrage and the Origins of Liberal Feminism in the United States, 1820–1930.* Cambridge, Mass.: Harvard University Press, 1996.

Mason, Mary Ann. *From Father's Property to Children's Rights: The History of Child Custody in the United States.* New York: Columbia University Press, 1994.

Mattaei, Julie A. *An Economic History of Women in America: Women's Work, the Sexual Division of Labor, and the Development of Capitalism.* New York: Schocken Books, 1982.

Matthews, Jean V. *Women's Struggle for Equality: The First Phase, 1828–1876.* Chicago: Ivan R. Dee, 1997.

May, Elaine Tyler. *Barren in the Promised Land: Childless Americans and the Pursuit of Happiness.* New York: Basic Books, 1995.

Melder, Keith E. *The Beginnings of Sisterhood: The American Women's Rights Movement, 1800–1850.* New York: Schocken Books, 1977.

————. "Ladies Bountiful: Organized Women's Benevolence in Early 19th-Century America." *New York History* 48 (July 1967): 231–54.

Miller, Jacquelyn C. "An 'Uncommon Tranquility of Mind': Emotional Self-Control and the Construction of a Middle-Class Identity in Eighteenth-Century Philadelphia." *Journal of Social History* 30 (fall 1996): 129–48.

Miyakawa, T. Scott. *Protestants and Pioneers: Individualism and Conformity on the American Frontier.* Chicago: University of Chicago Press, 1964.

Modell, John, and Tamara K. Hareven. "Urbanization and the Malleable Household: An Examination of Boarding and Lodging in American Families." *Journal of Marriage and the Family* 35 (August 1973): 467–79.

Murphy, Lucy Edersveld. "Business Ladies: Midwestern Women and Enterprise, 1850–1880." *Journal of Women's History* 3 (spring 1991): 65–89.

O'Connor, Thomas H. "The Irish in New England." *New England Historical and Genealogical Register* 139 (July 1985): 187–195.

Osterud, Nancy Gray. "'She Helped Me Hay it as Good as a Man': Relations among Women and Men in an Agricultural Community." In *"To Toil The Livelong Day": America's Women at Work, 1780–1980,* edited by Carol Groneman and Mary Beth Norton. Ithaca: Cornell University Press, 1987, 87–97.

————. *Bonds of Community: The Lives of Farm Women in Nineteenth-Century New York.* Ithaca: Cornell University Press, 1991.

Parker, Ida R. "'Fit and Proper'?: A Study of Legal Adoption in Massachusetts." In *The Origins of Adoption,* edited by David J. Rothman and Sheila M. Rothman. New York: Garland Publishing, 1987.

Perlmann, Joel, Silvana R. Siddali, and Keith Whitescarver. "Literacy, Schooling, and Teaching among New England Women, 1730–1820." *History of Education Quarterly* 37 (summer 1997): 118–39.

Pessen, Edward. *Riches, Class, and Power before the Civil War.* Lexington, Mass.: D.C. Heath, 1973.

———. "The Egalitarian Myth and the American Social Reality: Wealth, Mobility, and Equality in the 'Era of the Common Man.'" *American Historical Review* 76 (October 1971): 989–1034.

Porter, Susan Lynn. "The Benevolent Asylum—Image and Reality: The Care and Training of Female Orphans in Boston, 1800–1840." Ph.D. diss., Boston University, 1984.

———. "Victorian Values in the Marketplace: Single Women and Work in Boston, 1800–1850." In *Women of the Commonwealth: Work, Family, and Social Change in Nineteenth-Century Massachusetts,* edited by Susan L. Porter. Amherst: University of Massachusetts Press, 1994, 17–41.

Presser, Stephen B. "The Historical Background of the American Law of Adoption." *Journal of Family Law* 11 (1971): 443–51.

Reynolds, David S. "The Feminization Controversy: Sexual Stereotypes and the Paradoxes of Piety in Nineteenth-Century America." *New England Quarterly* 53 (March 1980): 96–106.

Rorabaugh, W.J. *The Craft Apprentice: From Franklin to the Machine Age in America.* New York: Oxford University Press, 1986.

Rosenberg, Charles E. *The Care of Strangers: The Rise of America's Hospital System.* New York: Basic Books, 1987.

Rosenberg, Rosalind. *Beyond Separate Spheres: Intellectual Roots of Modern Feminism.* New Haven: Yale University Press, 1982.

Rothenberg, Winifred B. "The Emergence of a Capital Market in Rural Massachusetts, 1730–1838." *Journal of Economic History* 45 (December 1985): 781–808.

———. "The Emergence of Farm Labor Markets and the Transformation of the Rural Economy: Massachusetts, 1750–1855." *Journal of Economic History* 48 (September 1988): 537–66.

Rothman, David J. *The Discovery of the Asylum: Social Order and Disorder in the New Republic.* Rev. ed. Boston: Little, Brown, 1971.

Rothman, Sheila M. *Living in the Shadow of Death: Tuberculosis and the Social Experience of Illness in American History.* New York: Basic Books, 1994.

Ruggles, Steven. "The Transformation of American Family Structure." *American Historical Review* 99 (February 1994): 103–28.

Ryan, Mary P. "A Woman's Awakening: Evangelical Religion and the Families of Utica, New York, 1800–1840." *American Quarterly* 30 (winter 1978): 602–23.

———. *Cradle of the Middle Class: The Family in Oneida County, New York, 1790–1865.* New York: Cambridge University Press, 1981.

———. "Femininity and Capitalism in Antebellum America." In *Capitalist Patriarchy and the Case for Socialist Feminism,* edited by Zillah R. Eisenstein. New York: Monthly Review Press, 1979, 151–68.

———. "The Power of Women's Networks: A Case Study of Female Moral Reform Societies in Antebellum America." *Feminist Studies* 5 (spring 1979): 66–86.

————. *Women in Public, between Banners and Ballots, 1825–1880.* Baltimore: Johns Hopkins University Press, 1990.

Schneider, Eric C. *In the Web of Class: Delinquents and Reformers in Boston, 1810s–1930s.* New York: New York University Press, 1992.

Scholten, Catherine M. *Childbearing in American Society, 1650–1850.* New York: New York University Press, 1985.

Schuyler, David. "Inventing a Feminine Past." *New England Quarterly* 51 (September 1978): 291–308.

Scott, Anne Firor. *Natural Allies: Women's Associations in American History.* Urbana: University of Illinois Press, 1993.

Sellers, Charles. *The Market Revolution: Jacksonian America, 1815–1846.* New York: Oxford University Press, 1991.

Shiels, Richard D. "The Feminization of American Congregationalism, 1730–1835." *American Quarterly* 33 (spring 1981): 46–62.

————. "The Scope of the Second Great Awakening: Andover, Massachusetts, as Case Study." *Journal of the Early Republic* 5 (summer 1985): 223–46.

Smith, Charles C. "Financial Embarrassments of the New England Ministers in the Last Century." *Proceedings of the American Antiquarian Society,* n.s., 7 (1891): 129–35.

Smith, Daniel Scott. "'Early' Fertility Decline in America: A Problem in Family History." *Journal of Family History* 12 (1978): 73–84.

————. "Family Limitation, Sexual Control, and Domestic Feminism in Victorian America." In *Clio's Consciousness Raised: New Perspectives on the History of Women,* edited by Mary S. Hartman and Lois Banner. New York: Harper and Row, 1974, 119–36.

Smith-Rosenberg, Carroll. *Disorderly Conduct: Visions of Gender in Victorian America.* New York: Oxford University Press, 1985.

————. "The Female World of Love and Ritual: Relations between Women in Nineteenth-Century America." *Signs* 1 (autumn 1975): 1–30.

————. *Religion and the Rise of the American City: The New York City Mission Movement, 1812–1870.* Ithaca: Cornell University Press, 1971.

————. "Sex as Symbol in Victorian Purity: An Ethnohistorical Analysis of Jacksonian America." In *Turning Points: Historical and Sociological Essays on the Family,* edited by John Demos and Sarane Spence Babcock. Chicago: University of Chicago Press, 1978, 212-47.

Solomon, Barbara Miller. *In the Company of Educated Women: A History of Women and Higher Education in America.* New Haven: Yale University Press, 1985.

Stansell, Christine. *City of Women: Sex and Class in New York, 1789–1860.* Urbana: University of Illinois Press, 1982.

Sterling, Dorothy. *Ahead of Her Time: Abby Kelley and the Politics of Antislavery.* New York: Norton, 1991.

Stout, Harry S. and Catherine A. Brekus, "Declension, Gender, and the 'New Religious History.'" In *Belief and Behavior: Essays in New Religious History,* edited by Philip R. VanderMeer and Robert P. Swierenga. New Brunswick: Rutgers University Press, 1991, 15–37.

Sweet, Leonard I. "The Female Seminary Movement and Woman's Mission in Antebellum America." *Church History* 54 (March 1985): 41–55.

Tate, Gayle T. "Political Consciousness and Resistance among Black Antebellum Women." *Women and Politics* 13 (1993): 67–89.

Thurston, Henry W. *The Dependent Child: A Study of Changing Aims and Methods in the Care of Dependent Children*. New York: Columbia University Press, 1930.

Treudley, Mary Gosworth. "The 'Benevolent Fair': A Study of Charitable Organization among American Women in the First Third of the Nineteenth Century." *Social Service Review* 14 (September 1940): 509–22.

Tyor, Peter L., and Jamil S. Zainaldin. "Asylum and Society: An Approach to Institutional Change." *Journal of Social History* 13 (fall 1979): 23–48.

Tyrrell, Ian. *Sobering Up: From Temperance to Prohibition in Antebellum America, 1800–1860*. Westport, Conn.: Greenwood Press, 1979.

Ulrich, Laurel Thatcher. "Housewife and Gadder: Themes of Self-Sufficiency and Community in Eighteenth-Century New England." In *"To Toil The Livelong Day": America's Women at Work, 1780–1980*, edited by Carol Groneman and Mary Beth Norton. Ithaca: Cornell University Press, 1987, 21–34.

———. "Vertuous Women Found: New England Ministerial Literature, 1668–1735." In *Women in American Religion*, edited by Janet Wilson James. Philadelphia: University of Pennsylvania Press, 1980, 67–87.

———. "Wheels, Looms, and the Gender Division of Labor in Eighteenth-Century New England." *William and Mary Quarterly*, 3rd ser., 55 (January 1998): 3–38.

Van Broekhoven, Deborah. "'Better than a Clay Club': The Organization of Anti-Slavery Fairs, 1835–60." *Slavery and Abolition* 19 (April 1998): 24–45.

———. "Needles, Pens, and Petitions: Reading Women into Antislavery History." In *The Meaning of Slavery in the North*, edited by David Roediger and Martin H. Blatt. New York: Garland Publishing, 1998, 125–55.

Varon, Elizabeth R. "Tippecanoe and the Ladies, Too: White Women and Party Politics in Antebellum Virginia." *Journal of American History* 82 (September 1995): 494–521.

———. *We Mean to Be Counted: White Women and Politics in Antebellum Virginia*. Chapel Hill: University of North Carolina Press, 1998.

Vinovskis, Maris A., and Richard M. Bernard. "Beyond Catharine Beecher: Female Education in the Antebellum Period." *Signs* 3 (summer 1978): 856–69.

Walsh, Mary. *"Doctors Wanted: No Women Need Apply": Sexual Barriers in the Medical Profession, 1835–1875*. New Haven: Yale University Press, 1977.

Wellman, Judith. "The Seneca Falls Women's Rights Convention: A Study of Social Networks." *Journal of Women's History* 3 (spring 1991): 9–37.

———. "Women and Radical Reform in Antebellum Upstate New York: A Profile of Grassroots Female Abolitionists." In *Clio Was A Woman: Studies in the History of American Women*, edited by Mabel E. Deutrich and Virginia C. Purdy. Washington, D.C.: Howard University Press, 1980, 113–27.

Welter, Barbara J. "The Cult of True Womanhood: 1820–1860." *American Quarterly* 18 (summer 1966): 151–74.

———. "The Feminization of American Religion, 1800–1860." In *Clio's Consciousness Raised: New Perspectives on the History of Women*, edited by Mary Hartman and Lois Banner. New York: Harper Torchbooks, 1973, 137–57

———. "'She Hath Done What She Could:' Protestant Women's Missionary Careers in Nineteenth-Century America." In *Women in American Religion*, edited by Janet Wilson James. Philadelphia: University of Pennsylvania Press, 1980, 111–25.

White, Ann. "Counting the Cost of Faith: America's Early Female Missionaries." *Church History* 57 (March 1988): 19–30.

Yellin, Jean Fagan and John C. Van Horne, eds. *The Abolitionist Sisterhood: Women's Political Culture in Antebellum America*. Ithaca: Cornell University Press, 1994.

Zboray, Ronald J. "Antebellum Reading and the Ironies of Technological Innovation." *American Quarterly* 40 (March 1988): 65–82.

Zboray, Ronald J. and Mary Saracino Zboray. "Whig Women, Politics, and Culture in the Campaign of 1840: Three Perspectives from Massachusetts." *Journal of the Early Republic* 17 (summer 1997): 277–315.

———. "Books, Reading, and the World of Goods in Antebellum New England." *American Quarterly* 48 (December 1996): 587–622.

———. "Political News and Female Readership in Antebellum Boston and Its Region." *Journalism History* 22 (spring 1996): 2–14.

Zelizer, Viviana A. *Pricing the Priceless Child: The Changing Social Value of Children*. New York: Basic Books, 1985.

Index

leadership in, 57; and women's
sphere, 46. *See also* Boston
Female Anti-Slavery Society;
Centre Missionary Sewing
Circle; Female Reading and
Charitable Society; Praying
Society; sewing; Worcester
Anti-Slavery Sewing Circle;
Worcester Female Association;
Worcester Female Samaritan
Society; Worcester Soldiers'
Relief Society; Worcester
Soldiers' Rest
social control, 84–85, 92, 137
spiritualism, 79, 118
Spurr, Mary Ann, 101, 154–55
Stanton, Elizabeth Cady, 168
Stone, Lucy, 55, 74, 164, 171
Stowe, Harriet Beecher, 61
Sweetser, Rev. Seth, 69–70, 80

taxation. *See* Calvinist Church;
Congregationalism; churches;
women and religion; Worcester,
city of
Taylor, Lydia, 23, 24, 67
Taylor, Samuel, 23, 67
Taylor, Sarah W., 62, 67
temperance, 36–37, 38, 65, 109, 110–11, 131, 163
Thurber, Caroline B., 95
Thurber, Charles, 95
Thurber, Lucinda, 95
Tolman, Lusanna W., 95
Trollope, Frances, 45, 53, 100
Trumbull, Louisa Jane, 48, 52, 98
tuberculosis, 105–8

unemployment, 132. *See also* Relief
of the Poor; Worcester Female
Employment Society
Unitarian (Second Parish) Church,
12, 21, 33; and Calvinist
Church, 25, 32, 39, 40

Waldo, Daniel Jr., 9–10, 29, 42;

election to office, 10, 16;
estimate of church taxpayers, 29;
support of church, 26, 42. *See
also* Calvinist Church; Waldo
family
Waldo, Elizabeth, 27, 28
Waldo, Rebecca, 10, 16, 21, 22, 42;
censured, 17; orthodoxy of, 14;
petition to First Church, 18–19;
wealth of, 11, 27–28. *See also*
Calvinist Church; Waldo family
Waldo, Sarah, 10, 16, 21, 22, 42;
censured, 17; orthodoxy of, 14;
petition to First Church, 18–19;
wealth of, 11, 27–28. *See also*
Calvinist Church; Waldo family
Waldo family, 12, 13–14, 33, 42
Walker, Sarah H., 109–10, 153
Washburn, Ichabod, 115
welfare: residency requirements, 174
Wetherell, Hester. *See* Newton,
Hester
Wheelock, Hannah C., 95, 97, 108
White, Nancy A., 49, 54–55
White, Tamerson, 145–48, 149, 153,
155. *See also* Worcester
Children's Friend Society
Wilmarth, Lydia, 166–67
women: and bankruptcy, 97–98; and
domesticity, 1–2, 189n. 1;
economic dependency of, 99,
178; and employment, 133, 146,
165–66; and gender spheres, 2–3, 46, 80, 189n. 2, 167–70, 181–82; and health, 104–6; and the
market, 64–65, 178; and poverty,
173–74. *See also feme covert*;
sewing; women and religion;
Worcester Female Employment
Society; Worcester women's
rights conventions
women and religion: and church
governance, 12, 13–14, 20; and
church taxes, 12, 22–23, 27–28,
31; and disestablishment, 22–23;
and feminization, 44, 191n. 4;